Punk Is Dead

Modernity Killed Every Night

Punk Is Dead

Modernity Killed Every Night

Edited by Richard Cabut
and Andrew Gallix

Winchester, UK
Washington, USA

First published by Zero Books, 2017
Zero Books is an imprint of John Hunt Publishing Ltd., Laurel House, Station Approach,
Alresford, Hants, SO24 9JH, UK
office1@jhpbooks.net
www.johnhuntpublishing.com
www.zero-books.net

For distributor details and how to order please visit the 'Ordering' section on our website.

Text copyright: Richard Cabut and Andrew Gallix 2016

ISBN: 978 1 78535 346 8
978 1 78535 347 5 (ebook)
Library of Congress Control Number: 2016951866

A CIP catalogue record for this book is available from the British Library.

Design: Stuart Davies

Printed and bound by CPI Group (UK) Ltd, Croydon, CR0 4YY, UK

We operate a distinctive and ethical publishing philosophy in all
areas of our business, from our global network of authors to
production and worldwide distribution.

CONTENTS

For my partner, Laura, and my children, Joseph,
Theo, Bernadette and Aniela
— Richard Cabut

For my son, William, and my parents who share many of my
punk memories
— Andrew Gallix

Besides.

ART probably doesn't exist — So it's useless to sing about it — and yet: people go on producing artworks — because that's how it is and not otherwise — Well — what can you do about it?

So we don't like ART and we don't like artists (down with Apollinaire!). HOW RIGHT TOGRATH IS TO MURDER THE POET! However, since we must swallow a drop of acid or old lyricism, let's do it quick and fast — for locomotives go fast.

Modernity too, therefore — both constant and killed every night

Jacques Vaché, *War Letters*, Letter to André Breton, 18 August 1917

Modernity killed every night.
Name for 430 King's Road: after Jacques Vaché (1974)

Jon Savage, *England's Dreaming: Sex Pistols and Punk Rock* (1991)

Punk's the Diamond in My Pocket

by Judy Nylon

I emigrated to London in 1970, carrying a black zipped overnight bag, and wearing over-the-knee platform boots, cut-off jean shorts and a black Borganza coat. Borganza is like longhaired velvet, so I looked pretty lush. I had no trouble getting the max time of six months on my passport stamp — there was just no history of people emigrating from the United States with carry-on luggage. Nobody knew I only had $250. I'd been in London before and had that inexplicable intuition that I was coming home. It never occurred to me to be apprehensive, I just set about meeting the people who would become my new world. I don't carelessly lose people: I'm still down with my first friends from those days. I went to the Speakeasy nights and shared the front half of a house in Chelsea that belonged to Donald and David Cammel (they had just made the film *Performance*). Their mother, Iona, who had studied what she referred to as 'systems of human perfection' with Aleister Crowley, lived in the back half of the house with Henry, her English bull terrier. I went to the Casserole at lunch and maybe passed by Parson's later. Chelsea is still my mothership. I was 5'10" with very short white-blonde hair and the sort of androgynous *sprezzatura* of someone born in the minor key. I'm not going to pretend I was ugly or an outcast; I found it easy to meet people who were interesting. I kept it real by silently remembering the family names of the four foster homes I'd grown up in. Even today, they are like remembering the names Matthew, Mark, Luke and John, reminding me that I belong everywhere and nowhere. I am often left out of punk histories because I fall between countries: I sort of represent the perennial thread that connects punk to the before and after of subculture. I don't identify with any particular class or flag, and don't rely on a single group for a belief system. I consider myself 'fourth world,' a hybrid of the other three.

I quickly had to sign on as a model to get the home office behind me. I hardly ever worked. Whatever I was, I was not much of a model. I eventually worked in the studios in Covent Garden as a freelance photo stylist for advertising. This was during the era of very cheap $250 return air flights on Freddie Laker. You could pick up a guitar cheaply in New York and carry it back to London where it sold for double the price. I also took photographic prints to Paris as a private courier. With hindsight, when punk started, what I brought to the party was my gradual insistence that we'd have the widest possible wingspan: inclusion, everybody in from all the margins, not exactly the same, but a scene. I was experientially prepared for this moment by the cards already dealt me in life. I'd thought about it. I've always been an internationalist, and as an autodidact, my real addiction is to learning more. There is no way I'd let punk be reduced to a coffee-table book of white English boys spitting. It is a fallacy that there was ever a pure London punk, Paris punk, New York punk or Berlin punk: many of us were very mobile. Somehow in the books on punk that I've read, the only one who ever took plane rides was Malcolm McLaren. Think about it: that's silly. My very existence would eventually come into conflict with Malcolm and Vivienne's version of punk as an advertising trend. If you look at the pictures of us all at the opening night of the Roxy in Covent Garden, nobody is wearing clothes designed by Viv. Eventually you'd start to see people who worked for her, or people she gave them to, wearing them because they looked cool. The trousers she gave me ended up being worn by John Cale on his *Helen Of Troy* LP cover. I don't know what happened to them after that. Those T-shirts that Bernie Rhodes made for their shop sold for £20 a pop, and the dole maximum was £45 or £50 per week. In the beginning, it wasn't about fashion; a few of us were visually-oriented, so having a look was a given. Nobody played well: it was about living differently. A collective cry from the heart seeking a way out of poverty, despair and boredom. My punk story is a diamond slice I can show you to help you imagine a rock too big for the frame.

Way before punk, my first female friend to hang out with in early-Seventies glam London was Gyllian Corrigan. We share a few funny stories. One night we went to a party thrown by Kit Lambert that became legendary because it hosted several layers of London together, before they were really aware of one other. Nureyev let us in the front door and Keith Moon was your host on the floor above. It was there that I met the New York Dolls when Billy Murcia was alive. On the Dolls' second trip to London, with Jerry Nolan on drums, Syl would introduce me to Brian Eno at a late-night party in the bar of Blake's Hotel. The earth shook — I thought I'd met my most complementary mind ever. He matched the bookish part of my nature perfectly, though he wasn't a guy I'd stand back-to-back with if I had to fight my way out of a bar in Naples. I'm not from the same Catholic background he was. For me pornography was neither deliciously forbidden nor very interesting. For him, I was possibly kind of exotic. I'd just come from assisting Catalan artist Antoni Miralda with a food-art performance on a train to the Edinburgh Festival. Eno's 'Back in Judy's Jungle' references the way he and I lived when he briefly moved in with me. He taught me to be more selfish and, as he once said, I taught him to be complete alone. I need to be alone for at least a few hours each day. I always have.

It didn't end with a fight, I just realized I couldn't see him without taking a loss. Two great things came of it all for me: I met John Cale, who was the only guy to ever ask me to be in his band, and then I met Chrissie Hynde when she came to Brian's flat in Maida Vale to interview him for *NME*. Looking at pictures, I can break the early days into time slots by hair colour. Before Brian, I was a platinum blonde, during Brian I had red hair like in the *Tiger Mountain* video and as I defected to punk, my hair went back to black. I shapeshift easily on the outside, remaining dead constant on the inside. Brian Eno and I are the same age, yet I fell on the punk side of Boring Old Fart. There was one interesting moment when I was hanging out with Paul Simonon and Eno was spending time with Paul's mother.

I already knew Kate Simon, but joining up with Chrissie in both London and Paris, and meeting Patti Palladin when she arrived in London, made us a crowd — a punk expat posse of bad-girl cousins. We were the first Americans that many London punks had ever known. It's hard to describe Sid's face when we ran out of gas in the East End late one night in Patti's pimped-out Morris Minor station wagon. She and I jumped out, pulled a length of hose out of the back and started sucking petrol out of someone else's tank. We're screaming at each other because the hose was too stiff and we couldn't find anything smaller and more supple. It was really down to shared knowledge in punk days. Things were in the air. You saw other people that looked like you would know them, around at the Roebuck or the Ship, or maybe the record bins and bookstores around Shaftesbury Avenue, or maybe just on the other side of the street anyplace, moving quickly, carrying guitars in gig bags. There's a youth antenna that we all had and we — Chrissie and I — developed it spending hours just walking the streets, taking it all in, with maybe a quid fifty between us for a shared order of monks vegetables, upstairs at the Wong Key. We were the girls that came late to gigs, when you could slip in free and stand at the back. Later we'd congregate around the soundboard. We were never all going to be in the same band like the Slits or anything, but every night wherever it was going on, we were all there.

Patti and I would become punk's first DIY home-recording-studio duo — as such we connect to what came after punk. She caught a Teac that fell off a lorry and I'd played around in Eno's pocket studio, so I had some ideas. We just felt our way forward with Snatch. Kate would shoot a lot of the best record covers and then end up holding the major photos of Bob Marley's golden days. Patti fell in with the Heartbreakers and ended up producing and singing duets with Johnny Thunders on the CD, *Copy Cats*. I moved onto experimenting with dub and punk until it crystallized into my *Pal Judy* LP. There's a lot of people saying 'we' when they write about punk, but those who had a job working for the record companies, or music papers, or clothes shops have a whole different level of immersion than those of us who didn't. What impressed me about Chrissie in those days was that she was living so far over the edge that she'd either get something to happen or be found dead trying. She was about thirty when she got into the studio with a band of her own. When it is like that you acknowledge all the other people who supported you. In punk, having backup was all-important if rarely mentioned. You can't get philosophical when you're in real danger of not surviving. The main hangout for the Yank girls was Covington Road, Jonathan Ross's house. It was through Jonathan's sharing of his home and his extended family that I was connected to the historical creative Chelsea, and I felt at home in it. I have been known to pull invitations to openings out of John Betjeman's trash bin (Betjeman was Jonathan's godfather). Hynde and I would show up for a free glass of wine on our way to some gig, to the puzzlement of many people there. We must have seemed like a reflection of their pre-war selves... Continuity. I'm glad to have been able to show Man Ray my *Violon d'Ingres*, a tattoo that shouts out that punk connected to what he did.

One really crucial thing about punk is that it is when the breakthrough came for females. Punk was the one culture, along the timeline, that succeeded where Surrealism, Dada, Beat and so on had failed us. I'd have been excluded, tagged as a muse and trimmed to a footnote, in any of them. Until the record companies stepped in, in London, where I was, at street level, punk was drenched in equality. Male punks might have been violent when pushed, but they were also engaged with feminism, vegetarianism and secularism in daily life. Nobody preached; they just walked it as a given. Any time I'm asked about some historical punk anecdotes I'm connected to, I make it my business to mention any other female who was there also. Otherwise you get stories about the same dozen guys from a few groups. The 'Not For Girls' tag line on *Sniffin' Glue* was a joke.

Introduction

Prose for Heroes

by Richard Cabut and Andrew Gallix

Our becoming is done. We are what we are. Now it is just a question of rocking along with things as they are until we are dead.
— Donald Barthelme, *Snow White*

This anthology of articles and interviews, featuring some of our most astute and active commentators and participants, is about punk's becoming — and about what it, and we, became.

The notion quickly emerges, via more than one of our writers, that at the very beginning punk was constantly in the process of forming. If the pertinent sense of punk is to be found anywhere, it is in this formative gap, this disjuncture.

Early fans and writers offer explorations of this blank zone inhabited by a Blank Generation — a term I use in the way Richard Hell originally intended: a void to be filled by whatever might be conjured and created.

Malcolm McLaren's biographer Paul Gorman describes the King's Road scene of the mid-Seventies, and how he was (probably) in the Roebuck pub on the very night Johnny Rotten first auditioned for the Pistols, round the corner in SEX.

Jonh Ingham, who wrote the very first music press interview with the Pistols, published in *Sounds* on 24 April 1976, examines the soaring influence of Patti Smith in a piece — 'The Divining Rod and the Lost Vowel' — which, when it appeared in *Sounds* in a different form, was lauded by guitarist and rock historian Lenny Kaye as the best on-the-road article he had ever read.

Cultural anthropologist Ted Polhemus — who, while organising a fashion forum at the ICA in 1975, stood as character witness for McLaren and Westwood in an obscenity trial involving one of their T-shirts — describes the intersection of style and subversion. He makes it clear that, as with all proper youth movement shakers, the Pistols offered not just a style but also a matrix via which fans could propose and propel their own styles.

Dorothy Max Prior, who also worked at the ICA at that time, muses on sex and punk in the Seventies — her private, and sometimes very public, acts connecting her with the larger social sphere. David Wilkinson does the same with his piece 'Ever Fallen in Love?' We are left with little doubt that it was desire, with its power and scope to shock and embolden, that shifted punk beyond the realms of the rational.

Cumulatively, these pieces hint that any sense of nostalgia we feel for punk might best be reserved for this period of becoming — which is, in some respects, marked by an innocence character- istic of childhood.

Punk at this time — before the Clash essentially — was not fixed in a standard left-wing stance but was, rather, a defiant and stylish boho response to the modern world of inertia and consumption. As Jon Savage points out, 'Punk was informed by utopian anarchism in its most recent form, the Situationists.' This not-uncommon notion is affirmed in this book by psychogeog- rapher Tom Vague in his piece 'King Mob Echo,' which points out the intense associations between punk and the Situs.

Prompted by Situationism, punks were not interested in restructuring economic systems, but in how fast modern society could be destroyed. Cool, or what! They were entirely reasonable in their demands for the impossible. They were not in the least afraid of the ruins. They wanted to sabotage the Spectacle... before it had sunk in that, as postmodern theorists had pointed out, the very idea of such subversion was a childish chimera.

Via negation, punks wanted to upend the world... before the PoMos *et al.* sneered (like punks!) at any supposed dissimilarities between the Real and the Spectacle... before the gist of meaning and truth became but a haze... before attention to a 'new kind of superficiality' and depthlessness, buzzing with numbing codes and signs, assumed theoretical urgency.

Before all of this, punk continued to become — consumed with boredom, and driven to feel, create and strive for meaning — and to live.

Here, both the annotated version of Tony D's 1980 'Sid Vicious March' piece from *Kill Your Pet Puppy* ('Learning to Fight'), and Penny Rimbaud's 'Banned From the Roxy' commentary, which Penny typed up by hand for us from its original source *International Anthem*, with an exclusive new introduction, point to a quest for truth and significance.

Sometimes, eventually, the aforementioned negation turned into self-negation, as described in art historian Neal Brown's article 'Camera Squat Art Smiler,' which is amongst those pieces that add something entirely lacking in too many narratives of punk: personality, humour — albeit a mad laughter — and lyricism. The self-negation, it is suggested, is a substitute for punk's original sense of unformed desire, impossible to attain, sustain or grasp.

Meanwhile, Jon Savage, with his extensive 'Punk Etymology,' underlines the fact that at the beginning — and at the end — is the word. Jon would like it stressed that readers should add their own punk culture finds to his list, to which he has written a fresh introduction. Modestly, Jon hasn't included any references to his own works, of which there are many, of course. Of these my own favourite, perhaps, is an article in *The Face*, issue 70, February 1986:

Regard it [punk] rather as an ambitious cultural movement that connected, as so few do, with the world outside, and like Dada and Surrealism, sought to turn it on its head. Or even better regard it as an attitude that can be captured at any time, in a laugh, a toss of the

head and the refusal to accept anything less than total possibility.
(Jon Savage)

— Richard Cabut

I can still picture a small advertisement for Better Badges in the back pages of some music magazine. This must have been around 1980. I believe it was in *Smash Hits* but have chosen to forget that rather embarrassing detail. A black-and-white ink drawing — possibly by Savage Pencil or Ray Lowry, but probably by someone else — featured above a chart listing their current bestsellers. It depicted a spiky-haired couple in full bondage regalia. If memory serves, the girl — I should say woman, really — wore a kilt and fishnets. I faintly recall a dainty chain hanging between one of her earlobes and nostrils. A safety pin was no doubt involved at one end or the other, possibly both, although by then safety pins were no longer in currency. Her companion was hunched over a walking stick. Or perhaps she had the walking stick and he was hunched over a Zimmer frame, unless it was the other way round. The visual punchline is that these hardcore punks were also OAPs. It seemed a totally incongruous conceit at the time, akin to a child struggling to picture itself as a grown-up. And yet, here we are. All the old dudes. Commemorating punk's fortieth anniversary, or, as is more likely, bemoaning it Victor Meldrew-fashion. Five days ago, social media alerted me to the fact that Paul Cook had just turned sixty. *Sixty!* The surviving Pistols were all born in 1956 save for Steve Jones (1955). Ironically, Sid was the youngest (1957). I discovered punk rock in 1976, when I was only eleven — *eleven!* — and 'officially' remained a punk for the following decade. It was a home for those who felt homeless; somewhere to fit in when you did not. It had the same impact on me as Surrealism or May 1968 had on many others. Those of us lucky to still be here are in our fifties and sixties, and the Better Badges cartoon appears prescient rather than absurd. Context is everything.

The Museum of London recently shared a picture of a group of punks on their Twitter feed. What immediately caught my attention was the date: 1975. I got in touch with them, pointing out that there had to be a mistake. Nobody, I explained, looked like that at the time. The style is already codified — almost a uniform. It could have been taken in 1978 at the earliest. Given that no band names or logos, or slogans, were painted on the backs of the leather jackets, this was probably before 1981. 1979 sounded just about right, the year when punk was thriving — largely unnoticed — underground, and we attempted to reconcile the Ants' dark glamour with the equally seductive puritan zeal of Crass. I was told, in no uncertain terms, that the photographer's wife was adamant and that, anyway, some people did look like that in 75. Eventually, Danny Baker got involved, confirming what I had said; the photographer's wife double-checked and realised the error of her ways. Beyond proving me right, none of this is very important in the grand scheme of things, but it is indicative of the way in which the past is subtly rewritten, every nuance gradually airbrushed out of the picture. Yet punk was lived — and how it was experienced is our primary concern here — in breathless weekly instalments. Not only was 1977 completely different from 1978, 1979 or 1980, but the mood kept changing throughout the year. Punk was still in its infancy during the early months. The period running from spring to early September — encompassing the Silver Jubilee and the 'Summer of Hate,' as the *NME* called it — constituted the movement's high-water mark. The autumn and winter got much darker, culminating in the Pistols' split in early 78. The movement was quickly reinterpreted retrospectively, from the vantage point of the early Eighties: anachronic mohican haircuts already crop up in Alex Cox's *Sid and Nancy* movie from 1986. If you believe certain punk memoirs, the streets of London, in 1977, were thronging with skinheads. They were not. Apart from pictures of Skrewdriver, I never saw one before 1978. By 1979, every other boy round our way sported a crop, braces and DMs.

> *Today, nostalgia is almost as unacceptable as racism. Our politicians speak of drawing a line under the past and turning our back on ancient quarrels. In this way, we can leap forward into a scrubbed, blank, amnesiac future. If [Walter] Benjamin rejected this kind of philistinism, it was because he was aware that the past holds vital resources for the renewal of the present. Those who wipe out the past are in danger of abolishing the future as well. Nobody was more intent on eradicating the past than the Nazis, who would, like the Stalinists, simply scrub from historical record whatever they found inconvenient.* (Terry Eagleton, 'Waking the Dead,' *New Statesman* 12 November 2009)

This book was partly inspired by the almost universal knee-jerk reaction against nostalgia. Without nostalgia, we would have no Homer or Proust. It is the wellspring of countless — perhaps all — great works of art. The cult of the future, upon which our system is predicated, seems far more pernicious to me. No future indeed! Besides, punk's cultural importance should, I think, be officially recognised in museums and galleries. After all, a case can be made for punk as the last great youth subculture in the rock 'n' roll mould. Jon Savage writes, in his introduction to *Teenage: The Creation of Youth 1875-1945* (2007), that punk's 'historical collage... marked the moment when the linear forward movement of the sixties was replaced by the loop.' Grunge was indeed essentially an offshoot of the American hardcore punk movement of the early Eighties. Britpop was a collage of earlier British youth styles. The early-Noughties wave of American bands that came in the wake of the Strokes harked back to CBGBs and post-punk... Punk should also be commemorated in museums because it was a summation of all the avant-garde movements of the 20th century. In fact, it may even have been the avant-garde's last stand (which would cast the title of this book in a new light). The movement brought about a revolution of everyday life, turning it into a permanent adventure and abolishing the boundary between artists and audience; art and life. Everything, from fanzines to clothes, became part of this total artwork that was punk. Boris Groys writes that 'the contemporary museum realizes the modernist dream of a theatre in which there is no clear boundary between the stage and the space for the audience — a dream that the theatre itself was never able to fully realize' (*In the Flow*, 2016). Having succeeded where theatre failed, punk should take pride of place in the contemporary museum he describes. The last reason I will invoke here is that punk was almost universally reviled at the time. It is time to take pride in our eventual victory.

My contention is that what we are commemorating is not so much punk itself as the past commemorations of punk. In a piece written on the occasion of the phenomenon's tenth anniversary, reproduced here for the first time, Simon Reynolds argued that it was punk's ubiquity — rather than its death or betrayal — which was stifling the progress of popular culture. 1986 was perhaps too close to take stock. It was the year I finally recognised that I no longer had anything in common with those people, who looked like me, but whose sole ambition in life seemed to be to fight or wallow in their own vomit, frequently combining both activities. If the Pistols had reformed to mark the anniversary, they would have been the biggest band in the world. There were doubtless complex contractual and personal reasons why this did not happen, but what is sure is that it would also have been seen as a travesty and a cop-out. By 1996 — and the Filthy Lucre tour — such qualms had been set aside, proving that something which was still alive in 86 was now dead as a dodo. Since then, the tripartite division of punk history (pre-punk, punk, post-punk) has become the norm. BBC Four's excellent *Punk Britannia* (2012) series follows this format, which is logical — chronological — but pays as much attention to punk's ancestry and legacy as to the explosion itself. In this model, punk increasingly becomes the squeezed middle.

Punk is probably the most analysed youth cult ever, but also one of the most resistant to academic analysis — a problem the following book has not quite solved.

Punk gigs had a very distinctive, surprisingly sweet, smell. It was a subtle blend of Crazy Color hair dye, hairspray, smoke and lager. That smell has completely evaporated. We should bring it back; bottle it. We need a phenomenology of punk.

The first punks I ever saw walked past me at Clapham Junction station. They looked like they had stepped out of the future.

I know exactly where I was when I read a certain piece in the music press or bought a given record.

I remember visiting Seditionaries for the first time, not only with my mum, but also my dear Auntie Jenny, who gasped, 'What have they done to our Queen?' My acute embarrassment has dissipated, but I still regret having hurt her feelings by exposing her to Jamie Reid's work without a word of warning.

I remember hiding my chains and safety pins under my jacket, during the summer of 1977, whenever I spotted Teddy Boys on the King's Road.

Across the road from the Electric Ballroom, 3 November 1979. Two sisters who were picked up by their parents after the Penetration gig. You were about my age, maybe a bit older. You certainly looked more punk, with your fishnet mohair jumpers, than I did at the time. I always found them too itchy those jumpers. Your parents arrived in their nice car. I imagined you being whisked away to some Peter Pan dwelling, all warm and cosy. A proper home. Your bedroom walls were covered in punk posters and press cuttings. You would lie awake a while, the concert still buzzing in your ears. If you're reading this, have a drink on me.

Once we were part of punk; punk is now part of us.

— Andrew Gallix

1

The Boy Looked at Eurydice

by Andrew Gallix

Retrofuturism, as we now call it, came out of the closet in the late Seventies due to the widespread feeling that there was indeed 'no future' any more. Whilst Johnny Rotten waxed apocalyptical, Howard Devoto screeched existentially about his future no longer being what it was. Time seemed topsy-turvy, out of joint; the future not something to look forward to, but to look back on. 'About the future I can only reminisce,' sang Pete Shelley on a dotty ditty dedicated to 'nostalgia for an age yet to come.' (Significantly enough, it was almost immediately covered — recycled — by Penetration.) This trend was knowing and 'ironic' in typical postmodern mode (à la Rezillos or B-52s), but also imbued with a genuine longing for a time — mainly the Fifties and Sixties — when the march of progress (in the shape of the space age and consumer society) seemed unstoppable. A time, crucially, when the future punks were still children, or twinkles in their parents' eyes. Twinkling little stars.

When we were young, we were very young. It was de rigueur. Kate Phillips, the first journalist to ever mention the Sex Pistols, focused almost exclusively on their youth: 'They are all about 12 years old. Or maybe about 19, but you could be fooled' (*NME*, 27 December 1975). 'We were 17; they were 25,' John Lydon recalls, dismissing the musicians on the New York scene as 'dirty old people.' Malcolm McLaren had fancied himself as the band's singer, rather than their manager, but, according to Nick Kent, his 'old paranoia' about 'being too old got the better of him.' After seeing the Pistols live for the first time, Richard Strange (Doctors of Madness) suddenly sensed that his time was up: 'I'm two years too old,' he lamented. Explaining that he was slightly younger than the Pistols and their entourage, Marco Pirroni feels the need to add that 'two years was a big gap, gigantic' at the time. Unlike Brian Eno, Judy Nylon 'fell on the punk side of Boring Old Fart' despite being the same age as him: 'There was one interesting moment when I was hanging out with Paul Simonon and Eno was spending time with Paul's mother.' Joe Strummer could have drawn the very same conclusion as Strange or Eno. Upon joining the Clash, he was deemed 'a bit old' by Glen Matlock (himself only four years his junior). Concealing his real age would be an essential part of the public schoolboy-cum-pub rocker's reinvention as a bona fide punk. A year on from the Pistols' acrimonious demise, Steve Jones confided in *Sounds*, 'I feel a bit old. I walk down the street and see these little punk rockers, about 13, and they don't even recognise me.' Already in his mid-thirties by 1980, Charlie Harper (UK Subs) screamed his desire to be 'teenage' as though it were a state of mind, or perhaps even the only way to be: 'Teenage / I wanna be teenage / I wanna be teenage / I wanna be.'

We were so young, we were so goddamn young. Sid Vicious boasted that he 'didn't even know the Summer of Love was happening' because he was 'too busy playing with [his] Action Men.' 'See my face, not a trace / No reality,' sang the Pistols on 'Seventeen,' the closest they ever got to a generational manifesto. Buzzcocks, who had barely reached adulthood, penned a paean to 'feeling almost sixteen again.' In a cheeky act of lèse-majesté — given that this was the single John Lydon had mimed to during his fabled King's Road audition — Eater wound back Alice Cooper's 'I'm Eighteen' to 'Fifteen,' thus reflecting the group's average age. The Lurkers, and others, glamorised the growing pains of being 'Just Thirteen'... I can still see that picture of two prepubescent, second-generation skinheads in a black-and-white photo spread — doubtless compiled by Garry Bushell — from around 1979. If memory serves, the humorous caption read:

'Hope I die before my voice breaks.'

Witold Gombrowicz's debut novel, *Ferdydurke* (1937), reflected the emergence of the 'new Hedonism' Lord Henry had called for in *Dorian Gray* as well as the shifting human relations Virginia Woolf had observed in the early years of the twentieth century. Outwardly, we strive for completion, perfection and maturity; inwardly, we crave incompletion, imperfection and immaturity. The Polish author suggests that the natural progression from immaturity to maturity (and death) is paralleled by a corresponding covert regression from maturity to immaturity. Mankind is suspended between divinity and puerility, torn between transcendence and pubescence. In 1941, Max Horkheimer declared that the Oedipal struggle was over and that Oedipus had won: 'Since Freud the relation between father and son has been reversed. The child not the father stands for reality. The awe which the Hitler youth enjoys from his parents is but the political expression of a universal state of affairs.' 'It's funny,' says Nicky in *The Vortex*, 'how mother's generation always longed to be old when they were young, and we strain every nerve to keep young.' Was the Vortex club named after Noël Coward's 1924 play, or was it a nod to Ezra Pound's 1914 essay? All we can say for sure is that, more than any other subculture before or since, punk was afflicted with Peter Pan syndrome. Oscar Wilde's famous aphorism — 'To be premature is to be perfect' — had found its ideal embodiment. Early gigs frequently resembled a St Trinian's prom night gatecrashed by the Bash Street Kids. The ubiquitous school uniforms — all wonky ties and peekaboo stockings — were designed to rub punks' youthfulness in the wrinkled faces of the rock dinosaurs and other Boring Old Farts. One could also flag up the recurring theme of onanism ('Orgasm Addict' and 'Teenage Kicks' being the prime examples) as well as McLaren's dodgy flirtation with paedophilia (from the early nude boy T-shirt through Bow Wow Wow) to argue that the Blank Generation was more clockwork satsuma than orange. Bliss was it in that dawn to be young. But to be a punk rocker was very heaven!

The critic Brian Dillon describes the surface of Robert Rauschenberg's *Erased de Kooning Drawing* (1953) as being 'startlingly alive, active, palimpsestic.' The same could be said of punk, whose myriad influences shone through despite the *tabula rasa* of Year Zero; the attempt to wipe the slate clean ('No Elvis, Beatles, or the Rolling Stones / In 1977'). By the early Seventies, mainstream pop music — which now boasted a relatively long tradition — was becoming increasingly self-referential and started plundering its back catalogue. The Fifties haunted glam rock, and even teenybopper outfits like the Bay City Rollers (not to mention the likes of Mud and Showaddywaddy). Meanwhile, a proper Teddy Boy revival was in full swing (its sartorial needs catered for by none other than McLaren and Westwood). Punk was the culmination of this excavation of popular music history and regression — via the hardcore rhythm and blues being played in British pubs, the rediscovery of Sixties American garage bands (*Nuggets* was released in 1972) and discovery of the Stooges et al. — towards a stripped-back, primitive version of rock 'n' roll embodied by the Ramones' *reductio ad absurdum* of surf music and bubblegum pop. A *regression* running counter to the so-called progression of prog rock.

Punk's enduring legacy notwithstanding, the original movement had nowhere to go: literally, *no future*. Going forward meant that it would no longer be an event, just another collection of professional bands releasing records at regular intervals and touring to promote them. Musical progression, for a genre that rejected virtuosity in favour of enthusiasm and inventiveness, would also prove problematic: 'We say noise is for heroes (heroes) / Leave the music for zeroes (zeroes) / Noise, Noise, Noise is for heroes (heroes) / Oh yeah' (The Damned, *Machine Gun Etquette*, 1979). As Chrissie Hynde has often pointed out, the curse of the punk was to turn — imperceptibly, but almost inevitably — into a muso. In those days, lest we forget, Paul Weller would get a lot of flak simply for tuning up on stage. Punk's spirited DIY approach to music was symbolised by those hasty sketches of three guitar chords that featured in the January 1977 issue of a fanzine called *Sideburns*: 'This is a chord. This is another. This is a third. Now form a band.' They were famously referenced on Stiff Records' poster for the Damned's tour, that same year, supported by one-chord wonders the Adverts: 'The Damned can now play three chords. The Adverts can play one. Hear all four of them at...' But what happens when the band you have formed can play those three chords as effortlessly as seasoned session musicians? How many times can 'White Riot' be imbued with the conviction, vitriol and sheer hormonal energy it warrants?

Simon Reynolds, who rates Plastic Ono Band's 1970 debut as a 'seminal proto-punk record,' provides a possible answer. Yoko Ono achieved the sound on that album by getting 'superbly skilled musicians' to play 'like brain-dead gorillas wearing oven mitts' (*Totally Wired*, 2009). Malcolm McLaren came up with another ingenious solution: sacking Glen Matlock, who had most contributed to the composition of the Pistols' repertoire, and drafting in Sid Vicious, who could not play for heroin, let alone toffee. In a neat instance of life imitating art, the manager's fanciful refrain about his protégés' lack of musical proficiency (which tapped into a long avant-garde anti-music tradition) became a self-fulfilling prophecy: 'Find yourself four kids. Make sure they hate each other. Make sure they can't play' (*The Great Rock 'n' Roll Swindle*, 1980). Neil Spencer's review of the Pistols at the Marquee — their first piece of exposure — highlighted the band's anti-music credentials: '"You can't play," heckled an irate French punter. "So what?" countered the bassman, jutting his chin in the direction of the bewildered Frog.' Incidentally, it was Matlock — probably the band's most accomplished musician overall, as we have said — who affirmed that they were about more than mere music. And then, of course, there was that clincher of a finale: '"Actually, we're not into music," one of the Pistols confided afterwards. Wot then? "We're into chaos"' (*NME*, 21 February 1976). Early punk had a distinctly Oulipian quality: lack of musical proficiency was exploited as a creative constraint. Not being great players generated a tension, an intensity — but also a fragility — that proper musicians can seldom replicate. The danger of walking a musical tightrope, fearing that it might fall apart at any moment, knowing that it will, and rejoicing in those sonic epiphanies when it all miraculously comes together. The best punk bands never went through the motions; the motions went through them. The American fiction writer Peter Markus has spoken beautifully about the flashes of brilliance that can be conjured up when amateur musicians make a virtue of necessity:

I'm a failed musician. As a kid I used to punk around with pals and find objects along our riverbank to bang on, bought pawnshop guitars and drums and broken-keyed organs and made music out of our not knowing what we were doing. It was pure accident, those moments when we found ourselves in the middle of some sound spell. We knew it when we came out of it, the times that we went there, the times we were somehow taken. I can count the times on one hand, but I hold those times in my hand still like stones or fossils that somehow manage to float, have found a way to displace space and gravity and have pushed back against the failings of memory and the thinning out of time. Those moments stopped occurring, it seemed, even then, once our hands seemed to know where they ought to go, what chords they ought to be playing, and it was this sense of knowing (or thinking that we knew what we were doing) that killed the magic of our song. (The Brooklyn Rail, 5 February 2015)

Punk was *carpe diem* recollected in cacophony — living out your 'teenage dreams,' and sensing, almost simultaneously, that they would be 'so hard to beat' (The Undertones). The movement generated an instant nostalgia for itself, so that it was forever borne back to the nebulous primal scene of its own creation. Its forward momentum was backward-looking, like Walter Benjamin's angel of history. The Wasps' introduction to 'Can't Wait 'Till '78' is a case in point: 'I mean it's still 1977, d'you know what I mean? Remember what happened at the beginning? Let's have a bit more of it, eh?' (*Live at the Vortex*, 1977). 1978 — Year One after Year Zero — is anticipated as a return to 'the beginning.' To quote the Cockney Rejects on their debut album,

I wanna go back to where it all began / And I wanna do a gig in my back garden / Wanna have a laugh before the press get in / If you give 'em half a chance / They'll kill the fucking thing. ('Join the Rejects')

By 1980, when that record was released, going back to 'where it all began' meant totally different — and even contradictory — things to totally different — and indeed contradictory — people. Every splinter group that joined the ranks of the punk diaspora (Oi!, the mod revival, 2-Tone, no wave, cold wave, post-punk, goth, early new romanticism, anarcho-punk, positive punk, psychobilly, hardcore etc.) was a renewed attempt to recapture an original unity, which the emergence of these very splinter groups made impossible. As Paul Gorman put it in a recent documentary, 'People began to play with, and tease out, the strands which were therein, and it was so rich, and so full of content, that one strand could lead to a whole movement.' When Garry Bushell claims that the Rejects were 'the reality of punk mythology' — which is precisely what Mark Perry had previously said apropos of Sham 69 — he is referring to a very restrictive, lumpen version of punk that excludes most of the early bands bar the Clash. (Even within the Clash, only Joe 'Citizen Smith' Strummer ever really subscribed to this view.) Many Blitz Kids felt that it was their scene — which was not only contemporaneous with Oi! but also its inverted mirror image — that captured the true spirit of the early movement. Each new wave of bands sought out this point of origin: punk prior to its negation by language, when it was still in the process of becoming. The moment when memory's exile would come to an end and literally *take place*. The moment that would coincide with the moment, which the philosopher Simon Critchley calls the 'now of nows.' His friend and collaborator, the novelist Tom McCarthy, explains that in cases of trauma, the brain often fails to integrate the traumatic event into memory's narrative thread: 'That gap, or absence, that few seconds of silence on the tape, become real; since everything else that is on the tape is fake, that gap must be real' (*How to Stop Living and Start Worrying*, 2010). That fabled gap — those weeks or months that everybody missed, even when they were there — became punk's ultimate reality. As Mick Jones remarks, 'By the time everyone had sussed it, it was already over.' Not accepting that it was over, trying to bridge that traumatic gap by reliving those 'few seconds of silence on the tape,' accounts for much of the movement's subsequent history.

Like the Faubourg Saint-Germain for the Proustian narrator, punk was always elsewhere. In the early days, in London, it was at CBGB in New York City (think of Eater's 'Thinkin' of the USA'). For those in New York City, it then became London. There was always somebody out there who was in the right place, or whose hair was spikier than yours — who seemed to be the real McCoy. The Silver Jubilee boat party, on 13 June 1977, was one of those rare occurrences when you could accurately pinpoint where punk was. It was there, on that drunken boat adrift upon the Thames. However, most people in the know remained stranded on the Embankment, like in that oft-reproduced picture where you can spot Richard Strange, Steve Strange and Kevin Mooney among a very English queue of lookers-on who had literally missed the boat. Even insiders such as Viv Albertine and Palmolive of the Slits: 'We turn up, but have no hope of getting on, I see Palmolive try and leap across the gang-plank but she's turned away' (*Clothes Clothes Clothes, Music Music Music, Boys Boys Boys*, 2014).

Expressing a desire to 'go back to where it all began' is all well and good, but where did it all begin, and how far back do you have to go to get there?

Where is a bit of a red herring. New York City had a head start, but it is obvious that punk would have remained a drug-drenched late flowering of the beatnik scene without Britain's contribution. If punk came from the United States, the United Kingdom was its destination; its manifest destiny. When former New York Doll Syl Sylvain failed to join the fledgling Sex Pistols, in London, Malcolm McLaren gave his white Les Paul to Steve Jones. This symbolic passing of the baton was echoed by the recruitment of Johnny Rotten in lieu of Richard Hell, who also remained on the other side of the pond. Rotten looked a hell of a lot like Hell — which is why he was auditioned in the first place — but he certainly was no lookalike, as Glen Matlock confirms: 'To this day Richard Hell thinks Johnny Rotten had nicked his look, and I can understand why, but he didn't, so it was kind of weird. Instead of having Richard Hell over from America we had Johnny Rotten from Finsbury Park.' The fact that he had developed a similar style (spiky hair and ripped clothes) was purely coincidental, proving that something must have been in the air.

Attempting to pinpoint *when* that 'something' first appeared is also a non-starter. Mark Perry realised that 'something [was] actually happening here' when the Ramones played London's Roundhouse and Dingwalls in July 1976: 'It wasn't just that one-off album.' Steve Diggle believes the Screen on the Green gig, at the end of the following month, was 'the first time where punk crystallised into this kind of movement': 'The Pistols, Clash and the Buzzcocks all played there. Siouxsie was in the audience, all dressed in a punk way. It suddenly all started to make sense. It started to take off. You could tell.' Do you go further back, to Television's early gigs at CBGB, or to the New York Dolls, or the Stooges, or right back to Dada by way of Situationism? The point of origin recedes as one approaches it.

Locating the end point of the first — authentic — stage of punk proves equally problematic. Was it when Sid Vicious lobbed a pint glass during the Damned's set, on the second night of the 100 Club Punk Festival (September 1976)? Vic Godard recalls that 'Before the 100 Club festival, punk was like a secret society. Afterwards it got hijacked by everybody.' Or was it when the Pistols, goaded by Bill Grundy, uttered some choice Chaucerian words on prime-time television (December 1976)? When the Clash signed to CBS (January 1977)? The closure of the original Roxy (April 1977)? The chaotic Silver Jubilee boat party (June 1977)? The Pistols' break-up (January 1978)? …Assuming, for the sake of argument, that punk died with Bill Grundy, the initial stage of the movement would only have lasted four months. Before August 1976, it was too small; after December, it was already too big. Blink and you miss it. 'The original punk thing ran out very quickly,' says Linder Sterling, 'but the fallout, as we know, went on and on and on. But in its initial purity, punk was probably just six months or so' (*Totally Wired*). In the now traditional tripartite retelling of the tale, punk is increasingly the squeezed middle, while the pre- and post-punk periods keep gaining ground.

The history of punk is, above all, the story of the traumatic loss of its elusive essence: that brief moment in time when a new sensibility was beginning to coalesce — sufficiently well-defined to be recognised by the cognoscenti; sufficiently amorphous to accommodate a wealth of conflicting impulses. A brief moment which may have ended, symbolically, with Jonh Ingham's 'Welcome to the (?) Rock Special' piece, published on 9 October 1976. Significantly, the article opens with a few crucial considerations on onomastics:

I was hoping to avoid mentioning the bloody word at all, but since Sounds *has so adamantly advertised this shebang as a Punk Rock special, I guess there's no avoiding it. In the context of the band [the Sex Pistols] and people mentioned in the following pages, I hate the word as much as they do.*

The debate surrounding the new movement's christening is often glossed over nowadays. McLaren, for instance, favoured 'new wave' in homage to the French cinematic *nouvelle vague* — a moniker that ended up describing punk's more commercial fellow-travellers and other bandwagon-jumpers. The fact that the noun that finally stuck (courtesy of *Melody Maker* journalist Caroline Coon) was second-hand — 'historically inaccurate,' as Ingham points out — made it all the easier to reject. To get a purchase on the new phenomenon it was necessary, at some stage, to name it, but the transaction could only be a rip-off: the word gave you punk by taking it away, replacing it with an increasingly grotesque caricature.

My contention is that punk died (or at least that something started dying or was lost) as soon as it ceased being a cult with no name — or with several possible names, which comes to the same thing. Reflecting upon Mapplethorpe's photograph of Patti Smith on the cover of *Horses* (1975), Ian Penman writes that 'One of the reasons the resulting image was so powerfully unnerving was the absence, back then, of any readymade ideological syntax with which to parse the experiment' (*London Review of Books*, 5 May 2016). When Caroline Coon asked John Lydon what punk meant, the latter replied: 'That's an open question. It always was. You can't put it into words. It's a feeling' (*Sounds*, 22 July 1978). Linder Sterling recently recalled how, upon witnessing the Pistols for the first time, she did not 'even have the language to describe what it [was]' — which is doubtless why the impact it made on her was so profound. In the beginning was the unword, when the unnamed cult remained a question mark to outsiders and insiders alike. John Peel began his first punk special show by observing that 'no two people seem to be able to agree exactly what punk rock is' (BBC Radio One, 10 December 1976). Things started going awry when everybody did agree. Punk — in its initial, pre-linguistic incarnation, when the blank in Blank Generation had not yet been filled in by that 'bloody word' — was the potentiality of punk. It escaped definition, could never be pinned down, as it was constantly in the process of becoming. Punk was a movement towards itself, made up of people who disliked movements and kept pulling in opposite directions. Devoto's brilliant parting shot, when he sabotaged the first stage of his career, springs to mind: 'I don't like music. I don't like movements.'

Michael Bracewell claims that 'one of punk's very first roles was to debate its own definition — to make internal dissent an integral part of its own identity.' Such self-reflexivity ensured that the nascent movement never quite coincided with itself. If the original spirit of punk is anywhere to be found, it is in this gap, this disjuncture — this grey area. One could even argue that punk was 'a thinking against itself,' to hijack Adorno's famous phrase: internal dissent *was* its identity. It turned its negative force against itself — alienated itself — in a bid to safeguard its otherness. Take Buzzcocks' 'Boredom' (on the *Spiral Scratch* EP, released in January 1977) which was so presciently contrary that it performed the feat of debunking punk clichés before they had even had time to become clichés. Or the self-destructive icono-clasm of *The Great Rock 'n' Roll Swindle* (1980). As with religious iconoclasm, one's relationship with punk was expressed through the destruction of its image and rejection of its name, both deemed inadequate.

A mere four years after the launch of Dada, Tristan Tzara declared that 'the real dadas' were now 'against DADA.' The real punks were also against punk, or at least the label. Being a true punk was something that could only go *without saying*; it implied never describing oneself as such (something akin to the Jewish prohibition on uttering God's name was at stake). Insiders would often claim that they listened to heavy dub reggae, krautrock, or just about anything but punk rock itself. Like Eurydice, punk could only be approached by turning away.

Punk's year-zero mentality (like all other attempts to start again from scratch) was haunted by a yearning to return to some original, prelapsarian state — back in the garage, when the cult still had no name, before they killed the fucking thing. Being born again is just that: being born *again*. Being borne back.

Punk fashion reflected this doomed quest for authenticity. The playful, postmodern plundering of rock history's wardrobe, the deconstruction and reassembly, collage and bricolage; the ambiguous semiotics and DIY aesthetics, gave way to a drab, off-the-peg uniform. The look was radicalised and codified until it finally ossified into mohicaned cliché — an evolution which mainly took place between 1978 and 1981. When Linder Sterling attended the Pistols' second gig in Manchester, there was, she says, 'an amazing sense of something incredibly new... yet still trying to take shape. Still in process.' She regrets that it soon became 'diluted and something other than itself' (*Totally Wired*). It was in fact by increasingly becoming itself that punk, paradoxically enough, lost its soul — that sense of feeling 'almost' sixteen again; of being on the cusp of an awfully big adventure.

Unreferenced quotes are frequently lifted from John Robb's excellent Punk Rock: An Oral History *(2006).*

2

Rummaging in the Ashes: An Interview with Simon Critchley

by Andrew Gallix

AG: Are you the only punk turned philosopher?

SC: No, we must be legion. We have to be. But I confess that I don't know many others. In fact, I don't know any who were punks in 1976-78. When I went to university in 1982 and in the following years, academia was still dominated by a middle-class hippie culture with a scattering of flouncy New Romantics and Cure-loving proto-goths. For me, punk was the way into whatever happened to me educationally. It opened the door, got me reading and thinking for myself. Everything I've done since can be traced back to what punk meant to me in 1976-78.

Could you tell us about your involvement in various punk bands?

It was nothing special. I had played bass guitar in bands from the time I was fifteen, in 1975. We were initially playing covers (some Bowie, Eno's 'Baby's on Fire,' even some bloody Status Quo!) and then moved into some awful imitation of progressive rock with seven-minute songs in multiple time signatures and long instrumental breaks. When punk happened, and it happened fast (I will come back to this later), we basically threw away all our old songs and I remember writing about ten songs in a weekend — all three-minute three-chord dystopian rants — and we had a new set, which we played in a pub the following week. I was the lead singer and bass player. We had all cut our hair and changed our clothes completely. I was living in what Americans would call the 'burbs,' in Letchworth and then in Hitchin, what I fondly think of as the Wasteland. As others have pointed out, punk was very much a suburban phenomenon, even though it was obsessed with the city, in a kind of grimy, alienated, J.G. Ballard way. I won't bore you with the details of the various bands I was in during my big punk years from 1976-78, except to say that they had terrible names like Rusty Crumpet, The Social Class Five, Panik (with a K, of course). There were other bands I was in, after about 1978, which were a lot better, like The Good Blokes, but that was after the initial surge of punk and things changed again and became a lot funkier. But my band did play the famous Roxy Club in Covent Garden. Sadly, we were rubbish and only about twenty people saw us.

When did you give up your bondage trousers, ten-hole DMs and Lewis leather jacket? Was that when punk died for you?

God, I could talk for ages about the daft clothes we wore, about the see-through plastic jackets, the black, shiny Smith jeans, red plastic sandals, elaborate patterns with safety pins, the mascara. I could talk about getting chased down the street repeatedly by hippies for wearing straight trousers and having dyed hair. But the get-up that you mention with the Lewis leather (of which I was very proud), along with Vivienne Westwood T-shirts from Seditionaries, was from around late 1977. I think my hair was dyed black too. Anyway, the thing that I remember was how fast fashions changed and how quickly we would all move from one look to another. We would beg, borrow or steal the clothes. But for me, the whole adventure with punk was over by mid to late 1978. I can clearly remember wearing a navy-blue Harrington jacket, straight Levi's, black Dr Martens shoes with no dye in my hair and no piercings (I took out my three earrings). Punk was over as far as I was concerned. I was listening to a lot of dub reggae and soul by that time.

In Very Little… Almost Nothing: Death, Philosophy, Literature
*(1997) you write beautifully about 'the sheer romanticism of early
punk: its pure consciousness of the moment expressed through
fragments of explosive and abusive noise, above which utopian heresies
were screamed or sneered.' Is it primarily because punk inherited the
idea — common to all avant-garde movements — that life can be transfigured through the power of the imagination, that you define it as an
avatar of Romanticism?*

The passage you are quoting from is from a long discussion of
early German Romanticism and I am trying to think through the
idea of Romanticism as our naivety, namely the idea that life,
politics and everything passes through the medium of the
aesthetic or the literary; the idea that the everyday can be transformed through a work of art, and into a work of art. And I am
trying to think about Romanticism in the context of responses to
nihilism, namely the devaluation of the highest values, the death
of God and the rest. The spectacular energy of punk, for those
early months especially, allowed us to push back against the
pressure of reality with the force of the imagination, in little
three-minute musical droplets of Wordsworthian sublimity.

*You also describe punk as 'a working through of the creative possibilities
of boredom that resist any easy translation into pleasure' and go on to
assert that 'Boredom as the self-consciousness of naïveté is the
Grundstimmung of punk.' Could you explain this?*

I am alluding to Heidegger here, for whom anxiety is the
Grundstimmung, the basic attunement that allows the world to
withdraw and fall away, and allows for the possibility of the
creative nothingness of freedom. Heidegger also talks, in the late
1920s, about 'profound boredom' as another possible basic
attunement, and I was trying to link that to the theme of boredom
that runs like a red thread through early punk, notably in the

Buzzcocks' *Spiral Scratch* and the opening track 'Boredom,' as Howard Devoto sneers. But I'm also trying to make a distinction between Situationism and punk. The debt that punk owes to Situationism is clear, especially in the manipulations of Malcolm McLaren: 'cash from chaos.' But the difference is important. Situationism was a diagnosis of the society of the spectacle that believed that liberation was possible through pleasure. As Raoul Vaneigem says, 'we have a world of pleasures to win and nothing to lose but our boredom.' Punk was different. 1977 was the inversion of the emancipatory drive of 1968. We were bored with pleasure, with the sterile hippie pleasures that had been retailed to us for the previous decade, especially sex (we were very anti-sex and thought it was reactionary – remember Johnny Rotten's remark that sex was just two minutes thirty seconds of squelching noises). We wanted to stay with boredom and use boredom as a tool for a more minimal and more overtly nihilistic form of Romantic naivety. All forms of Situationist *détournement* would always be recuperated by the music and culture industry that punk sought to subvert. But that didn't mean ceasing from all subversion, but to go on *détourning*, to go on making and listening to music, in the full awareness of the naivety of what we were doing and its limitations. We were not going to change the world and the world was rubbish anyway, just another council tenancy.

What do you make of the idea that punk was a Gesamtkunstwerk, *in which fanzines, clothes, record-sleeve artwork, members of the audience etc. were as important as the bands themselves?*

I am not the biggest fan of the idea of the *Gesamtkunstwerk*, which is always linked to a kind of nationalist aestheticism in my mind, but there is no doubt that punk was an assemblage of different media, not just music. Fanzines like *Sniffin' Glue* were vital. In fact, early on, there was not even that much to listen to: 'New

Rose' by the Damned, 'Anarchy' by the Pistols, the *Spiral Scratch* EP, then the first Clash album. The music trickled out at first and then became a flood. The trickle was much cooler.

The transformation of life into art, the abolition of the boundary between artist and audience; tropes like blankness, boredom and no future… Could punk be viewed as a kind of postmodern summation, or recycling, of all the preceding avant-garde movements? Was it perhaps even the avant-garde's last stand?

Another thing I don't like is the term postmodernism, which is a word which I've never consciously used. But I think it makes sense to see punk as a kind of exhaustion of the avant-garde. Some people have tried to tell the story of rock and roll, from the Mississippi Blues and Elvis through the Beatles and the Stones and on to punk, as a kind of an arc, where punk is already a return to what is primeval and essential about rock and roll, a kind of iconoclastic reformation movement against the decadence of Seventies progressive rock. Perhaps punk completes a cycle of popular culture that comes to an end in 1977. Perhaps this cycle is simply doomed to repeat itself. I am thinking here of hipsterism as a very conscious archiving of that cycle, within which we still move. Maybe this is why punk is still so strangely relevant and nobody cares about Barclay James Harvest.

Philosophy, you have often said, begins in (religious and political) disappointment. Could a parallel be drawn with punk, which was born of the twin failures of the consumer society (following the first oil shock) and the counterculture?

Absolutely. My idea that philosophy — by which I simply mean thinking, conceptual articulation — begins in disappointment, comes straight out of my experience with punk. We were not flower children or even revolutionaries. The 1968 dreams of liberation had been shown to result in shallow complacent hedonism. And this was also reflected in the drug culture. We didn't want to experience another world, we didn't take LSD or hallucinogens. We took speed in order to experience the degradation and flat tedium of a collapsed world with greater intensity. The only drug I ever had a problem with was speed, because it was so much fun. But it can really mess you up. Oh, and amyl nitrate was fun too. We used to buy it from sex shops in Soho (when there were still sex shops in Soho).

There was a religious fervour to punk. A spate of instant conversions occurred at early gigs: people like John Mellor (Joe Strummer) or Stuart Goddard (Adam Ant) would see the Pistols and see the light. You too experienced 1976 as 'Year zero.' When you heard the Ramones' debut, it was as though every other record you had ever listened to 'had been erased.' Two years later, there was another abrupt turning point in your life, when you almost lost a hand while working in a factory. This industrial accident erased 'big chunks' of your memory (à la John Lyndon following meningitis). You were 'wiped clean,' as you put it. It is tempting to see the latter event as an echo, or continuation, of the former. As someone who was twice born again during those years, was punk's significance this opportunity it offered to reinvent oneself and start afresh?

That's a good question. Yes, there was a kind of iconoclasm to punk, a fundamentalism almost. It was like a Protestant Reformation without God; what I called later 'atheist transcendence.' We wanted to see reality for what it was in all its ugliness (the high-rise car parks, the council estates, the tedium of television) and tear away the decadence and fallenness of the culture industry that surrounded us. Yes, hearing the Ramones' first album late one night at a friend's house was a Year Zero moment. Everything else seemed irrelevant. Apart from the three bands who everyone was suddenly listening to independently, but somehow at the same time: the MC5, Iggy and the Stooges and the Velvet Underground. I remember finding the Stooges' second album, *Fun House*, late in the summer of 1976. Our keyboardist found the Velvet Underground's first album, and the guitarist found the MC5's *Kick out the Jams*. The only other thing that survived was Bowie. Always Bowie.

About the industrial accident that 'the Critchley character' talks about in *Memory Theatre*: that happened in September 1978 when I was eighteen years old and it was a total memory wipe, from which I've never really recovered. I was listening to Jilted John on the factory radio when it happened. It felt like I'd been wiped out, physically and mentally. I mean, it was awful. But the accident also gave me a lot of spare head space to fill with books and songs and other imaginings. The effect of trauma is a feeling that everything is unreal, a kind of a fake. That feeling has never left me.

Brian Dillon describes the surface of Robert Rauschenberg's Erased de Kooning Drawing *(1953) as being 'startlingly alive, active, palimpsestic.' Is punk's richness also due, in part, to its palimpsestic quality — to the fact that its myriad influences shine through despite the attempt to wipe the slate clean?*

Sure, that makes sense. Punk was about the erasure of the dominant, dinosaur-rock environment. It was about wiping that away. But what was revealed was another, complex palimpsest of musical influences, like the MC5. But also — importantly, although we didn't really even realise it at the time — punk was all about race and racism. We were implicitly revolting against the racism of white dinosaur rock: idiots like Eric Clapton. This became explicit in Rock Against Racism and the Anti-Nazi League (I used to go on their marches). My first experience in a non-white environment was through punk, where we would go to reggae sound-system parties and usually be the only white boys there. Somehow, being a punk meant that we were seen as being all right, acceptable. Bob Marley popularised this movement with his 'Punky Reggae Party.' In a sense, there is nothing whiter than punk, but it opened up new possibilities in listening to black music, the kind of thing that I simply didn't have access to before punk happened.

If we leave aside punk's enduring legacy, the original movement had nowhere to go — no future. Going forward meant that it would no longer be an event, just another collection of professional rock bands. As a result, punk was backward-looking, like Walter Benjamin's angel of history; haunted by the nebulous primal scene of its own creation. Each new wave of bands sought out this point of origin: punk prior to its negation by language, when the cult with no name (or several names) was still in the process of becoming. The moment when memory's exile would come to an end and literally take place. *The moment that would coincide with the moment. 'The now of nows,' as you write in* Memory Theatre *(2014).*

During a conversation you had with novelist Tom McCarthy, the latter explained that in cases of trauma, the brain often fails to integrate the traumatic event into memory's narrative thread: 'That gap, or absence, that few seconds of silence on the tape, become real; since everything else that is on the tape is fake, that gap must be real' (How to Stop Living and Start Worrying, *2010). Is the search for punk's 'now of nows' — those weeks or months that everybody missed — akin to 'that few seconds of silence on the tape'?*

I think that's a great thought. My industrial accident was like that gap, when reality sliced through everything, metal through flesh, making everything suddenly seem fake. Punk was like Benjamin's angel of history with a prohibition on the future because there was no future, as the Pistols said. The past was a new palimpsest of possibilities in the process of emergence, the creation of some new idea of heritage, and punk was devoted to that now of nows when one would be lifted up and out of the everyday in order to see it all more clearly, with greater intensity and lucidity. Punk was lucid, it always seemed to me.

Central to your philosophical work is a critique of the notion of authenticity. I wonder how that applies to the punk days when street credibility was so important and being called a poser was, as you have pointed out, the 'highest form of abuse'?

Absolutely, the worst thing one could be was a poser. Everyone feared that. But I don't think punk was about authenticity. It was about exposing the layers and layers of inauthenticity that make art possible. That was the Warholian element in punk. But — and this is important to me — punk was about an experience of truth, of felt, heard truth, that was made possible through inauthenticity, mediation and fakery. This is something that I tried to write about in my little book on Bowie, namely that his music is inauthentic all the way down. It is a series of borrowings, a series of acts of ventriloquism through the adoption of multiple personae. But this is the only way in which truth can be heard. Indirectly, as it were. I really think that authenticity is the great curse of popular music. It is a question of liberating ourselves from the ideology of authenticity in the name of a felt and heard truth.

In the International Necronautical Society's 'Declaration on the Notion of "The Future"' (2010), you declared: 'We resist this ideology of the future, in the name of the sheer radical potentiality of the past, and of the way the past can shape the creative impulses and imaginative landscape of the present. The future of thinking is its past, a thinking which turns its back on the future.' What do you make — particularly in the context of the commemoration of punk's fortieth anniversary — of the almost universal knee-jerk reaction against nostalgia? As though nostalgia were some sort of conservative crime against the future and progress. As though we could have had The Odyssey *or Proust without it…*

Although my good pal Tom McCarthy was too young to be a punk, in my mind the INS was a project that was completely consistent with the punk aesthetic, especially as that was filtered through figures like Genesis P-Orridge and Throbbing Gristle and their inspired assault on culture. Obviously, Stewart Home — who was a punk — was a direct influence on the INS. About nostalgia, I hate it, but it is unavoidable and I get whimsical when I think back to the punk years and how everything suddenly became possible. Bliss was it to be alive at that time and to be young was very heaven. But the message of punk is very simple: anyone can do it. The basic point that punk was making was that anyone could form a band, write songs, play instruments (even badly) and go out and perform and make a statement, articulate a musical proposition. It was a beautifully uncomplicated experience. You would just put your gear in a van and go and find a gig and play for beer. We did that one night in Luton and met Gary Numan, wearing Turquoise boots — what an idiot!

A mere two years after publishing his 'Dada Manifesto' (1918), Tristan Tzara declared, 'the real dadas are against DADA.' It seems to me that, in similar (anti-)fashion, the real punks turned against punk as soon as the phenomenon started coinciding with itself, thus becoming instantly recognisable. I'm thinking of the way punk (at its best) turned its negative force against itself — alienated itself — in a bid to safeguard its otherness: Buzzcocks' prescient debunking of punk clichés ('Boredom'), for instance, or the self-destructive iconoclasm of The Great Rock 'n' Roll Swindle. *From this perspective, could punk be viewed as 'a thinking against itself'?*

Like I said already, punk did not last very long. For me, it lasted about eighteen months and there were so many changes in that time alone. Because of the acute awareness of the fact that punk would eat itself, as it were, that it would become a creature of the very music industry whose codes it subverted, we knew that it was going to be short-lived. And that was fine. It was only after the initial impetus behind punk had died that people started to defend the idea of true, authentic punk. This completely missed the point. In fact, the punk bands that I liked were always a bit crap and didn't last, like the Vibrators or the Radiators From Space or Johnny Moped or the Lurkers. Punk fed on its own energy and expired like a firefly. It was beautiful.

I remember Jordan pointing out in The Face — *this must have been in 1981 — that the Exploited's then ubiquitous 'Punk's Not Dead' slogan (itself a response to Crass's 'Punk is Dead') was self-defeating. The more leather jackets it adorned, the more it proved that punk* was *dead. Only it was not, not completely: it was dying, and in a way it has been dying ever since. It might be useful, at this juncture, to hijack Maurice Blanchot's distinction between* la mort *(death) and* le mourir *(dying), which you have defined as 'the impossibility of death'; 'being riveted to existence without an exit.' Joe Corré's recent decision to burn his punk memorabilia — worth an estimated £5m — in protest at the phenomenon being treated like a 'fucking museum piece' is, in my view, the latest example of punk's* mourir. *The irony of Punk London being supported by Boris Johnson will be lost on no one, of course, but isn't it important, if we want to pay homage to what punk once was — when it was truly alive — to accept that it is no more?*

Maybe punk was always dead, always already playing in the ruins of an essentially dead culture, trying to flog a dead horse. But it was a lively death, and we had a lot of fun rummaging in the ashes and blowing on one or two embers to heat them up. I must say that I find the idea of the commemoration of punk particularly distasteful, and that punk can be archived and celebrated in museums pretty awful. That said, I think that punk marked a beginning point for a sequence of possibilities and movements in popular culture that continues to this day. The basic credo of punk is autonomy, as the Buzzcocks sang on their first album. You can do this, anyone can do this. It's a beautifully simple DIY aesthetic which I think can be traced through a whole series of pop-cultural movements, from early hip-hop, to acid house and the Nineties dance scene, right through to overeducated Brooklyn hipsters fiddling at their laptops.

When we talk about punk, we are, I feel, increasingly commemorating its past commemorations — a tired narrative at odds with the excitement and sense of adventure we felt at the time. How could we defamiliarise punk — see 'ourselves as strangers' once again? How could we tap into the 'sheer radical potentiality of [punk's] past' and experience it as an event?

I think it is simply a question of keeping one's ears open, listening to new stuff all the time and not lecturing young people about how great it was to be alive in the late 1970s. I try not to do that (and probably fail). One thing I have consistently tried to do is to listen to new music and not dwell on the past. I am constantly being fed music by friends and acquaintances and I remain stubbornly optimistic about what music can do and what music can mean. Maybe that's my version of nostalgia. When Bowie died early in 2016, I got asked to do a lot of interviews and stuff because I'd written a little book on Bowie that was really a fan's book, written from a fan's perspective. It was really sad that Bowie died, but what was brilliant was meeting a good number of younger people for whom Bowie meant as much as he did for me. It just doesn't matter that they weren't there in the 1970s. I feel the same way about punk. There is something transmissible about it that defies the dead hand of commemoration.

Does your interest in anarchism — most obvious in Infinitely

Demanding: Ethics of Commitment, Politics of Resistance *(2007)* *and* The Faith of the Faithless: Experiments in Political Theology *(2012) — originate in punk? Did you find an echo of punk at the University of Essex and in Deconstruction* (The Ethics of Deconstruction, *1992)?*

Yes, absolutely. Everything goes back to that punk moment for me, of being wiped clean and beginning again. The bands I played in were a lot of fun and we tried really hard. But we never made it and that's fine. We weren't good enough. I was really lucky to have the chance to translate what I was doing with music into the discipline of words and the world of philosophy. Luckily, because I didn't have to pay fees and my mother was pretty poor, I got to go to university for free and read a lot of books. I learned to try to sublimate what was happening to me in music into words. But it all flows from the same place. Punk is about that moment of refusal and revolt when you see the world for what it is and try and do something, make something, make something resound and sound; maybe even make something shatter and break. This is the romantic naivety of punk, which I would still defend. I still think this is possible, in music, in politics, in writing and thinking. Maybe I'm hopelessly deluded, but there is something about a punk attitude that is incredibly important. I'm always looking for it in the eyes of the people I meet: a spirit of defiance, refusal and vertiginous, dizzying freedom. I see it a lot.

3

King Mob Echo

by Tom Vague

The semi-mythical origin, hidden history and philosophy of punk rock can be traced back to the Situationist International, a political art movement that came to prominence in the May 1968 events in Paris, largely via the Sex Pistols' manager Malcolm McLaren and the designer Jamie Reid — and through them to the Gordon Riots of 1780. The connection was first made in *Sex Pistols: The Inside Story* by Fred Vermorel, with the postscript: 'If the Sex Pistols stemmed from the Situationist International, their particular twist of radical flash and burlesque rage was also mediated through a band of hooligan pedants based in the Notting Hill Gate area of London. This was King Mob.'

The King Mob group members Dave and Stuart Wise duly elaborated, in their pamphlet *The End of Music — Punk, Reggae: A critique*, that

> part of the genesis of punk goes back to the English section of the Situationists and the subsequent King Mob – a loose affiliation (hardly a group) of disparate though confused revolutionary individuals in England in 1968. King Mob lauded and practised active nihilism... Better to be horrible than a pleasant altruistic hippy. As a kind of undialectical over-reaction to hippy, Chris Gray had the idea of creating a totally unpleasant pop group — those first imaginings which were later to fuse into the Sex Pistols and a spoof, hip, in depth, sociological report of utter degeneration in the subcultural milieu to be published by Penguin books and then exposed for the farce it was.

Before the Situationists there were the Lettrists, who pioneered psychogeography, drifting around Paris in slogan-daubed clothes in the early Fifties. The first British Lettrist/Situationist was the Scottish-Italian Beat writer Alex Trocchi, the author of *Young Adam* and *Cain's Book*. When the Situationist International was founded in 1957 the only British member was the artist Ralph Rumney — representing his London Psychogeography Association in the Italian section. Rumney was one of the first members to be excluded, for taking too long to complete his psychogeography report on Venice. He later married Michele Bernstein, Debord's ex, who ended up living in Salisbury and related to punk more than the other Situationists. In the mid-Sixties Trocchi became a key figure in the burgeoning hippy counterculture, and started to depart from the SI party line as he launched his Project Sigma, 'based on the Manifeste Situationiste.' As Trocchi was excluded, his beatnik/hippy take on Situationist theory was superseded by the short-lived English Section of the SI, consisting of Chris Gray, Tim Clarke, Donald Nicholson-Smith and Charles Radcliffe. Gray published the first English translation of an SI text, Raul Vaneigem's *Basic Banalities* as *The Totality for the Kids*, while Radcliffe edited *Heatwave* magazine, featuring 'The Seeds of Social Destruction' youth revolt round-up of Teddy Boys, ton-up kids, Beats, ban-the-bombers, ravers, mods and rockers. Debord's definitive Situationist text *The Society of the Spectacle* was followed up in 1967 by Raoul Vaneigem's *The Revolution of Everyday Life*.

The King Mob group formed out of the English Section of the SI — who were expelled from the Paris-based radical intellectual group for attempting to communicate Situationist theory 'in a more hip streetwise style.' Fred Vermorel has a funnier but less believable version of the Anglo-French split in the SI:

In an idle moment, Chris boasted he could call on at least 30 trained and combat-hardened street fighters in the Ladbroke Grove area

42

alone. Hearing of this exciting development, Guy Debord rushed across the channel to inspect the troops. He was directed by an embarrassed Chris to the home of one Dave Wise and bursting in discovered Dave lying on a sofa watching Match of the Day *with a can of McEwan's Export. Such idle truck with the state's one-way communication system (ie. Dave's 6-inch telly) annoyed Debord, who became furious when Dave informed him that his guerrilla combat unit was him and his brother Stuart. Denouncing Dave's modest library as ideologically suspect and throwing books all over Dave's flat, Debord raged back to Paris.*

Vermorel claimed to be a card-carrying Situationist, as the International became defunct in 1972, and to have introduced Malcolm McLaren to their ideas.

Before the May 1968 events in Paris, the leading English Situationist Chris Gray launched the *King Mob Echo* underground paper, with an accompanying graffiti campaign and 'King Mob guerrilla theatre' Situationist stunts, including the storming of Powis Square Gardens and a fake Father Christmas giving away presents at Selfridges.

King Mob was a reference to the Gordon Riots of 1780, when the revolutionary London mob burned down Newgate prison, nine years before the storming of the Bastille. The post-Situationist group took the name from the *King Mob* book by Christopher Hibbert, subtitled *The Story of Lord George Gordon and the Riots of 1780*, published in 1958. John Nicholson, the author of *The Great Liberty Riot of 1780*, refers to 'King Mob of Georgian England,' encompassing all of the Georgian period.

When I was compiling the *King Mob Echo* Dark Star books, Chris Gray told us: 'I didn't quite understand what it is you've sent me. Is this one book or two? Because, if it's meant to be just one book, there seems to be undue stress on the Gordon Riots, whose link with the Situationists is tenuous to say the least of it.' However, I think the connection was established by Malcolm

McLaren and Jamie Reid developing Chris Gray's idea in punk rock. The 18th-century roots of punk are clear in that time of more or less permanent riots, risings and revolutions — if we choose to see punk in a riotous mode — depicted by Hogarth and Dickens in his Gordon Riots novel *Barnaby Rudge*. The riots are named after Lord George Gordon and were ostensibly against the Catholic Relief Bill. As the Gordon Riots developed a revolutionary dynamic independent of the Protestant cause, all the prisons of London, Catholic chapels, gin distilleries and hundreds of houses were destroyed. In the most notorious incident, the mob stormed Newgate prison on the site of the Old Bailey. In Christopher Hibbert's *King Mob* book, the destruction was led by punk-rock time-bandits:

Many of these figures could be seen standing perilously, in postures of arrogant, abandoned recklessness, on ledges, the tops of walls and astride window-sills on those parts of the building not yet too hot to touch. Now hidden by gusts of sulphurous smoke, now brightly lit in a cascade of sparks, they shouted obscenities at each other and made vulgar gestures as they urinated into the flames.

Two centuries later, in an interview for a King Mob feature in *Dazed & Confused* magazine, Malcolm McLaren didn't need much encouragement to portray the Situationists as the 1968 equivalent of the 'well-dressed men,' said to have been behind the Gordon Riots:

They used to hand out copies of the King Mob Echo *at Vietnam demonstrations, marches, where there used to be such a motley crew of students but there was always this set that seemed to be so much better dressed than all the others and they became known as the English Situationists and later King Mob. In demonstrations they definitely stood out as the dandies of the revolution.*

At the first Vietnam War demo in London, the King Mob contingent were renowned for disrupting the Trotskyite chant of 'Ho, Ho, Ho Chi Minh,' with 'Hot chocolate, drinking chocolate.' The first issue of the *King Mob Echo* paper came out in April 1968, before it all kicked off in Paris. After the cover of *International Times* 26 featured the Situationist comic-strip 'In our Spectacular Society,' *IT* 30 — the Notting Hill 'Interzone' issue — was illustrated with King Mob graffiti.

In Notting Hill, an 'Open the Squares' demo was diverted by King Mob members, disguised as pantomime animals, towards the Powis Square gardens, thus bringing about the occupation of the area as a community space. *IT* 41 featured their 'Notting Hell' flyer for a campaign in defence of the Powis Square Six, who were charged with causing 'malicious damage' to the gardens' gates. As Russian tanks crushed the Czechoslovakian uprising, King Mob twinned Powis Square with Prague's Wenceslas Square and made an appeal that sounds like a punk-rock gig: 'Powis (Wenceslas) Square in Notting Hell for the Devils Party — the Damned, the Sick, the Screwed, the Despised, the Thugs, the Drop-outs, the Scared, the Witches, the Workers, the Demons, the Old — give us a hand, otherwise we've had it.'

The 1968 writing on the walls of Notting Hill, largely attributed to King Mob, included: William Blake's 'The tigers [tygers] of wrath are wiser than the horses of instruction'; 'The road of excess leads to the palace of wisdom [changed to 'Willesden']'; Coleridge's 'A grief without a pang, void, dark, dreer, a stifled, drowsy unimpassioned greif [sic]' from 'Ode to Dejection'; 'All you need is dynamite'; 'Burn it all down'; 'Dynamite is freedom'; 'Belsen lives'; 'Religion = Opium'; 'God is dead'; 'Kars kill'; 'The only race is the rat race'; 'Revolution Now'; 'Rachman was right'; 'Christie lives'; and 'Viet Grove.' Most famously, hoardings alongside the Tube line between Ladbroke Grove and Westbourne Park were sprayed with: 'Same thing day after day — Tube — Work — Diner [sic] — Work —

Tube — Armchair — TV — Sleep — Tube — Work — How much more can you take — One in ten go mad — One in five cracks up.'

After the attempted assassination of Andy Warhol by the radical performance artist Valerie Solanas, King Mob issued their own hit list in solidarity, featuring Mick Jagger, Marianne Faithfull, David Hockney, Miles and Twiggy. Malcolm McLaren said he was particularly inspired by their attacks on a Wimpy burger bar on Ladbroke Grove. At Christmas 1968, in their most famous Situationist stunt, the group occupied the toy department of Selfridges department store on Oxford Street. One of them, dressed in a red coat and white beard, proceeded to give away presents to children, until the staff were forced to requisition the gifts. The stunt was inspired by New York's Black Mask 'mill-in at Macy's' in 1967 and re-enacted by McLaren in *The Ghosts of Oxford Street* film. King Mob also presented a 'Miss Notting Hill 69' carnival float, featuring a girl with a giant syringe attached to her arm, and removed the security gates at the LSE sit-in.

The former Situationist Charlie Radcliffe turned up again as the 'official political advisor' on Jefferson Airplane's *Volunteers* album, featuring the New York Motherfuckers' manifesto: 'We are everything they say we are and we are proud of it. We are obscene, lawless, hideous, dangerous, dirty, violent and young.' In the early Seventies, Radcliffe wrote for the underground paper *Friends* on Portobello Road, where he became involved with the late dope smuggler Howard Marks. In 1972, an attempt was made to put Chris Gary's 'totally unpleasant pop group' idea into practise by Marks and Dennis Irving, who set up Lucifer Records to release songs entitled 'Fuck You' and 'Prick.'

At the same time, King Mob (the Situationist group and the Gordon Riots book) inspired Malcolm McLaren and Jamie Reid's art-college film project, *The History of Oxford Street*. The first treatment featured the pop-Situationist Gordon Riots synopsis: 'The middle class started it against the Catholics. Then hundreds of shopkeepers, carpenters, servants, soldiers and sailors rushed into the streets. There were only a few Catholic houses to smash so they started to smash all the rich houses.' According to Jamie Reid:

> We didn't have the techniques or the skills to pull it off, but it was potentially a very interesting project and gave us our first taste of an idea we later developed with the Sex Pistols. The result of the Gordon riots was that afterwards Oxford Street was redesigned in such a way as to prevent the populace getting easy access into the important parts of the City.

Reid also co-founded the Suburban Press pro-Situationist underground paper in Croydon, where he said, 'My job, graphically, was to simplify a lot of the political jargon... Even though it's hung round my neck ever since, I was never involved with the Situationists to the fullest extent because I couldn't understand half of what they had written.' Meanwhile, back in the States, the pro-Situationist Point Blank group produced a pamphlet called *Space Travel: an Official Guide for San Francisco Commuters*, featuring 'Nowhere' buses as a *détournement* of the 1964 Merry Pranksters' 'Further' bus trip. Jamie Reid recalled that the buses' artwork was 'printed up by Suburban Press as a poster in 1973 and sent to Point Blank.' Suburban Press were also responsible for 'This store welcomes shoplifters,' for an Oxford Street sticker campaign.

After the Angry Brigade blew up the Biba boutique on Kensington Church Street in 1971, Malcolm McLaren paradoxically opened his own clothes shop, Let It Rock at 430 King's Road, with Vivienne Westwood. In 1974, the shop became SEX, although one name mooted had been Modernity Killed Every Night — a phrase used by the Surrealist Jacques Vaché (a Johnny Rotten-esque figure) in his *War Letters* to André Breton, quoted in the King Mob 'Art schools are dead' leaflet and published in the Wise brothers' *Icteric* magazine. Vaché also came up with:

'Knowing that there is no future that is possible or desirable, I experience the solace one feels in going back to sleep when the alarm clock has sounded.' Another shop-name idea was the porn-magazine quote: 'The Dirty Stripper who left her undies on the railings to go hitch-hiking said you don't think I have stripped off all these years just for money do you?' The foam walls were sprayed with lines from Alex Trocchi's porn novel *School for Wives*, the pro-Situationist 'What counts now is to get out of the suburbs as fast as you possibly can,' 'Does passion end in fashion?' and Rousseau's 'Craft must have clothes but truth loves to go naked.' In the window there were sketches of Lettrists wearing slogan-daubed trousers in early-Fifties Paris.

1974 also saw the publication of *Leaving the 20th Century: The Incomplete Works of the Situationist International* by Chris Gray, assisted and helped by the Wicked Messengers and Suburban Press. Jamie Reid, who did some of the graphics, has said, 'I never really read it, but I loved the one-liners, like the corpse metaphor.' Although it was by far the most accessible Situationist publication, sales of the original edition were slow until the punk connection was made in 1977. McLaren and Westwood proceeded to relaunch 430 King's Road as SEX, using *Leaving the 20th Century* as their blueprint for punk rock. The Situationist technique of *détournement* was utilised to transform Let It Rock clothes into pro-Situ salon couture: Wembley rock 'n' roll T-shirts were customised by over-dying and the addition of rips, zips, studs and clear-plastic pockets, containing nude women playing cards with SI/May 68 slogans, echoing/recuperating 'Ten Days that Shook the University,' and Fifties silk ties had confrontational slogans like 'Lesbian' printed on them.

British punk rock was inaugurated with the first SEX T-shirt, designed by McLaren, Westwood and the future Clash manager Bernie Rhodes: 'You're gonna wake up one morning and know what side of the bed you've been lying on!' This amounted to an updated *King Mob Echo* pop stars and artists hit list, also including the Angry Brigade targets Robert Carr and Biba (or a Seventies version of Wyndham Lewis's Vorticist *Blast*). The pro side featured the first mention of 'Kutie Jones and his Sex Pistols,' as well as Valerie Solanas and her 'Society for Cutting Up Men,' Ronnie Biggs, Jamaican rude boys, Point Blank, Buenoventura Durutti (spelt wrong), the Black Hand Gang, Alex Trocchi's *Young Adam* and Olympia Press.

In late 1974 McLaren went to the States to relaunch the New York Dolls with a pro-Situ motto/manifesto — 'What are the politics of boredom? Better red than dead' — and attempted to get Richard Hell of Television to front the Steve Jones band. As the Sex Pistols came together in the SEX shop, McLaren and Westwood produced increasingly confrontational T-shirt prints, featuring Trocchi's 'groaned with pain' quote from *School for Wives*, images of a boy from a paedophile magazine, a naked black footballer, the 'Cambridge rapist' mask, tits, and the 'after Tom of Finland' cowboys. Following the arrest of the SEX shop assistant Alan Jones for wearing the cowboys T-shirt, the shop was raided and McLaren and Westwood fined for 'exposing to public view an indecent exhibition.' At the same time, in the summer of 1975, a SEX Karl Marx patch shirt was exhibited at the ICA, the Pistols' ransom-note lettering was devised, bondage trousers were invented and the suitably Dickensian-looking John Lydon became Johnny Rotten.

As the Pistols rehearsed on Denmark Street, on the site of the St Giles rookery, and played a lot of their early gigs in the Gordon Riots zone, Chris Gray's 'unpleasant pop group' idea was perfected, channelling King Mob's 'twist of radical flash and burlesque rage.' Or, as the Wise brothers saw it, 'a musical situationism was born in dressed up rebel imagery.' Sid Vicious invented the pogo at the 100 Club on Oxford Street, echoing Maypole Hugh's 'no popery dance' of 'a rather extreme and violent nature' in Dickens's *Barnaby Rudge*. Jah Wobble and Shane MacGowan also assumed Dickensian roles.

For Vivienne Westwood's classic couturier situationniste creation, the 'Anarchy' shirt, old Let It Rock stock round pin-hole collar shirts (as worn by Lenin) were turned inside out, dyed with concentration camp-style stripes and stencilled with Situationist/May 68 slogans — 'Only anarchists are pretty' (from Point Blank), 'Be realistic demand the impossible,' 'Prenez vos désirs pour la réalité,' 'A bas le Coca Cola' — then accessorised with Karl Marx and inverted swastika eagle patches and 'Chaos' armbands. Couturier situationniste Malcolm McLaren subsequently presented the Sex Pistols to Paris, where they played the Chalet du Lac club, with Johnny Rotten as a bondage-suited reincarnation of Fantomas — a still from Louis Feuillade's 1913 film had featured on a cover of *King Mob Echo*.

In *England's Dreaming*, Jon Savage writes of a Situationist cabal at the SEX shop. Fred Vermorel, in an interview with this book's co-editor Richard Cabut for *Zigzag* magazine, claimed that: 'The whole Pistols thing was basically a Marxist conspiracy, which sounds ridiculous but that's what it was. You had Jamie Reid, Sophie Richmond and Malcolm sitting around talking radical politics, about how to radicalise this and that, how far can we go with this and that.' In 'The End of Music,' the Wise brothers described Reid and Richmond as 'two pro-Situs' who 'became roadies for the Sex Pistols,' adding that 'Rotten and co were fed lyrics from these formidable sources now on the side of reaction' (also referring to Fred Vermorel).

After the Pistols played at the 100 Club on Oxford Street, they signed to EMI in Manchester Square at the western end (around the corner from Lord George Gordon's house on Welbeck Street), and the office of McLaren's Glitterbest management company was at the eastern end in Dryden Chambers. As the first Pistols' single 'Anarchy in the UK' was promoted with Jamie Reid's *détournement* of a Union Jack flag with rips, safety pins and press-clipped blackmail lettering, the accompanying fanzine featured: 'Anarchy needs co-ordination, Where is Durruti? and his Black

Hand Gang,' pistol/bank note and 'Army Careers' illustrations from Suburban Press/*Leaving the 20th Century* and the Point Blank 'Nowhere' buses.

In 1977 SEX was renamed Seditionaries, with a new Situationist-influenced design by Ben Kelly, featuring blown-up photos of Dresden being bombed and Piccadilly Eros upside down, and a Biba-style bomb hole in the ceiling. Vivienne Westwood entered her most radical phase, creating tartan bondage trousers, Spiderman jackets and parachute shirts. She laid out the Seditionaries urban guerrilla manifesto in the muslin 'Destroy' shirt: swastika, inverted cross, decapitated Queen's-head stamp montage and 'Anarchy in the UK' lyrics. (As Jon Savage put it, 'Surrounded by the same Situationist rhetoric that had led Detective Inspector Habershon to the Angry Brigade, the Sex Pistols seemed to be urban guerrillas themselves; unpredictable, deeply destructive, everywhere.')

Around this time, Malcolm McLaren is said to have been told that Guy Debord wanted to meet him in a Chelsea pub. The Pistols' tour manager Nils Stevenson recalled that he returned from meeting a French representative of Debord, saying it was one of the worst things he had ever been through. In his *Vacant* memoir, Stevenson used Karl Marx's 'events and personages occur twice, the first time as tragedy, the second time as farce,' to illustrate the connection between Chris Gray and McLaren: 'Gray's proto-punk impulse was tragic in the sense that while he articulated it and understood its power, he didn't or couldn't do it. And Malcolm's later attempt to carry it out was farcical because he never realised that the Sex Pistols could play and were in fact rather good.'

The sleeve of the Pistols' second single 'God Save the Queen' featured Jamie Reid's classic *détournement* of Cecil Beaton's portrait of the Queen, as the bandaged head with safety-pin Atelier Populaire poster from Paris May 68. At the time of the Queen's silver jubilee, Malcolm McLaren as Lord George Gordon was arrested after the Pistols' Thames boat trip alongside the Houses of Parliament, as radical well-dressed men in Westwood clothes were attacked by the pro-Queen mob.

For the third Pistols' single, 'Pretty Vacant,' Jamie Reid reused the 'Nowhere buses' from the American Situationist Point Blank pamphlet, with one changed to 'Boredom.' The artwork for the fourth single, 'Holidays in the Sun,' was a Belgian tourism brochure comic-strip *détournement*, but that was scrapped after legal action and replaced by a holiday beach picture and 'Nice Drawing' from *Leaving the 20th Century*, along with the Suburban Press slogan, 'Keep warm this winter make trouble.' According to the first Situationist mention in *NME*: 'The back sleeve illustration, by the way (also scrapped, since "Holidays" is now going out in a plain white wrapper), depicting a nice middle-class family at luncheon, was based on a late-Sixties pamphlet put out by the International Situationists — a bunch of French radical loonies (or not) whose credo was permanent revolution.'

The Gordon Riots punk connection was further established in the 'Oliver Twist manifesto' flyer for the last Sex Pistols gig in England at Christmas 77, featuring a street urchin sketch by Charles Dickens's illustrator George Cruikshank and a scrawled missive, paraphrasing 'Now the Situationist International' in *IS 9* via Chris Gray's *Leaving the 20th Century*:

While contemporary impotence rambles on about the belated project of 'getting into the 20th century,' we think it is time to put an end to the dead time which has dominated this century, and to finish the Christian era with the same stroke. Here, as elsewhere, it's about breaking the bounds of measurement. Ours is the best effort so far to get out of the 20th century.

After the *Never Mind the Bollocks, Here's the Sex Pistols* album featured the 'EMI' track, with 'Don't judge a book just by the cover, unless you cover just another' line from Suburban Press, the working title of the Pistols film *Who Killed Bambi?* came from a Suburban Press image using a newspaper report of jewel thieves killing a poodle called Bambi. As the punk-rock revolution ended, McLaren and Reid set about producing their version of Chris Gray's 'spoof, hip, in depth, sociological report of utter degeneration in the sub-cultural milieu' — *The Great Rock 'n' Roll Swindle* film and album. The first post-Pistols 'Swindle' single, 'No One is Innocent,' echoed the 1890s bomber Ravachol, on being sentenced to death for bombing a bourgeois cafe, which was taken up by fellow anarchist Emile Henry.

The posthumous Sid Vicious single 'C'mon Everybody' came in a 'Vicious-Burger' sleeve, referring to Raoul Vaneigem's corpse metaphor ('People who talk about revolution and class struggle without referring explicitly to everyday life, without under-standing what is subversive about love and what is positive in the refusal of constraints, such people have a corpse in their mouth'). On the back cover the 'Rot'n'Roll' manifesto accompanied a Gordon Riots reenactment still from the *Swindle* film. The 'Friends of Vicious' T-shirt featured a black hand-mark reference to the Black Hand Gang, and the 'Vive Le Rock' shirt (from the Wembley rock 'n' roll festival) was accessorised with pro-Situ slogans: 'We are not in the least afraid of ruins — Buenaventura Durruti,' *The Anarchist Cookbook*, 'The Famous Molotov' and 'Ours is the best effort so far to leave the 20th century in order to join the punk rock disco.'

The Great Rock 'n' Roll Swindle film came out in 1980, on the two hundredth anniversary of the Gordon Riots, opening with Malcolm McLaren in rubber black mask as Fantomas from the cover of *King Mob Echo*. In a flashback to '1780: The Gordon Riots — The London mob created Anarchy in the UK,' effigies of the Pistols, guitars and paraphernalia were burnt by a New-Romantic mob, as McLaren, dressed as Lord George in a red tartan bondage suit, destroyed evidence that he was behind it. 'Swindle' products sold in the cinema foyer included Sex Pistols popcorn, Rotten bars, Gob ale, Anarkee-ora and Piss-lemonade, echoing the *King Mob Echo* 2 beer-bottle label. Jamie Reid was disappointed that the film didn't contain more Gordon Riots material as was originally intended. The Pistols' pro-Situationist designer commented, 'As far as I'm concerned, I thought the best Sex Pistols product was *The Great Rock 'n' Roll Swindle*. I think in a way we jumped too far ahead of ourselves. It was meant to be a loud and blatant statement about consumerism and who buys pop records and what a pop group is — just a factory churning out things for people to buy.'

4

Glam into Punk: The Transition

by Barney Hoskyns

By late 1975, New York was poised on the brink of punk rock, with Johnny Thunders' band the Heartbreakers already formed and a new undercurrent of groups dispensing with almost all traces of glam. Prominent among them were the Ramones. 'I can remember we were rehearsing and they were down the hall, they hadn't played yet,' recalls the New York Dolls' David Johansen. 'We told them, "Oh, God, you guys suck so bad, forget about it!" But I was like that with everybody. I'd say to Chris Frantz, "You're really a nice kid, you should get into some kind of business." I'd say, "With that guy singin', you're not gonna get anywhere." So what do I know?'

'Glitter rock was about decadence — platform shoes and boys in eye make-up, David Bowie and androgyny,' Legs McNeil wrote in *Please Kill Me!* '[It was about] rich rock stars living their lives from Christopher Isherwood's Berlin stories. You know, Sally Bowles hanging out with drag queens, drinking champagne for breakfast and having *ménages à trois* while the Nazis slowly grab the power.' Compared to what was happening in the real world, McNeil argued, 'decadence seemed kind of quaint.' Punk wasn't about decay, it was about apocalypse now.

In some senses, this was too simplistic. While Dick Hebdidge was right in his *Subculture* to argue that 'The punk aesthetic... can be read as an attempt to expose glam rock's implicit contradictions' — and that 'the "working classness"... of punk ran directly counter to the arrogance, elegance and verbosity of the glam-rock superstars' — even he conceded that the dog collars and bondage tartan trousers were really just another set of costumes, a kind of inverted dandyism through self-defilement. 'Punk thus represents a deliberately scrawled addendum to the "text" of glam rock,' Hebdidge concluded, 'one designed to puncture glam rock's extravagantly ornate style.' Punk, in a nutshell, was glam ripping itself apart.

Even the Ramones were descended directly from glam. 'I was into dressing up in my own style,' says Joey Ramone (a.k.a. Jeffrey Hyman), who sang in a Queens glam band called Sniper. 'I had a black satin jumpsuit made of stretch material with a bullet chain hanging around the groin with the zipper open, and elbow-length black leather gloves and a chain. I had pink-lavender boots with six-inch platform heels, a leather jacket, black sunglasses, long hair. It was pretty androgynous, but in those days you could let go. Still, a lot of people wanted to kill me.'

'Joey really got into the glitter thing,' recalled his brother, Mickey. 'He was stealing all my mother's jewellery, her clothes, her make-up and her scarves. I thought it was great that Joey was in a band, but it was really dangerous to hitchhike down Queens Boulevard looking the way he did. In platform boots he was over seven feet tall.' Joey did eventually get beaten up, but not before Sniper had become mainstays of the main local club, the Coventry. 'It was a real glitter crowd,' said Mickey Hyman. 'Everyone was into the Harlots of 42nd Street.' Both the Dolls and Kiss were regular attractions at the Coventry.

In the summer of 1974, with glam on the wane, Joey formed the Slade-Stooges hybrid that became the Ramones. Within weeks, the band had distilled the essence of Seventies hard rock down to two-minute blasts of proto-punk bubblegum — Brill Building meets nihilist metal. After the Velvets and the Dolls, they were the next stage in the continuum that defined New York's punk sensibility. And when Joey put his mom's make-up back in her boudoir and invested in some ripped Levis and sneakers, the city's romance with glam was over.

'Just as Nirvana would come along and blow away the hair bands, so the Ramones came along and blew away the glam bands,' says Bebe Buell. 'And then Malcolm McLaren took our Dolls and Ramones and turned them into the Sex Pistols.'

5

The Divining Rod and the Lost Vowel

by Jonh Ingham

2016

Patti Smith's first album, *Horses*, arrived in Britain in late 1975 saddled with the weight of expectation. For most people it was the first document from the new groups in New York busy deciding what modern Seventies music should sound like. These bands were little more than names that worked the imagination: Television, Talking Heads, Blondie, the Ramones. Great Britain was a Jurassic landscape in Dickensian thrall, the nation happy for the innards of Bleak House to ooze across the country like primeval tar, sucking down and drowning anything modern. The people who literally and metaphorically owned the land deemed that three TV channels and one popular music radio station (for most of the country) was enough media for modern culture, filtering it for safety through the bog of Light Entertainment, a concept dreamed up to ensure that frivolity was polite and frothy and harmless.

In spite of this, the decade had started strongly with T. Rex, Bowie, Mott the Hoople, Roxy Music, Slade and Gary Glitter, but as these teen titans crested into the downside of their creative arc, or moved to Manhattan the better to concentrate on the hearts and minds of young America, nothing had grown to replace them. From Wick to Camden Town, it looked used up. Worn out. Into this tar-pit land came the occasional report and photos from the stirrings in New York at CBGBs. They were intriguing, but no beacons of hope. The occasional self-produced singles from some of these bands, hunted down in specialist record stalls, were not promising. But *Horses* came with the imprimatur of a major record label. Everyone could buy it.

Born in 1946, Patti Smith was old enough to know the world before rock and roll. The world before 'teenagers.' She read and heard poetry when it was the de facto place to go for rhyme-powered truth, when poets dreamed they could change the world, before it was overwhelmed by the iambic pentameters of Chuck Berry and Lieber/Stoller. She understood, in a way that anyone born after 'Hound Dog' never could, the salvation offered by the passion of Little Richard, the sexual promise of the Rolling Stones, the white heat of the Who and Hendrix, and the raw spirit of bands like Them. Her poetic tradition flowed from Blake through Byron and Rimbaud to the Beats and those with the beat: Chuck Berry, Dylan, Jagger and Richards, Tim Hardin, Lou Reed, Jim Morrison... And slowly she started searching for the horizon between them.

At first, she thought of herself as a poet. Then, at an important reading, she decided to bring to her poetry 'the frontal attack of rock and roll.' She asked rock critic Lenny Kaye to add guitar. It worked. He stayed. They started to map a new territory, speaking opium poetry with a rock-and-roll mouth. Keyboards were added, another guitar, drums. It included her in the CBGB tribe, the only female group leader besides the lip-gloss-and-platinum Debbie Harry, whose gossip-point was that she used to be a Playboy bunny, about as far as you could get from the skinny, androgynous, crumple-haired Smith.

It's only in the future that we can see what really happened in the present. In 1975, what we think we see is a woman with a Brian Jones haircut and a thumbed-up *Season In Hell* making an extraordinary music that barely has cult status. What we learn, years later, is that in bedroom sanctuaries and mental safe houses and on imaginary guitar-land stages, a revolution is starting with an act as simple as a needle on a record.

The misfits and the square pegs are hearing secret alphabets, saying, come, go with me, here are some maps, everyone is a tourist, everyone an immigrant, everyone a stranger. You will get lost, you will have your wallet stolen. Don't drink the water. Go further! We have remedies and folk songs rearranged and games that kings forbid. Don't waste the dawn. Progress. The world moves! You are not invisible. Princes and thieves have constructed pyramids in honour of your escaping. What names they have given them! The Frug, the Pony, the Jerk, the Watusi. The Mashed Potato. With raw iron soul they can be yours. Just answer this: are you worthy to enter? Then gather at the marina and shove off.

In 1971, Smith had co-written *Cowboy Mouth*, a two-part play with Sam Shepherd. Her character kidnaps the other and tries to remake him into her image of a rock-and-roll saviour. She fails. But life improves on art. People were gathering at the marina: *Horses* was making the people who dream of being somebody, but won't ever be somebody, into somebody. Michael Stipe called it Ground Zero for a new music, 'the defining moment in my life.' That's nice — and there's no underestimating how many young men put *Horses* into their music arsenal alongside the Sex Pistols, the Clash, and the Ramones. But it was women who were most inspired to claim the music and the life as their own — to look artist-thin cool in a black leather jacket and junk-store discoveries, to write songs about easy sex and free money, to make three chords soar in feedback joy; to ignore and dismiss the whole male ideal of a female musician — the floaty dresses, the big mascara eyes and the bedroom lips, the sculpted pop hairdo and the straight chanteuse hair, the songs about waiting for her man, getting her man, losing her man, standing by her man... All those... rules. Power is never given, Smith's art said. Be responsible for your own experience. The rules are what you make them. You can do the impossible; it's there for the taking.

By the 1990s, so many sassy female groups and musicians existed that a clichéd tag like Riot Grrrl couldn't corral them all. Stipe was right. *Horses* was Ground Zero, its influence spreading like virulent half-life radiation. First of all the punk groups: the Slits, the Raincoats and the Bush Tetras; Siouxsie and the Banshees, X-Ray Spex (Oh bondage up yours! indeed), Exene and Phranc and the early Go-Gos in LA. Then Chrissie Hynde. Chrissie was a woman you saw around the city, living in a cheap room with a mattress and a guitar, writing songs. She was shy but boy did she have attitude, and you never thought for a minute that she wanted to be a star like Joni Mitchell or Carly Simon; she wanted to be a star like Mick was a star or Dylan, in control and calling the shots. Which she became. And then: Courtney Love, Kim Gordon, Polly Harvey, Shirley Manson, Missy Elliott and Queen Latifah, tough-minded business people like songwriter Dianne Warren... Still they come: the Yeah Yeah Yeahs, the Kills, Meg White, Beth Ditto, Adele... each generation continuing to give voice, expression and confidence as the owners of their own destiny.

In May 1976, the Patti Smith Group came to Europe on a mad, one-country-per-day tour; their first time on the road. England's two punk groups the Sex Pistols and the Damned were a few months old, and the converted knew every London punk by sight. I was a writer at the music weekly *Sounds*, living the new sensation and spreading the gospel, so a tour of duty with the group was a natural. However, after the clear-cut manifestos of Malcolm McLaren, the Patti Smith Group was not so simple.

1976

London. A few minutes before the Patti Smith Group is due for a run-through on the TV music show *The Old Grey Whistle Test*, Lenny Kaye sits on the drum podium, fingers idly walking the unplugged fretboard of a black 1957 Fender Stratocaster guitar. Modestly famous for compiling *Nuggets*, an archive album of Sixties ephemera that shows the most important music often happens in the margins, Lenny has recently made the transition from rock critic to rock critic's wet dream, a full-time musician.

Even though the group will only play for eight minutes, all their guitars — the Gibson Firebird, the Les Paul Sunburst Finish, the Cherry Red — are reverently displayed with rock-and-roll piety. This is it, kids, what two thousand years of Christian civilisation has strived to perfect: the electric guitar.

Drummer Jay Dee Daugherty appears, immaculate in white stovepipe jeans and braces, and after checking his kit picks up a guitar. On the monitor a film clip of Paul McCartney starts crooning 'Yesterday.' Lenny underpins him with flashy guitar fills. Then from the other side of the podium comes a stumbling run. Never taking his eye off the monitor, Jay unleashes a shaky melody of quaking, out-of-tune notes.

Ivan Kral and Richard 'DNV' Sohl appear and they pick up guitars. It seems you just can't start the job without being sanctified by the six-string. The band is without attitude, low-key, discussing what and how they will play. This is their second television appearance, and it has taken much time to decide the two songs, and one of them, 'Land,' normally goes for twenty minutes.

Patti walks across the studio floor, quite small and incredibly thin. Fiorucci jeans hug pencil legs over boxer's boots. An ochre-coloured Indian shirt that could double as a dress might have been pulled out of Keith Richards' laundry bag. Her shipwrecked hair obscures Bob Dylan 'Don't Look Back' Wayfarer sunglasses. That is just clothing; what the eye continually falls on is a supple houndstooth cashmere Yves Saint Laurent jacket, a prize from her belief that when you have some money you should spend it on something very expensive that will make you feel good through the times with no money.

The Old Grey Whistle Test is British TV's one concession to the belief that rock has become an adult art form. Master of Ceremonies 'Whispering' Bob Harris treats music with reverence and expects his musical guests to do the same. A few months before, he famously followed an appearance of the New York

Dolls with an apology for their musical noise. Flash clothes, flash moves, flashbulb excitement — these have no place on *The Old Grey Whistle Test*, so having the Patti Smith Group on the show is an unusual choice.

In the confines of a stage barely big enough for the group to stand, Patti creates great theatre: whipping off her shades exactly as the pulsating intro breaks into 'Land of a Thousand Dances,' suddenly dropping on her knees in front of Lenny as though to eat his guitar. The cameramen leap quickly, but by the time they focus these TV moments have passed. When they draw to a close, there is an electric, tangible atmosphere — no one moves or speaks except for the whisper of Harris from the other side of the studio.

Between takes, Harris talks to her. He seems nervous and it's easy to see why; a close encounter is like a double-barrel shotgun pressed to the temples. Barrel one: she wears the New Yorker's archetypal belief that they rule the world as only non-native New Yorkers do. Barrel two: she has that confidence, that rock-and-roll arrogance, so rare in the modern musician, that in stars we call charisma. I mean this as a positive. She's lively, fast, funny and uninhibited in the way stars are. Watching a video of Jimi Hendrix laying waste to 'Hey Joe' and 'Sunshine Of Your Love,' she whoops and hollers and encourages the boy to rock and roll. Later, Lenny, DNV and writer Paul Gambaccini are discussing old New York doo-wop hits like true music obsessives and spontaneously start singing a classic tune; suddenly she improvises a verse over it with an ecstatic smile, making it both theirs and her own.

Because musicians naturally gravitate to clubs, we are sitting at a table in the Speakeasy, a basement Mecca that's been cosseting rock stars since the 1960s. Cultural giants have rocked on its stage and found sustenance at its bar. Cameras are banned and journalists discouraged. Shenanigans and indiscretions, the métier of the rock star at play, are thus given license and privacy.

On this Tuesday night none of these things is happening. Then a tall man enters, sees Patti and warmly says hello. It is obvious from the strut of self-confidence that he is a rock star but his acne-scarred face is anonymous. After he leaves Patti reveals: it is Gene Simmons of Kiss, they of the greasepaint faces. In a rock world that values as essential qualities credibility and heartfelt truth, the clownish vaudeville turn of Kiss looks like an easily dismissed joke. It's not as if they've troubled the Top Ten. In an approving tone Patti divulges that last year Gene Simmons made three million dollars. It's hard to decide which is stranger; that she is a friend of Kiss or that he made so much money.

Being people who are constantly in proximity to wealth while having none, we marvel at Gene's good fortune.

'I never keep money,' says Patti. 'I spend a lot in one day and then scrimp for months.'

'I'd like to have enough money that I didn't need any more,' says photographer Kate Simon.

'Honey,' comes the reply, 'a woman always needs money.'

Paris. Two days later. The band has performed in Copenhagen the night before and their equipment is late. Finally, both coincide at the Elysée Montmartre, where the hoarding advertises 'The Dirtiest Show in Town.' Group is separated from tools by enough crowd spilling into the streets for the police to demand the doors be opened or the concert cancelled. Unknown to the group, a second, early show has been added, so without a soundcheck they perform their debut Paris concert.

It's a tawdry place, originally a ballroom, with gingerbread ceiling and a minstrel gallery. From the stage Patti surveys the room and reckons this is the kind of place where Nijinsky must have danced.

'It's a strip joint,' yells someone in the audience.

'Well, Nijinsky did a lot of stripping,' she smiles.

Expectantly we watch to see what magic the Patti Smith Group is made from. About the fourth song Patti starts to improvise in verbal cut-up, the music drowning out sentences and thoughts, but others leaping clear: 'Don't you know the blackest thing in Harlem is white?' Between numbers she works hard to establish rapport, making silly jokes, encouraging the audience to make noise and be wild. The reading of Jim Morrison's 'American Prayer' leads into 'Ain't It Strange.' It builds, Patti beginning to wail, punching fists and dancing around the stage like a dervish. 'This is no avant-garde project of me / I'm still trying to be your valentine… / Everything I've done has been with one object in mind / Deep in my heart I know rock and roll will be beyond poetry / Beyond soul / Deep in my heart of me I see a glorious future for me.'

One of their best songs: 'Radio Ethiopia,' the station for those so over-infatuated with reggae they start speaking Rasta-ese, building from a dubular base to a soaring rock riff and then on into space. Patti chanting: 'I take Rimbaud, Artaud, Verlaine / You take Buddy Holly, Jimi Hendrix, Jim Morrison.' Triumphant: 'It's like one big cultural exchange!' Mantra-like: 'I take Artaud, you take Jim / Now I'm back to remerge them.'

The audience is devotional, cheering, calling out, throwing books to her. It is just hot and sweaty and smoky enough, and the band just good enough, to convince yourself you feel part of the great beast, the vampire animal come to feed its soul with electric megawatt rock-and-roll input. But really, we all want to make it more special than it actually is.

Unsatisfied with her audience she berates them. 'Oh come on man, this is Paris!' When the cheering and celebration dies down, she yells over the music, 'Paris means nothing to me, Paris is just a word,' and then they blast into 'Land' and 'Gloria.'

As the audience fights its way out after the last strains of 'My Generation,' two Americans expound to each other.

'Wow,' he says. 'She was too much woman for me.'

'Yeah,' she breathes ecstatically. 'It was too much, man.'

With the benefit of a soundcheck, the second set is fantastic.

Lenny and Ivan work in unison, trading bass chores and often ignoring them, keeping things together with tight, slashing rhythms. Ivan remains more or less where he is while Lenny utilises a rocking sidestep to launch into guitar-hero evocations. DNV maintains an almost motionless pose, keyboarding by feel with long, elegant fingers, staring intently at Patti the entire time. Jay kicks the proceedings along with an expression near weeping.

Patti bounces around the stage in her boxer boots, floating like a butterfly, punching the air with her fists, the only clues that one of her icons is Muhammad Ali. By 1976, adoring Ali is a given, but Patti's identification seems to go deeper.

When Ali first burst into the boxing world as Cassius Clay, the Establishment didn't respect him as a fighter. Most thought he couldn't box — a heavyweight was meant to wade in and flatten the other guy and Clay skittered around the ring like a stone across water with his hands at his hips, dancing, dancing, leaning back just far enough when the opponent launched a punch for the glove to miss, then connecting with a flurry of hard punches before floating away out of reach. He was so fast, so pretty, he was the greatest. But as he became World Champion, adopted Islam as his religion, changed his name, Ali demonstrated that he was more than just the world's most famous athlete — he was a black man who refused to play the white man's game, who stood up and demanded, in a hostile world, to be regarded on his own terms as a beautiful, successful human being. And he did it, largely, by an intuitive ability to improvise, to react to situations with speed and wit, 'the lead actor in his own American drama,' as biographer David Remnick put it. Patti is old enough to have watched this drama unfold as it happened and it's tempting to think she sees parallels in her own life, not only in the fight for acceptance, but also in how the improvisation within the ring matches her own performances.

During 'Ain't It Strange' she starts dancing with Lenny, grabs onto the organ and arches her back, then whirls around in circles until she collapses on the floor. Staggering up to the mike, she grabs it and hauls the next verse from deep within her. She begins reading 'An American Prayer' over the most evil guitar/bass/drums run. 'We are ruled by TV... Give us one more hour to develop our art and perfect ourselves... This is Radio Ethiopia... and you're on.' As a primal rock riff starts, she picks up her guitar and watches Lenny's left hand intently. She begins playing, stops and clues in again, gives up, and repeats the process with Ivan and then spins to the microphone.

'Deep in the heart of any man is the fear. The fear of temporary loss of control!' It's a triumphant cry, followed by the pick tearing down the neck until she finds the proper fret and scrapes the top string to oblivion. She drops to her knee by a monitor and administers more marrow scraping. The circle of photographers leans in as close as possible, clicking madly.

For the encore the band stand in a line, DNV standing blank-faced with a fag hanging from his insolent lips, picking bass guitar with well-developed one-finger style. They play a perfect version of 'Time Is On My Side,' followed by the obligatory 'My Generation.'

Post-gig interviews are conducted in a dazed, exhausted atmosphere. *Rock & Folk* writer Philippe Manoeuvre disdainfully asks about all this Rimbaud shit. Patti ignores the implication of a homeboy dismissing his own poet, replying that it's not the poetry so much anymore as the life.

Ah yes, the life. In 1976 the conceit of the Artist as a Romantic, living life for Art, life imitating Art, still appeals to those who see themselves as creatively outside the commercial mainstream but still want Top Ten success. The fascination is so strong that musicians even adopt their names — Tom Verlaine! Phil Rambow! — and you have to admit, it does look, well, romantic. Shelley drowning off the Tuscan coast and his friend Byron cremating him on the beach, brains boiling out of the broken skull into the flames; the preening opium addict Cocteau, with a library's worth of inspirational texts, images and some of the century's most startling and original films to steal from; a poet here, a painter there, and above all the poster boy, the teen prodigy Rimbaud, with a drug lover's manifesto espousing a long disordering of the senses — 'For he arrives at the unknown!' — abandoning art at nineteen, shot by his lover Verlaine, then roaming through Algeria and Ethiopia to an early death. It's a pantheon to aspire to. Even rock bands who see an icon in Andy Warhol and instead practise the concept of artist as businessman, like the Rolling Stones, very ably disguise it behind a screen of romantic outlaw chic.

The Stones are another of Patti's icons, especially Keith Richards. But then he's practically everyone's icon; as early as 1964 *Fab* magazine called him 'the mainspring of rhythm and blues,' and by 1975 *Sounds* journalist Barbara Charone had updated it to: 'when Keith Richards opens the door, rock and roll walks into the room.' Keith personifies the romance of excessive times, summed up in the 1972 Annie Leibovitz image of him passed out on a backstage chair, pink-tinted hair a stranger to a comb, long Moroccan scarf draped around him, ruffled shirt open to the waist, silver cocaine snorter on a chain around his neck. He looked cool.

Between 68 and 72 the Stones produced probably the most compelling work of their career. Not just big statements with difficult questions and answers like 'Midnight Rambler' and 'Sympathy For The Devil,' but also gems like 'Bitch,' 'You Got The Silver' and 'Moonlight Mile,' vivid panoramas both simple and sophisticated (sometimes in the same song) with often brilliant lyrics. If Keith was a truthful compass, the road of excess did lead to greatness.

And here was the crux of Patti's dilemma. To achieve career-sustaining success, she had to be a poet in a rock-and-roll world. Whether the profound simplicity of Little Richard (awopbopaloobop!) or the pop complexity of Smokey Robinson

(America's greatest living poet, according to Dylan) or the verbal cathedrals of Dylan himself, all those fabulous meters and cadences were wedded to a beat. Patti had to be in a band.

'I've always had Lenny because I needed someone to lean on,' Patti told *Rock & Folk*. 'But what if one night we were both in trouble? So we got DNV. And if DNV was in trouble then we were both in trouble, so we needed another one. One night we were all in trouble and we said, "We've got to get a drummer to keep this thing all together".'

In her conversation with *Rock & Folk* Patti ties up some threads: Keith touring the panelled mansions and concrete arenas of America, Rimbaud touring the hash brothels of Africa, Patti touring the (what exactly?) of Europe.

Paris Arista Records Man takes the band to dinner at La Coupole, dining epicentre of the Left Bank literati. Throughout the meal, Patti collapses against the seat, head back, eyes closed, exhausted. When the others decide that Arista Man can take them to the brand-new Club Sept she returns to the hotel. We don't know it yet, but she hasn't slept since London.

Club Sept is: very trendy! Very exclusive! Barred to us! But in a world of diminished culture, France still respects a poet, and eventually our motley group is allowed through the nameless door in the nondescript wall. Around a small dancefloor, small tables are filled with suited businessmen drinking cocktails with beautiful women checking themselves in the mirrors along each wall. The DJ is playing the music that you're imagining. When New York rockers dream of nighttime in Paris, this is not the *bite* they carouse in.

As dawn tinges the sky, Ivan and Richard walk back to the hotel. In the middle of the Champs Elysées, Richard 'Death In Venice' Sohl strikes a pose. 'Paris at dawn!' he exclaims. 'I feel like a photo in French *Vogue*!' As a subscriber to 'rented chic' — that is, clothes with holes in them — it's not likely. The veteran of a classical background who didn't discover rock until age sixteen, he's not a devotee to the magic pulse in the way that, say, director Paul Schrader was transfigured on seeing his first movie at seventeen. Reckons the band moved into rock and roll 'because we grew up. As we keep growing we'll move out of it.'

Back on the avenue at nine am, Ivan ritually films the Arc de Triomphe with the Bolex 16 mm camera that is constantly by his side. A Czech who learned to play guitar at eleven and had a smash-hit record the same year, he would spend dissident time in New York trying to develop a career and going to Patti Smith gigs, wondering why they didn't need a really good guitarist, until they asked him to join.

The band gathers in the hotel lobby. Patti arrives last, wearing yesterday's clothes and looking even worse than the night before. Two people hold her up so she can stand. The band look shocked but no-one addresses her or her condition. In whispers we learn that she didn't sleep last night. On the way to the airport, she pukes. In the waiting lounge she collapses in her seat, Dylan shades in place, Keith scarf around her throat, Ali boots splayed out in front of her. Surrounding her is rock and roll on the road: Lenny asleep, a roadie stretched full out on the seats, people looking dishevelled and dazed. Passengers gape and gawk. It's hard to see how this road of excess is leading anywhere, least of all greatness.

Brussels. Five concerts in five countries in five days. It's ludicrous. The band has been working solidly since Christmas, this Continental jaunt the madcap finale to no doubt necessary overwork. Arista Man says, too, that Brussels won't be an important gig. 'It's not a major stop on the map but you have to fly over it to go from Paris to Amsterdam so you might as well drop in and play.' Right. Just another honky-tonk on the road map of Europe.

Lying on her bed all afternoon, Patti talks at length, appearing to say the first thing that comes to mind, contradicting herself every few minutes. It's an opaque exchange — a conversation needs the chemistry of interaction — but, leaning into the bathroom mirror, she starts chatting with sparky precision. Perhaps it's from washing her hair. In those few minutes of mental and physical clarity as eye make-up is applied and lipstick glides on it's easy to see why she's been a muse to Robert Mapplethorpe and Sam Shepard; she glows with a unique, luminous beauty.

Patti is mimicking Dylan at his worst in *Don't Look Back*: wired, white, sunk inside her own oblivion, dancing on the perimeter with Rimbaud and Jimbo, where there are no stars, stoned immaculate. It's ironic she bows down to Muhammad — Ali is supremely self-disciplined whereas the rest of her gallery of gods are anything but. Jimi Hendrix, Jim Morrison, Brian Jones, Keith Richards, all have the same life-on-the-edge-of-the-cliff quality. Creating ecstatic visions by destroying the body is a cliché of the worst order, but there's no denying its fascination. If you're the perfect artist (or perhaps just lucky) you can make the perfect statement: take it right to the edge, like Mr Dylan in 66, then halt. I was there — I looked into the abyss and have returned, stronger, heavenly with its brilliance, one of the elite. I'm not the average artist going just far enough to say I've been there.

It's bullshit. It doesn't make you stronger and the amount of great, or even good, art that's come from it is far outweighed by the damage it rationalises.

Or perhaps she's just dealing with personal problems. Or coping with the road. Who's to know? The only one with the answer isn't saying.

The concert is in a lecture theatre at the university. The stage is six inches high. Fifteen hundred seats ring it in a tiered semi-circle. The audience fills every inch of space from the edge of the stage — sitting on the stage — to the back corners. It's probably the most perfect viewing situation ever.

The dressing room is subdued, Lenny preparing guitars, Jay

changing into a white suit. Jay is the fashion plate of the group, a taste developed in his native Santa Barbara. He's the only member to have the conventional background of high-school groups (including the deliriously named King Tut and the Space Queers), graduating to the big time with the Mumps when its leader Lance Loud was made famous by the TV show *An American Family*. Relocated to New York, he used to run into Ivan all the time at Patti Smith gigs, 'because we both liked seeing her so much, and we'd both be wondering why they didn't need a really good guitarist and a drummer.' Ten months ago he signed on.

As we talk, he says something that will become a punk mantra over the next two years.

'The important thing to remember is that we're our own best fans. There's always an audience, though we didn't start out to please anybody but ourselves. This band hasn't forgotten what it's like to be out there. We're intent on breaking down the barriers between the two. You don't really realise what you're doing; you just go out and do what you have to do. Everybody has his own personal vision — rehearsals frequently turn into group therapy sessions. We're just passing through rock. We're in a constant state of flux, and I'd say that now we're beginning to leave rock. Europe has given us a big lift. The audiences are much more prepared to accept us. They've put life back into our old songs, given them new emphasis. After a while, singing "Gloria" loses all meaning.'

With stage time imminent, Patti ropes in the band. 'You guys, tonight's your night to really push me. Like, if I loosen out on the songs, pretend it's an instrumental. On "Radio Ethiopia" really listen to the ways you can interact. And don't forget the feeling that goes with — [she duplicate's the song's great riff]. Listen. If you hear someone taking a solo, complement them. If you hear a leak or trouble, use your own initiative to make it good. But interact, that's the important thing. Don't go off on your own stream so much you don't know what's happening.'

We go to a concert hoping it will be memorable. That it will be a moment — talked about for years afterwards. Moments happen. You don't choose them. Band and audience and expectation and the sublime all concentrated into a point, a here/now when music lifts beyond chords and amps and swagger to make a connection with the gods and become a walk in heaven. A moment just happens. Tonight is a moment. Tonight is pure, ecstatic, passionate, inspiring.

The feeling of communication among the band flows strongly. Lenny has so much space, he's doing moves that surprise even him. Acting as Patti's foil, he dances with her, plays for her. When Patti straps on her guitar, she watches his hands intently, taking lessons. She cocks her head and then moves a couple of feet, resting her head on Lenny's shoulder for a minute while he blitzes the audience. The circle of photographers leans in as close as possible, clicking madly. As she begins to improvise she shuts her eyes and gropes for the words, listens to an internal voice as a groove starts, opens her eyes and stares intently into the distance as the words tumble out, then closes her eyes and breaks into a big smile, floating and stinging.

The audience responds from the beginning. She speaks to them in halting French, beaming at Lenny when she gets it right. After 'Free Money' they go berserk. Patti encourages the noise, then calms them down. 'Radio Ethiopia' is inspired. Tonight, instead of using its normal base upon which to improvise, they kick it out of the way and just soar. At the intro to 'Land' the audience starts cheering. The opening riff of 'Gloria' brings renewed cheering and a mass sing-along. Jay concludes 'My Generation' by kicking apart his kit and storming from the stage. No-one leaves, chanting and cheering for more. In Brussels, that minor honky-tonk on the map between Paris and Amsterdam, Patti Smith gets her first taste of outright adulation. For ten minutes, 1,500 people go absolutely nuts.

Elated fans buzz around the dressing-room door, wanting to get in. 'You are a friend of Patti Smith?' asks a kid. 'Do you know what sign she is?' 'Is Patti fragile?' asks another. The band sits around a table, looking shattered. Patti is triumphant. She is being interviewed by local radio.

'Rock and roll is a logical step from poetry, but do you think that all ze poets of this age should be into rock and roll?'

Patti launches. 'Well, as I said on the album cover, the word "Art" must be redefined. The new children are so aware, you know, the beauty, culture, sculpture, drugs, mathematics, sex, death. Children now are units of sensation long before they were... even in my youth. Kids have many, many levels. And I just think that the old definition of anything, the definition of poetry, the old definition of rock and roll is... is... *la mort*. It doesn't apply anymore. Things are changing too fast. Rock and roll is getting such universal appeal, such universal alchemy, that we're getting more power. Rock and roll is getting more powerful than anything before because it's art that communicates to all men. It doesn't exclude anyone, there's no hierarchy. Nobody's cooler than anyone else.'

Her eyes are closed, the speech somewhat blank, certain phrases coming after slight hesitation.

'It's all... it's like... When Jim Morrison said, "We want the world and we want it now," he was merely asking for what we're going to be taking anyway. So whether or not we have it right now by having it handed to us doesn't matter. Eventually we are going to get it anyway. Rip it back. Reform it. Reform having two — you know — "re-form" and "reform."'

Her eyes snap open and she stares into the distance with an expression that says, I said that? It's impossible to know whether it warms her or scares her.

'Yes,' responds radio guy, 'but ten years ago the people in rock were very much younger, the Stones, the Beatles were kids...'

'Well I'm a kid,' she replies positively. 'We're all kids. You're a kid until you stop kidding around. You're a kid until you choose to be otherwise. America has been drenched with the myth of Peter Pan so I have this syndrome that says, "You won't grow up."' She laughs.

In fifteen minutes she answers four questions, rambling in an insistent monologue that is hard to interrupt. Inconsistencies slide by.

'What is ze difference between "star" and "image"?'

'Tonight the people were the stars. To them I was the star. Which is alright if you want to believe in it. I believe in constellations. They're stars, we're stars, everything forms when we're all linking together, having a perfect moment. Like a big bell, you know.'

'Do you think you are a star?'

'No.' She's very definite about that. 'I'm just talking metaphorically. "Star" is a Sixties word... It's void. All these words have multi-definitions. We're trying to break the language barrier. I'm not interested in semantics —'

Lenny cuts in. 'Any time you say something to something that makes it what it is. [Eh?] And that means you limit what it is. [Oh.] And we're against being labelled as anything because then that just means it's another place we can't go. We want to go every place, to speak every language, we want to play every song. And anything that takes place outside the bearing of the group — how famous we get, how many records we sell — that has no bearing. All we want to do is do what we do and take it a step further and see how far out into space we can go. [Glad that's clear.]'

Then radio guy's girlfriend asks the million-dollar question — whether it's strange that people today are so interested in self-destruction.

'Well, self-destruction is obviously negative. If you self-destruct... [her voice dies out as she thinks, then comes back forcefully] ...but the way a snake self-destructs, you know, when he takes the old skin off — he destroys the old skin, but you come out with a new skin, a more developed skin, a more illuminated skin. So it's like a double thing. It's like a rebirth... You know... Like death and resurrection being so linked that one doesn't become more fantastic than the other, I guess, if you experience both... [her voice now less sure] ...I guess that's what it's all about.'

Brussels Arista Man takes the band to a restaurant for dinner, just as you know Amsterdam Arista Man will tomorrow night. To do that, they have to push through a cheering crowd around the band's bus. For them, the Patti Smith Group are stars. Who cares what Patti thinks? As she wrote in *Cowboy Mouth*: 'They created a god with all their belief energies... the old God is just too far away. His words don't shake through us no more... Any great motherfucker rock 'n' roll song can raise me higher than all of *Revelations*.'

At the restaurant Lenny is cajoled into chatting up two statuesque women who clearly know who he is and want his advances, while Patti is at her most comatose, a screen registering few life readings. Afterwards, everyone returns to the hotel. They have to be up early in the morning for Amsterdam.

With photographer Kate Simon I work through the contradictions of Patti's excess, the music it produces and the person (or lack of it) it creates. Our soundtrack is Neil Young's recently released *Tonight's The Night*, a deeply unpopular album full of its own contradictions, mixing dissonant howls about addiction with stoned celebrations of reefer and the first release that shows he is his own artist, not ours. At least one thing is certain: regardless of what happens offstage, Patti and her band have played wonderful music of vision, passion and purpose and if that's so, perhaps the end justifies the means.

I close the curtains about five-thirty. Across the airshaft, the lights in Patti's room are still on.

6

Malcolm's Children

Paul Gorman talks to Richard Cabut

Paul Gorman, Malcolm McLaren's biographer, chats to Richard Cabut about his subject as both Lebenskünstler *and trickster, whose output might be described as a* Gesamtkunstwerk.

Malcolm McLaren was the enabler. That's how Glen Matlock has described him: 'The great enabler.' Something was going to happen whether it was called punk rock or not, but it wouldn't have taken the form that it did without McLaren. The attitude came from him, from his approach to his art and his life.

A Gesamtkunstwerk. A total work of art, a synthesis of the arts, comprehensive artwork, all-embracing art form.
— Oxford English Dictionary

Wagner used the exact term 'Gesamtkunstwerk' in his 1849 essays 'Art and Revolution' and 'The Artwork of the Future,' where he speaks of his ideal of unifying all works of art via the theatre. He also used in these essays many similar expressions such as 'the consummate artwork of the future' and 'the integrated drama'. Such a work of art was to be the clearest and most profound expression of a folk legend — a deep, unified statement of cultural truths.
— Wilson Smith, *The Total Work of Art: From Bayreuth to Cyberspace*

Gesamtkunstwerk is the term Young Kim, McLaren's widow, uses to describe his integrated artistic approach. This started for him in 1969, when he foreswore painting — although there is nothing new in that; many artists have done the same, including Asger Jorn and the other Situationists. McLaren admired them because, among other things, they wanted to find new forms of expression and were interested in presenting the whole deal — a *Gesamtkunstwerk*.

One of the interesting things about the shop manifestations at 430 King's Road was that they were all of a piece: the interior, the exterior, the clothing, down to the labels, which McLaren designed and had made in Portugal by a specialist maker. All was unified behind an overarching concept. When that sort of approach is applied to popular culture — when it all fits — that is when things start to pop.

My book about Barney Bubbles — *Reasons to be Cheerful: The Life and Work of Barney Bubbles* — is a case in point. His career took off as a graphic designer for Conran for four years before entering the music business, but he already had five years at Twickenham Art School under his belt. Bubbles art-directed Hawkwind who were years ahead of everyone else in handling the *whole deal*. Bubbles designed their album sleeves, a succession of logotypes which appeared on posters, music press adverts, badges and T-shirts, painted the equipment, formulated astrological signs dictating where each member should stand on stage, body-painted the naked dancer Stacia, and later made films to be projected with spin-off group Hawklords.

McLaren was a product of a similar multidisciplinary art-school education to Bubbles. In his case, McLaren attended eight different art schools where he tried his hand at life drawing, fine art, environmental installations, urban interventions, filmmaking, painting and performance. So, it's not that surprising that when he opened his first shop, Let It Rock, it was not going to be like Granny Takes A Trip. That was a far simpler proposition — a place with a cool psychedelic atmosphere — but the incarnations at 430 King's Road under McLaren's direction had more depth and application. It was intended to be a

Gesamtkunstwerk from the get-go.

McLaren searched for the music to fit the attitude as expressed by the shop spaces and the clothing designs with Westwood. Rock 'n' roll was rebellious but at the same time it was nostalgic, and this was as boring as his initial Ted customers' attitudes were conservative. When the Sex Pistols project was underway, everything else was in place because of this integrated approach. McLaren often talked about this. It's a fascinating creative approach, and a powerful way to propagate what came to be in certain respects a myth.

One of the things that turned McLaren on was popular mythology — especially those aspects of it that he had encountered as a kid. Cowboys, Native Americans and, of course, pirates, which came into play later on in his life. Play being the apposite word, because he thought people should be childish and tap into openness. In this respect, he perceived punk as a mythological process, one that he turned over to the end of his life.

In fact I just came across a regional Californian newspaper from 1987, which reports that while he was living in LA and working in the film business there, Malcolm gave talks to students about the myths of punk at Pasadena's Design and Arts Centre. These are in line with the tales he told in Soweto in the early Eighties during the making of *Duck Rock*, sitting outside drinking palm wine and smoking, and entertaining the township dwellers with stories of the Sex Pistols.

In the last decade of his life in particular McLaren gave many lectures — communication, talking, was part of his *Gesamtkunstwerk*. Although to say that the interview was his true art form, something that has been suggested, is flip. In my view his great achievements are the LPs *Paris* and *Duck Rock*, the 2008 film installation *Shallow 1-21*, the early-Eighties fashion collections with Westwood — and punk rock, which I guess we are still trying to get our heads around.

Lebenskünstler: 'Life artist', someone who masters life in a somewhat eccentric way.
— Hongfire.com/forum

McLaren would recognise, and probably subscribe to, the concept of the *Lebenskünstler*. He took hold of, say, the music and film industries and applied art practice to each — but an unusual, not easily recognisable art practice. He came out of it having lived an art statement. People around him came out of it with their heads spinning: what the fuck has happened here?

The actor Lauren Hutton — who was McLaren's girlfriend in the Eighties — says she told him he had the 'psychology of a serial killer' and subsequently urged him into therapy (after all he was living in California at the time). The therapist identified his issues with the absence from his life of a father figure. Peter McLaren had deserted his family when Malcolm was eighteen months old. That departure was of course a very important and formative event. I have a copy of the card he sent to his father after they first met when McLaren was forty-two. It is, not surprisingly, extremely poignant. The key to McLaren's outlook is this lack of an authority figure, and instead being brought up by his contradictory and capricious grandmother. Most of his subsequent work can be framed in that light.

He came to reconnect with his father in unusual circumstances. When McLaren visited England to promote the *Waltz Darling* album in 1989, he used the interviews to talk about the search for his father. He had taken to the promotional trail to push a record, and here he was baring his soul about his dad. It could be written off as 'punk,' but it's more than that. This was personal and touching, but also a brave disavowal of the commercial process.

McLaren was Baudelaire's carefree *flâneur* talking about his obsessions and so processing life in an artistic way. He also promoted play power, urging people to 'be irresponsible, be everything that this society hates.' Play was at the centre of much Sixties critique and I'm sure he would have been aware of Richard Neville's *Playpower* book (they later shared the same agent, Ed Victor).

In fact, McLaren absorbed the great anti-authoritarian works of the Sixties — *The Anarchist Cookbook, Steal This Book* and so on. He was straightforward about that, a child of the Sixties as much as Jagger was, but interpreting the information in a different way. He was also interested in Marx, but aware that you could no longer apply Marxist theories in a relevant and interesting way — but he also knew that you could apply the attitude.

It would have definitely been him who personally sprayed 'Modernity Killed Every Night' on the interior walls of 430 King's Road when it became SEX in 1974. Such people as Jacques Vaché were well known to McLaren since Fred Vermorel had introduced him to the Situationist International and King Mob in 1967/8. He knew the associations between Modernism, nostalgia, the past, and the phrase about Modernity was on point. After all, he shifted away from the revivalism of Let It Rock (1971-72) and Too Fast To Live Too Young To Die (1973-74) because these were nostalgia trips. There's the theory that punk was the bookend to Modernism, which is interesting especially if you look at Malcolm's outlook and output. For instance, he hated T-shirts because of their Modernist connotations — I've got a quote from him saying that they really gave him the horrors — and that's why he *détourned* the T-shirt in avowedly anti-Modernist fashion. In this respect, in a clothes shop, 'Modernity Killed Every Night' is a bold statement. It means turning everything upside down. So, his use of the swastika on the Destroy T-shirt — which was part of the armour of living in 1977 — he made it fluorescent, put a statement on top, used it as just one symbol of power in a collage meditation on the subject: a perfect circle, The Queen, Christ on the cross... This wasn't the banal swastika-wearing of Sid Vicious or Johnny Thunders, both of whom were turned on by shock tactics for the sake of them. Not that McLaren didn't delight in the response to the swastika; this was only one aspect of his decision to use it.

> *The trickster exhibits a great degree of intellect or secret knowledge, and uses it to play tricks or otherwise disobey normal rules and conventional behaviour*
> — G.P. Hansen, *The Trickster and the Paranormal*

In a *Daily Telegraph* interview in the Noughties, McLaren posited that the word 'Svengali' would feature prominently in his obituary. The first major *NME* piece about the Sex Pistols, on 27 November 1976, wasn't an interview with the band, but with McLaren. He discussed much that he talked about subsequently, the shop at 430 King's Road, the experience of working with the New York Dolls, the fact that he didn't listen to contemporary popular music in the Sixties and, instead, was informed by radical politics. The piece was headlined: 'The Colonel Tom Parker of the Blank Generation.'

After the Grundy incident, McLaren refused to let Yorkshire TV interview the band directly and answered questions on their behalf. The reporter asked, 'What kind of example are the Sex Pistols setting to children by being sick onstage?' And he came up with that dramatic statement, designed to start fires: 'People are sick everywhere. People are sick and tired of this country telling them what to do.'

This approach found ultimate expression in *The Great Rock 'n' Roll Swindle*, which I still think is a great conceit: a ruined movie that was taken away from him. He never forgave Julian Temple because his own version would have been worse commercially, but better artistically. Maybe it would have turned out to be a deliberately atomised document in the form of *Shallow 1-21* (2008) and *Paris: Capital of the XXIst Century* (which he completed weeks before his death in April 2010).

In his life McLaren gained very little personally in terms of finances from the whole experience, and what he did receive was consistently ploughed into the next project. Sometimes, his ambitions exceeded the strength of the material. For instance, the *Chicken* magazine project to promote Bow Wow Wow in 1981, in which he intended to use images of scantily-clad youngsters. This was at best injudicious. To understand it, one has to acknowledge McLaren's point that the selling of pop culture revolves around preying on the young. He also knew far more than the record companies about the sales potential of pubescent kids and what would sell. This was true in 1996 when he predicted in an interview that music sales would be swallowed by free downloads. And it was already true in 1981. At that time prepubescent kids, driving record sales and buying *Smash Hits*, dominated the consumption of pop culture. *Chicken* magazine was both Malcolm's take on that pre-teen influence, and a slap in the face for the record business.

He was vilified as a money-grabbing manager (it didn't help that the portrayed himself as 'The Swindler'). Yet, Bernie Rhodes — who can in some ways be considered his rival in music business terms for a brief period in early 1977 — signed the Clash to one of the most onerous and unfair contracts in record-business history, for ten albums with a seriously low royalty. The members of the Clash were broke for most of the group's existence and for some time afterwards. Money wasn't McLaren's imperative and in the end he had a few grand in the bank and a nice old-school Mercedes, but owned no property — he had spent what he had. What a great way to live!

In some ways the trickster persona was itself a trick. He told me that he thought people would understand that the Svengali business was a pose.

Another time, McLaren expressed the interesting belief that, after the Sex Pistols, everyone became interested in *the process*. When you think about *The Voice* and *Pop Idol*, all those people know about the process — about A & R, mentors, and managers. And McLaren initiated this awareness and interest — making advances and record contracts a key part of the front-page news about the Sex Pistols. Peter Grant didn't do it. Neither did Andrew Loog Oldham, who only became interesting in retrospect. But right from the beginning, Malcolm was right there giving the media a double-page spread wearing his great Karl Marx-patch Anarchy shirt.

> *Frequently the Trickster figure exhibits gender and form variability. In Norse mythology the mischief-maker is Loki, who is also a shape shifter. Loki also exhibits gender variability*
> — G. P. Hansen, *The Trickster and the Paranormal*

Malcolm defiantly enjoyed the sexual ambiguity he exuded. The first time I met him, in August 1975, was with my brother, who is gay. Malcolm was with some of the Sex Pistols, and wore a black ciré shirt, black leather pants and great black calfskin ankle booties. He was elegant, nicked all my brother's fags and spoke in a very affected way while not really inhaling the cigarettes — it was a statement. Every time I met him subsequently until his death, he made the same statement. He knew about the ambiguity, and enjoyed it. He talked to me about going up to Soho at the age of thirteen and doing that North London Jewish mod thing — like Marc Bolan — putting rouge on his cheeks. I don't care to speculate on whether he was a non-sexual person or not. I do know he was interested in and loved women and always attracted them, particularly beautiful women. His partners were all great-looking and fiercely attractive. But it's also true that if you call your shop SEX, and put the name up in the street in big pink rubber letters, you're not that interested in sex, but in making the statement about it. I think that says something about McLaren at that time, in the mid-Seventies, when he had absorbed the teachings of Wilhelm Reich and with Westwood had decided one form of attack on established values would be to blow the lid off British sexual repression.

The English will have to accept one day that punk is their most valuable contribution to 20th-century art and culture. They will see it is as being as fundamental as the invention of the motorcar, as impactful as any painting by Picasso. They will have to accept that punk was sexier than sex itself — and that it changed lives.
— Nigel Farndale, 'Malcolm McLaren: Punk? It Made My Day'

Over the course of time, Malcolm himself went through phases in his attitude towards punk. It is interesting that, in the final few years of his life — when he had become a formal visual artist showing his filmworks and become part of the international art discourse — he was ready to talk about punk and his position as the prime mover in setting the scene.

What he did, I feel, is create an attitude, a creative attitude — DIY, anti-corporate and not for sale. These are the three things that define punk. They offered a sense of authenticity in a world ruled by what he would come to call Karaoke Culture.

Authenticity is a word Malcolm employed in later years, although its use could be misconstrued. Rather than merely a cheap marketing term, authenticity to him meant in some ways a return to the rigour of the Arts and Crafts values he had encountered at art school in the 1960s. Authenticity in that context meant craft, it meant hard work, and it meant a lifetime as an artist — where everything you do as you live and breathe is art.

Of course, the anti-corporate thrust was already in the air, particularly in the mid-Seventies. A few years earlier, Robert Fripp had split the gigantic King Crimson, cut his hair and formed a three-piece wearing little T-shirts — he summed it up as small, intelligent and mobile. Right from the start, Malcolm adopted a scorched-earth policy, attacking both the establishment and the so-called alternative of the time — he called Iggy Pop a hippie and employed John Lydon because he wore an 'I Hate Pink Floyd' T-shirt — these are supposed to be the out-there creatures of the time. Of course, he took this from his definite links with King Mob who looked at the avant-garde as yet another iteration of the Spectacle.

Eventually, he succeeded in shaking up society politically and socially as well as musically. I was a teenager at the time, a sentient being interested in politics. I remember the Heath government very well and I remember the elections in October 1976. I remember what society was like and there is no doubt that there was a sea change before and after punk — a question of values, political values in particular. I agree with the theory that Margaret Thatcher is one of the outcomes of punk. Bob Geldof put it well: 'She set about the status quo of received opinion with her handbag and thwacked it into submission.' And in a way that is exactly what Malcolm McLaren set out to do, in line with his nihilist statement on a BBC One magazine programme at six-thirty pm on a Tuesday night in December 1976: 'In order to create you have to destroy.' This was uttered looking at the ground, avoiding the interviewer's gaze, as though to say: I am not going to engage with you. And during the 1984 *South Bank Show* special on the making of *Fans*, McLaren emphasised that working with the music industry 'goes against the grain for someone arrested for burning flags outside the South African embassy.' He understood that engaging with any institution on their terms goes against the grain of individual expression. I think McLaren has made us and successive generations feel the same way, and hopefully question how we deal with the established order. In that way, we are all his children.

7

Boom!

by Ted Polhemus

In the mid-Seventies I was finishing my graduate studies in anthropology at University College, London, had started on my first book (*Fashion & Anti-fashion*), was living with my girlfriend and future wife Lynn Procter in north London (at one point on Wilberforce Road in Finsbury Park, not all that far from John Lydon's family's home in the shadow of the Arsenal football ground) and working part-time at London's Institute of Contemporary Arts. Founded in 1946 by Herbert Read and Roland Penrose, the ICA (especially during the mid-Seventies) excelled in outraging the conservative press, while simultaneously biting the hand of the British Arts Council which provided much of its funding. The highlight of this provocation came in October 1976 when the ICA opened COUM Transmission's *Prostitution* exhibition which featured, most famously, performance artist Cosey Fanni Tutti's used tampons. Questions were asked in Parliament about Arts Council funding for such filth and the exhibition was closed prematurely but, although rarely acknowledged as such, this exhibition had staked out the aesthetic and ideological parameters of that subcultural volcano which, although still lacking a name, was about to blow: punk.

Some months prior to the *Prostitution* exhibition, encouraged by the wonderful Sir Roland (who would occasionally find time to recount tales of his fellow surrealist artists Man Ray, Dali or, my own hero, Duchamp over a coffee) I began work on organising what was perhaps the ICA's first exploration of the interface between art and fashion. *Fashion Forum*, as it came to be called, would be a series of informal discussions with established and emerging London-based fashion designers. Following on from successful evenings with the likes of Ozzie Clark and Zandra Rhodes, I was determined to turn my attentions to opening a peephole on what the future might hold for British fashion. In particular I'd noticed a strange little shop at the 'wrong' end of the King's Road called SEX and, despite its forbidding black, mysterious facade, I steeled myself to take a look inside and see if I could find someone to lure into appearing at the ICA.

The only person to be seen in SEX on the day I braved entering was a curious man called Malcolm McLaren who, in a state of considerable and mounting agitation, explained to me that unlike the ICA, which was a hopelessly bourgeois and insipid institution, he was a true 'Situationist' artist and that my bourgeois institution and I could piss off. In truth I had never heard of the Situationists (I would look it up later: Marxist revolutionary arts movement originating in Paris in the Fifties; their principle UK event, in 1961, taking place, strangely, at London's Institute of Contemporary Arts) and I left SEX disappointed that I'd failed in my mission.

But I had left my ICA card with Mr McLaren and it came as a surprise when he phoned me some weeks later to propose a 'deal.' It seemed the police had raided the SEX shop and busted them for selling obscene T-shirts — in particular one which featured an illustration borrowed (licensed?) from the homoerotic artist Tom of Finland, showing two exceptionally well-endowed cowboys who had forgotten to put on their trousers. McLaren's deal was this: if I would appear as a character witness at their forthcoming trial — vouching for their importance as serious, creative British fashion designers (none of which I felt would be stretching the truth) — then his partner Vivienne Westwood and their extraordinary, often fetishistically attired shop assistant Jordan would take part in my *Fashion Forum* programme (but not, I noticed, McLaren himself who was presumably still too committed a Situationist to appear at the bourgeois ICA).

I'd never attended a trial before and I expect this one was not exactly typical. For starters, although Britain has a long history of laws governing what one could and couldn't wear (most such sartorial laws, dating back to the Middle Ages, prohibiting the wearing of certain colours or fabrics deemed suitable only for the true aristocracy), it was most unusual for a British court in the 20th century to turn its attentions to such things as T-shirts. But then these were no ordinary T-shirts. At one point, if my memory is correct, the prosecution alleged that the two cowboys' penises were touching. 'No M'Lud,' protested the defence counsel, and after someone had found a ruler, the precise gap between the two offending sets of genitalia was duly recorded. A big bone of contention (so to speak) was whether one of the offensive T-shirts had in fact been displayed in the small window at the front of the shop, where innocent people passing by might have been shocked to discover that cowboys have something other than their horse between their legs. My memory is that when specifically questioned on this point by the defence counsel, none of the policemen who had raided the shop would swear to having actually been the one to remove the offending garment and thereby protect the public from the sight of engorged male genitals. Under oath I said my bit — not very well, jumbling my words, but it probably made no difference. McLaren, Westwood and SEX lost the case, were fined and, in the process, gained their first taste (as history records, not their last) of juicy publicity.

Some weeks before the scheduled SEX *Fashion Forum* event I had another phone call from McLaren. As a sideline to the shop, he was putting together a band called the Sex Pistols who, he assured me, were going to be bigger than Elvis. Would I, he wondered, like to have them play at the ICA? Sounded good to me, but when I made inquiries I was told that the ICA lacked the appropriate music licence — and so it came to pass that the Sex Pistols would debut elsewhere.

On the evening of the *Fashion Forum* event we had a packed house: Malcolm and his Sex Pistols were nowhere to be seen, Vivienne and Jordan looked splendid in their skin-tight rubber wear, and at one point in the evening fire alarms started going off throughout the ICA. As the host and presenter, I no doubt should have made everyone leave the building, but the sound of the alarms seemed distant and so I just carried on. A little later, precisely on cue in the midst of a discussion about rubber fetishism, three firemen dressed in fetching black and yellow rubber strolled into the room and, as if on a catwalk, up to the front to tell us that it was a false alarm. Later, the rumour circulated that Malcolm McLaren had instructed some or all of the Sex Pistols to run around the ICA setting off the fire alarms. Malcolm McLaren indulging in such a childish and (if the fire services had been genuinely needed elsewhere) possibly dangerous event? Surely not.

Religiously attending all the *Fashion Forum* events, and seated prominently right at the front of the one celebrating SEX, were the always visually enthralling threesome of the fashion designer Zandra Rhodes, the cult film director Derek Jarman and his partner the jewellery designer, artist and creator of the yearly *Alternative Miss World* event, Andrew Logan. Somehow, Jarman and Logan had acquired one of those huge old derelict warehouses which fronted onto the Thames just to the east of Tower Bridge. Today, this same warehouse is one of the most expensive and desirable properties in London — housing on the ground floor one of Terence Conran's swish restaurants and adjacent to the prestigious, small but perfectly formed Design Museum — but in the mid-Seventies anyone wanting to live in London's crumbling Docklands was completely unheard of. How times change.

When the huge, but ultimately unsustainable, Biba department store in Kensington closed in 1975 (hardly more than a year after it had opened with much fanfare) Logan and Jarman managed to acquire the facades of the fairyland castles which had adorned Biba's children's department. These same Disneyland-style battlements, together with the remains of some sets used in Jarman's pioneering film *Sebastiane*, now served to divide up the cavern-like interior of this warehouse on the south bank of the river.

Energetic, generous hosts as well as partygoers, Jarman and Logan held a Valentine's Ball in their warehouse on 14 February 1976. Jordan — bleach-blonde-bouffanted, racoon-eyed, curvaceously packaged in fit-to-bursting black fetish gear; always in my opinion the most potent, creative stylistic force at SEX — was said to have had her clothes ripped from her on a makeshift stage by a very out-of-it John Lydon aka Johnny Rotten. But, if it happened, sadly I missed it.

There was eventually a raucous, short but hardly sweet, performance of sorts from the Sex Pistols — one of their first — but it was hard to distinguish what was tuning-up, brawling or the gig itself. Apparently, there were some journalists from the *New Musical Express* at the event and (according to Jon Savage's superb *England's Dreaming: Sex Pistols and Punk Rock*) McLaren was determined to spark something press-worthy and suitably Situationist. My own recollection is that, as poor Derek and Andrew looked on fearfully, the one certainty which emerged from the chaos was that the young upstart Rotten and the middle-aged Situationist entrepreneur McLaren loathed each other. How, one wondered, would this dysfunctional band ever get off the ground? (In Tama Janowitz's 1986 short-story collection *Slaves of New York* there is an only slightly fictionalized account of me — born in Neptune, New Jersey, resembling 'a young Andy Warhol' and 'a bit creepy' — meeting the story's narrator in the Tate Gallery and then, after a meal, taking her and my wife Lynn to this famous party near the Tower of London. Strangely, while history remembers the evening for the antics of the Sex Pistols, Janowitz recalls that the party featured exotically dressed guests flipping pancakes. Or has my memory mistakenly merged two separate parties at the same exceptional location into one? By the way Tama: I loved the book but you might have pointed out that the large pile of 'various sexual devices' in our living room was there because Lynn was writing an article about sex aids for a magazine.)

Around this time, my wife and I became friendly with a vivacious, enticing young woman named Max, who was newly arrived in London from somewhere in the sticks. Like the always stylistically innovative John Lydon, Max cruised charity shops and sampled and mixed and deconstructed a unique, post-apocalyptic, postmodern style which was all her own. Always in-the-know about such things, and determined to position herself right at the centre of the coming subcultural storm, Max (and Jordan, who was also a friend at this time) kept Lynn and I up-to-date on the latest adventures of the Sex Pistols. One day, Max phoned to tell me excitedly that the Pistols were that very night playing at a tiny and little known club on the Finchley Road, which was just a few blocks from where Lynn and I lived in north London.

It's little surprise that this gig, one of the Sex Pistols' very first, is so little written about — even in Jon Savage's remarkably comprehensive (but for lack of an interview with myself) *England's Dreaming*. Hardly surprising because, aside from Max, myself and perhaps fifteen other fans of the group, there was no one else present except for the dozen or so regulars at the club, who incongruously appeared to be comprised of bright-eyed European au pair girls and heavily tanned Mediterranean guys with big-collared, well-ironed shirts opened down to their chests, to reveal a lot of gold jewellery nestled amongst the hair.

The Sex Pistols were on good form. The minute dancefloor in the shabby club felt enormous due to the lack of people. Up on the little stage the extraordinary persona of Johnny Rotten took form right before our eyes: scary, bent in what seemed like every sense of the term, leering, angry, utterly compelling. Here were

Richard III, Pinkie, Wilde and the young John Lydon all rolled into one amazing character from whom you simply couldn't take your eyes. At one point in the short set, between songs, a pretty Swiss or maybe French au pair girl ventured hopefully across the empty room and with a sweet smile and in a charming accent asked Mr Rotten if they might turn down the volume just a little. Hunched, coiled above her, the demented smile which spread slowly across Johnny's face like a plague was a wonder to behold — something which even Olivier, Richard Attenborough (who plays Pinkie in the 1947 film adaptation of *Brighton Rock*) or Wilde at his most petulant would have struggled to equal. Obligingly the band cranked up the volume still further, until the uproar blotted out even the rumbling of the underground trains below us. The au pairs fled, and only a dozen or so of us remained. No one knew it — there were no press present, no cameras — but the world had changed.

Not just a new music, but an entire, wall-to-wall new subculture was beginning to coalesce in London: flotsam bobbing and clumping together swept up by a surging tide of a new, long overshadowed generation's teen angst. But even throughout most of 1976 this was still a far cry from a coherent, easily identified subculture like, for example, the mods and rockers of Sixties Britain. You did see some of this new crowd wearing the ripped-up and safety-pinned-back-together style which John Lydon had experimented with even in the days before his reincarnation as the iconic Johnny Rotten — the style which would soon become the cartoonists' stereotype. But there were lots of other completely unrelated, often contradictory stylistic experiments going on at the same time and within the same loosely bounded group of a few hundred or so adventurous/demented souls. This was a come-as-you-really-are party — a celebration of diversity which, at least early on, deliberately and determinedly strove to avoid the conformity of any or all subcultural 'uniforms.'

The only stylistic feature shared by most members of this

emerging subculture was a passionate eclecticism — rooting through countless charity and second-hand shops like Acme Attractions on the King's Road (or, more cheaply, the Oxfam shop in your own unfashionable part of town or suburban backwater) to find the most unlikely combination of garments and accessories, and then whacking these together in the most startling and disconcerting of ways.

For example, down on the King's Road on a Saturday afternoon you might see a group of teenage girls wearing the traditional British schoolgirl uniform of blazer, white shirt and tie, but put together with, say, an itsy-bitsy shiny black PVC or leather mini skirt, which showed off more than it concealed of slutty, ripped-up fishnet stockings and a cheap garter belt from a sex shop, worn up high on the thigh. But this was only the start: hair might be in any and all primitive/futuristic florescent shades. And on the girls' feet you might find a chunky pair of classic Dr Marten's work boots, manly and proletarian footwear which would have been right at home on any of Christopher Lydon's construction sites. Around the neck — to *really* freak everyone out — a chunky black leather collar and lead as available from your local pet shop.

This car crash of semiological oppositions — innocent schoolgirl / cheap whore, ancient primitive / futuristic extraterrestrial, macho / feminine, classy / down-and-out tramp — was often to be seen amongst this emerging subculture of what Peter York would later classify as 'Them.' But nothing, not even this penchant for what we would today term postmodern sampling and mixing, was 100%. For nothing was taboo — with the single exception of rigorously and religiously avoiding anything reminiscent of the denim flares worn by the hirsute leftover hippies and other Boring Old Farts who still prowled the streets and still (despite being well past their use-by-date) saw themselves as the epitome of youth culture.

Throughout the exceptionally hot, long summer of 1976 this

ill-defined but powerful, newly emerging London subculture had no name for itself and was still to spark the sort of widespread moral panic which would come later. But it did have a geographic focus at the 'wrong' end of the King's Road by day and, in the dead of night, a strange tiny club called Louise's on Poland Street near the top of Soho. Long one of London's few lesbian hangouts, throughout the summer and then the fall of 76, Louise's cheek-to-cheek dancing dykes and their pretty girly partners began to find themselves rubbing shoulders with this bizarre new subculture which would soon be labelled punk.

Near the door on the ground floor as you entered you might spot the always elegant French woman, Louise herself, sat at a little round table sipping champagne with her friend the artist Francis Bacon. Downstairs, from November of 76 when the Sex Pistols had released their first single, 'Anarchy in the U.K.,' you would find the unfortunate girl who was the DJ struggling to satisfy the demands of, on the one hand, her regular lesbian clientele's requests for slow, schmaltzy dance classics and, on the other, the riotous 'Them' crowd's requests for the Sex Pistols' solitary recording to be played repeatedly until worn down to nothing.

Then on 1 December EMI's big, chart-topping mega group Queen dropped out of an interview on Thames Television's live *Today* show, and EMI decided to sling their new signing the Sex Pistols into the slot. Clearly rattled by the appearance, style and up-yours attitude of the Pistols and their little coterie of friends, the (some said tipsy) presenter Bill Grundy encouraged them in swearing and, as soon as the programme went off the air, the telephones were ringing non-stop with complaints — one man phoning in to say that it had all been so upsetting he had smashed his TV set to smithereens. So finally the Sex Pistols broke out of obscurity and a tsunami of publicity now broke over this newly christened bunch of no-good, dirty 'punks.'

A few days later, I passed John Lydon on the stairs of Louise's.

Always feeling a bit of a Boring Old Fart Boomer interloper in this world of antsy Seventies youth culture, and not wanting to be seen as someone latching on to this sudden media buzz, I gave John a little nod and was continuing on my way when he backed me against the railing of the stairway and demanded to know 'What? Now I'm famous, you don't speak to me anymore?' How very like John Lydon to need to cloak a friendly (and, for my part, much welcomed) gesture within an atmosphere of belligerence.

Throughout 1977, the aforementioned party giver and cult filmmaker Derek Jarman was devising and filming his own cinematic articulation of this new mood of cynicism and despair, which had settled like dirty, slushy snow over England's once green and pleasant land. Scooping together many of the most intriguing, larger-than-life emerging personalities of the now widespread punk subculture, Jarman situated them within a story which time travels from the distant past into a decidedly dystopian future. Made like all his films on a tiny budget, *Jubilee* (1978) features Jenny Runacre as a Queen Elizabeth I who, with the assistance of her occultist John Dee (Richard O'Brian), sees into the future to a time when her ill-fated successor and namesake Elizabeth II gets unceremoniously and arbitrarily mugged in a car park; a time when Britannia is ruled by gangs of feral, dysfunctional (or, perfectly functional in a dysfunctional time) punky teens and an insane pop media mogul (part Malcolm McLaren perhaps; as with so much of this film's perceptive predictions of the future, part Simon Cowell).

Jordan (from SEX) stars in *Jubilee* as a sort of prim history teacher-cum-kinky/kitsch pop phenomenon Amyl Nitrate, who finds her fifteen minutes of fame singing an operatic 'Rule Britannia' in the guise of a barely dressed, see-through-knickered, stocking-and-suspendered Boudicca, the Warrior Queen of the Iconic, who led an ill-fated revolt against the Romans. Toyah Willcox as Mad plays with fire. Adam Ant, the Slits and Siouxsie and the Banshees shine. Murder, mayhem, dingy cafes, anarchy in the UK and bingo are the order of the day. Tellingly, in one scene of smouldering street desolation we spot a graffiti scrawled across the ruins of a wall: 'Post-Modern.'

A scrappy but underrated film, *Jubilee*, like *Blade Runner*, envisions a time when the once smoothly efficient machine of modernism — of fashion, 'direction,' rationality, form-follows-function design and a technology which solves all problems — clatters crashing to a halt and the centre no longer holds. Like punk, *Jubilee* itemises all the essential features of a postmodernism which had previously only been sketched out in the form of esoteric theory. The perception of time as a straight, single line of perpetual progress is replaced by a quantum NOW within which, segueing back upon itself in endless fractal layers, are to be found semiotic traces, stains — or maybe just the shadows — of other lands, mythologised subcultures, primitive peoples, B-movies, historical eras, wet dreams and future fantasies. Then *Jubilee* — and, more broadly, punk — playfully sampled and mixed all these eclectic parallel universes into unlikely, deliberately contradictory and unstable combinations — in the end, prophetically, giving us a pretty damn good vision of postmodern life in the 21st century.

The other point about the blossoming new post-Boomer punk era which *Jubilee* grasped so well was its deliberate, determined, drooling childishness. Sick to death of the grown-up maturity, technical skill and slick professionalism which characterised the Boring Old Farts' pompous prig rock, these new upstarts were determined to regain the crude but enthusiastically sketched teen dreams and nightmares of the original rock 'n' roll. Musically, famously, the punk route was: learn three chords and start a band. Stylistically, we saw exactly the same process in the way that most punks expressed themselves visually — not by becoming professional designers, but instead by rummaging through charity shops and jumble sales and then, like children playing at dressing-up, parading around in the most unlikely of garments, accessories and make-up in a parody of adult appearance. Or, regressing in age, we saw teenage girls posing as prepubescent schoolgirls gone really, really bad in their deconstructed traditional school uniforms. And, for both sexes, there were infantile 'bum flaps' which mimicked nappies. In *Jubilee* we see a *Lord of the Flies* type world in which unchaperoned, disturbed (mostly female) children run amok and trash their once glorious, now not so, United Kingdom.

The crass childishness which is depicted in *Jubilee* (and which is at the heart of punk) is the exact, deliberate and carefully deliberated opposite of the beard-stroking, educated, technically-accomplished, grown-up world where the Boring Old Farts had reduced the old anything-goes spirit of rock 'n' roll to a limp, ageing shadow of its former self. The undisciplined, bratty little monsters of punk positioned themselves in precise, exact opposition to the leftover hippies. Instead of slick, mature, educated but vapid professionalism, deliberately childish and amateur, but gutsy and heartfelt, rock 'n' roll for one and all. Instead of Love and Peace, 'bovver boots' and Up Yours. Instead of gently flowing, naturalistic locks adorned with flowers, the eyeball jarring, glow-in-the-dark artifice of Crazy Colour fluorescents. Instead of the Age of Aquarius, No Future.

Or, the way Malcolm McLaren and Vivienne Westwood told it, punk was simply the creation of two extraordinarily creative Renaissance people — Situationist artists, revolutionary designers, patient nurturers of musical talent, far-sighted visionaries — namely themselves. Indeed, if filmed on his own, McLaren was inclined to brush aside even his former wife's contribution to claim (as he did in a 2009 BBC documentary) that punk was born 'in my little shop.' This view presumes that history is shaped not by great economic, demographic, cultural or political forces but simply by the actions of a few all-important individuals — in this case Malcolm McLaren single-handedly firing the shot which did for Archduke Ferdinand and thereby started the First World War.

Not only is this view a reductionist distortion of how history happens — and actually did happen in 1976 — but it also fails to give credit where credit is surely due to the startling, unprecedented creativity of hundreds and then thousands of teenagers like John Lydon, my friend Max, the always extraordinary Jordan, Siouxsie Sioux, and so very many others whose contribution was great but whose names were never known to us; kids who reinvented themselves and then had the balls to ride home on the bus.

8

The Flyaway-Collared Shirt

by Paul Gorman

In 1973, one of my older brothers was hired as a shop assistant at Domidium, at 348 King's Road, on the site ahead of the curve of World's End where the Bluebird Epicerie is now situated as part of the café complex drawing its clientele from the moneyed of Chelsea.

Domidium sold ethnic, post-hippie: Indian mirrored cushions and Moroccan rugs, that stuff. The first time I visited, having jumped off the 31 at its last stop in Langton Street, I walked past the glam emporium Granny Takes A Trip, where I knew Ronnie Wood and Keith Richards bought their gear. Just where the road bends inward I encountered the slogan Too Fast To Live Too Young To Die emblazoned above the small shop front at number 430. On one side, across a window, on the back of a leather jacket, was studded the name of the outlet's previous incarnation, Let It Rock.

My hero, Alice Cooper, had talked in *NME* about James Dean's line: 'Live fast, die young and have a good-looking corpse,' so I understood the ethos, but however intrigued, I was too afraid to enter; especially alone. It seemed to my untutored eye to be a Teddy Boy joint, although the establishment was by that time moving away from neo-Edwardianism, pushing leather jackets, jeans and T-shirts in homage to the Ace Café's Ton-Up Boys. Whatever, I steered clear. Coming from north-west London I had good reason to fear Teds. They were worse than the hardcore Finsbury Park youth at the gigs I and other great-coated teenage heads attended at The Rainbow. One time there, I watched as some twenty Teddy Boys, bequiffed, brocade-waistcoated and middle-aged, rushed the stage and trashed seats in fury after a woefully short set by Chuck Berry. Then, in the pub around the corner, they snarled and spilt jugs of beer if any of us so much as glanced at their glitter socks and Showaddywaddy drapes. Teds came from Harrow and Colindale, had jobs, Ford Consuls and accompanied women with haystack beehives, forcefully applied make-up, skinny legs, short fur swing coats and old-fashioned spike heels. I knew this because Nigel Owen, who lived next door to my family in Hendon, was the bassist in the Flying Saucers, and when he wasn't trying out Charlie Feathers licks in his bedroom, brought home a series of these dolly birds in the early hours, much to the consternation of his poor old mother.

My brother's appearance changed over the months of his employment at Domidium. From feather-cut he went to a hennaed rocker quiff, Italianate, by Pasquale & Jack, whose shop squatted above the stalls of Berwick Street market; the sign was still in the first-floor window last time I passed, though they have long since departed. Soon, Tim had a single gold earring, straight 501 button-fly Levis and tooled pointy-toed cowboy boots from Terry de Havilland's Cobblers To The World. With those, he wore American fuel-pump attendant shirts and a black-and-yellow corduroy elasticated-waist bomber jacket with 'Rockets' emblazoned on the back from The Emperor Of Wyoming.

Sometimes, he wore a most unusual shirt in black Aertex-type material with a flyaway collar cut high on the neck, cap sleeves and thick waistband. He told me he had bought this, and his drainpipes, at 430 King's Road, which soon changed image and name again, to SEX, picked out above the shop in pink rubber letters and spray-painted with slogans in gold. Here, he also picked up a pair of custom-made jeans with plastic pockets and a pink T-shirt with zips over the nipples, blazoned with pornographic text stolen from an Olympia Press porn book by the Beat poet and junkie Alexander Trocchi. Tim once lent the T-shirt to Veronica, a posh cookery writer of his acquaintance. She wore it to a party, and he never saw it again. Tim also coveted, but never bought, the white quilt-topped brothel creepers sold by the couple who ran 430, Malcolm and Vivienne. He came to know them while queuing to cash money in Barclays, or drinking in the local pub The Roebuck or the Last Resort wine bar.

At this time, Chelsea was a hodgepodge of extraordinary characters. I recall one middle-aged man, balding with a comb-over, who dyed his very long and curly beard a vivid hue of green and strolled up and down the thoroughfare with a parrot on his shoulder for no other reason, apparently, than to liven things up. An ancient self-proclaiming lesbian regularly paraded in immaculately cut tweed suits, with a silver-tipped cane, men's shoes and a trilby sat atop her Brilliantined hair. One young man, name of Philip, was nicknamed 'Bette Davis' due to his ludicrous jet-black curly coiffure. He combined that with a collarless shiny Beatles suit from Acme Attractions and an unending stream of catty asides. Another, with large Bambi eyes and Twenties slicked hair, was a model everyone called 'Piggy.'

It was not uncommon to note the presence in local cafes and shops of other exquisites such as the artists Derek Jarman, Duggie Fields and Andrew Logan. Janet Street-Porter would be here, Edna O'Brien there, drug deals occurred at Jean Junction, I was told, though was never party to them. Lunchtime drinking marathons were held in shabby places like The Man In The Moon and The Markham. On more than one occasion Marianne Faithfull could be observed in the World's End pub throwing back glass after glass after glass of red wine as though she were dying of thirst. The Trafalgar, a very seedy hole, featured blowsy strip shows on weekdays. Tim slipped in there for a pint one day and a kerfuffle broke out: one of the strippers became indignant when she noticed a punter furtively release his cock from the confines of his trousers and vigorously manipulate it as she shimmied and sashayed. 'Well what d'you expect me to do?' the bloke reasoned, as he was ejected into the noonday sunlight.

Gene Krell, exotic frontman of Granny Takes A Trip, told me the height of aberrant behaviour was scaled when the owners of furniture outlet Sophisto-Cat — Aussies 'Ace' Bourke and John Rendall — bought a lion cub from the pet shop at Harrods, and kept it on a chain in the shop during opening hours until the local authorities were alerted by frightened customers. Around this time, Trevor Myles had taken over the pop art Mr Freedom, and the design team Electric Colour Company decked his shop Paradise Garage in homage to Americana, complete with bamboo lettering, a Fifties gas pump, Birds of Paradise and a tiger-striped, flock-covered Mustang permanently parked outside. Meanwhile, one of Trevor's associates, the tortured John Lloyd, adorned his emporium Alkasura with religious artefacts and stalked World's End garbed in a monk's habit, complete with cowl. Lloyd, ever unstable, committed suicide via self-immolation on a building site in full view of the passing public.

Just a couple of months before that tragic event, over the August bank holiday of 1975, Tim commandeered me to assist him in the decoration of the off-King's Road flat of one of his customers, a Batik artist and opera singer called Thetis. If rumour were to be believed, she had once arrived home to find her brother — a priest — furiously masturbating beneath one of her artworks: a life-size print of Christ on the cross. Thetis didn't really mind speculation about that. What she didn't want leaking out was the fact that her real name was Susan. The job took us a week and Thetis wasn't at all pleased with the end result. By painting the sunlit place in eggshell finish gloss, all the surfaces gleamed insistently, creating a blinding effect for the occupant during the hours of daylight.

Every night after work we repaired to The Roebuck, the hub for the shopkeepers and restaurant workers in the immediate area. The staff at the pub didn't pay much heed to the fact that I was an all-too-obvious underage drinker, allowing me to sit back and learn how to swallow Guinness and smoke Senior Service, all the while observing the antics of its denizens.

One evening we were joined by the ginger geezer Malcolm, who wore a black ciré T-shirt, black leather jeans and dainty black calfskin ankle boots and assiduously relieved my brother of every spare untipped cigarette. We talked about straight Levis (I had just acquired my first pair; McLaren had been stocking them since the early Seventies) and when I caught him sneaking the last cigarette from my brother's packet I couldn't control my giggles. He looked at me fiercely. Then nonchalantly lit it.

Behind him was a collection of young men, about four or five years older than me. I took them to be French. They had the look of the Continental students who were our 'paying guests' at home in the mid-Sixties: skinny T-shirts, mohair jumpers, elephant cords or blue jeans, baseball boots and unkempt grown-out crops. I don't remember any green hair, but I can see the profile of one in particular now if I close my eyes. Disdainful, with an unwavering gaze of deliberate disorientation.

They left — I gathered much later, to audition the surly quiet one in front of the SEX shop jukebox — and the evening swirled around me.

At one point, an aggressive black man pleaded with Timothy to give him Francis Bacon's telephone number. Timothy had never met Bacon, although he was once invited to attend the great man's famously filthy South Kensington studio by the drunken painter, Sir Francis Rose. Very taken with Timothy's appearance at The Devonshire Arms, Stratford Road, Rose had made a date to escort my brother to Bacon, who, he insisted, would want to paint his portrait on the spot. Timothy stood him up.

Later that night, in The Roebuck, an untypically observant barman attempted to have me removed but relented under pressure from my new friends. Somebody I took for Freddie Mercury in my derangement — who I now believe to be John Cale — held court imperiously at another table. Upon closing time my brother was copiously sick over his blue boiler suit in the back of a black cab outside a flat in Maida Vale. The cabby ordered him to clean it up. I drifted indoors and put on the Wailers' *Natty Dread*. My brother entered, turned green at the insistent bass-heavy throb, and was sick again.

In time, he gave me the black shirt, which had become too small for him. I wore it with my Big Smith jeans and black suede brothel creepers in the late summer of 1976. Dressed in that outfit, one night, I told Tim I was going to see the Damned. 'You'll love it,' he pronounced. 'Visconti's a genius. You should see *The Leopard* too.' He looked crestfallen when I informed him that I was off to see a new group, not the film.

I also urged the shirt on my first girlfriend. She wasn't impressed because it didn't go with her dungarees, but did take my short-sleeved Acme summer shirt. One time she borrowed it to wear to a party and I never saw it again. I myself last wore the cutaway-collared shirt in 1978, to a terrible show by third-rate new wavers (the Tourists? the Members?) at The Music Machine near Mornington Crescent. Uniformed Sid-a-likes sneered that it made me look 'a poof.' Like I cared, but still...

Everyone I knew, and/or admired, moved on from punk as soon as it was given a name. There was no room for the green-bearded man, the suited lesbian or the Francis Bacon obsessive. The richness of that scene had been traduced to the saleable gob 'n' pogo archetype: spiky hair, permanent sneer, brothel creepers, Lewis Leathers. McLaren's commentary about the commodification of culture had itself become commodified. Maybe he intended it that way. Still, I kept the shirt.

In time, I came to know Glen Matlock and interviewed him for my book *The Look*. Unfairly maligned in the received history of punk, Glen is, after all, the Sex Pistol whose innate design instincts enabled him to recognise the extraordinary achievements of McLaren and Westwood years ahead of the pack, from future bandmates and style magazine writers to *Vogue* to the NY

Met and the V&A. Talking about the items he sold as an assistant at 430 King's Road between 1973-75, Matlock mentioned unprompted the flyaway-collared shirt, pointing out it had been half-inched from a design in a catalogue for outrageous Fifties Soho menswear outlet Vince Man's Shop.

I have tracked down a photograph of just one other such shirt from Let It Rock: the white version, worn by guitarist Chris Spedding with Levis and winklepicker boots in photographs promoting his 1975 hit 'Motor Bikin'.' But I've never seen another in black, not worn by any of the Pistols or the scenesters, nor in the footage or photographs I have scanned or the private collections and public archives I have trawled.

For a while the shirt was encased on my office wall, but recently it has been sprung from captivity and featured among exhibits in a series of Malcolm McLaren-related shows I have organised with his widow Young Kim. It was also among garments I loaned for a major fashion story by photographer Alasdair McLellan for *Man About Town* magazine. Super-stylist Olivier Rizzo — whose world-renowned work includes his position as in-house stylist at Prada — chose the flyaway-collared shirt for one of the most potent images in the shoot: a beautiful, slim male model in unzipped jeans from The London Leatherman and World's End Pirate-era hat, wears it with a safety pin fastening the neck. It may be fanciful, but it seems to me that in this single image, McLellan and Rizzo convey something of the garment's magic. That's because, for me at least, this small piece of cloth speaks volumes about a world forever lost, filled with deliciously deranged creatures indulging in the exciting and the forbidden, forever.

9

SEX in the City

by Dorothy Max Prior

The names, all of the names. The Bird's Nest, The Trafalgar, The Horns, The Lord Nelson, The Three Kings, The Arabian Arms, The Westminster Arms, The Windsor Castle, Scamps, The Falcon, The Tidal Basin, The Temple Bar.

I'm called all sorts of things when I'm working, depending on where I am and the mood I'm in. Sometimes I want people to remember me, and sometimes I don't. But I'm doing well, and I get requested and rebooked. I forgot to think up a name for myself when I started working, and hurriedly choose D (for Dorothy). As in O, story of. But everyone thought I meant Dee. So I'm sometimes Dee, and sometimes Dee-Dee, or Dee-Light. Or Lola, that too. Times they are a changing, and I'm now mostly booked as a stripper or a cabaret dancer rather than a go-go dancer. When I first work for Gemini agency, I just go where I'm sent. A few months in, I've proved myself, and I'm popular, so I can be a bit more picky. No more evening work — unless it's a quality cabaret or party booking. So no seedy clubs or pubs, especially no to that dodgy joint in New Cross with no stage, where they get you to dance on the pool tables and suggestively pass you beer bottles, and definitely no stag parties. And no private parties at the Westminster Arms, which is the New Scotland Yard pub. They more or less own it, and what happens at the evening lock-in parties — well, vice squad or what? Pubs at lunchtime are a different thing though — they're actually the heart of the trade, and lucrative too. The best ones are in the City, the East End and the Docklands — although there are a few elsewhere that are music venues by night and have striptease and go-go dancing at lunchtimes. No club licence needed, often not even blacked-out windows — anyone can just wander in off the street. Some of the girls work in both the pubs and the Soho clubs, but I don't like the club scene. You have to do as you're told, running from one club to the next — often there's five or six run by the same people and they want you to do the whole lot of them in one afternoon or evening, show after show after show, dashing around with your coat thrown over your costume and stiletto shoes chucked into a bag. And the club owners are a conservative bunch: you're expected to look a certain way, and dance to the music they choose. The pubs, on the other hand, are your own playground. The girls are usually booked as go-go dancers rather than strippers, with an expectation that the afternoon will finish with one or more striptease acts. We make most of our money not from the dancer's fee, but from going round and collecting tips. The usual thing is to troop around the bar in costume with a pint jug in hand. If you strike lucky, there'll be a second or third jug of silver, and hopefully paper. Copper gets given back, with a smile: you obviously need it more than me, love. Some girls are very tough and hassle heavily over the money. I've seen girls look at what's in the jug and change their mind about a final strip. I'm usually pretty sweet and un-pushy, and it works for me. Some men like the sugar-and-spice girls and some like the pushy broads. It's all in the game. You win some, you lose some.

I like using the Kinks' 'Lola' as an entrance track, so it works to use the name too, adds strength to the story. Because striptease — burlesque-style striptease, anyway — is always about story-telling. First, you need the character; your onstage persona for this particular ten-minute act (three tunes is the norm: the intro, the tease and the finale). Some girls have one persona played out in slight variations every time they perform — wild leather-clad rock chick, slinky diva in evening dress and feather boa, schoolgirl innocent — others are actors taking on different roles, often with a number of names, to the point where they can be rebooked a week later at the same venue and not be recognised.

So, yeah, here I am — Dee-Dee, Dee-Light, Lola, whatever. I've got three or four main routines, with costumes for each. Very much within the burlesque tradition — the strip without the tease is not my cup of tea — but with a contemporary Seventies vibe. There's talk that we'll soon get forced out of business by the growing trend for much more explicit striptease, in which costume and music are almost incidental, but for now, although go-go dancing is falling by the wayside — the days of turquoise bikinis and white vinyl boots have long gone — 'exotic dancing' is still holding its ground.

So if it's the Kinks' 'Lola,' the entrance is in a blue satin cheongsam, with feathery fans, very flirty and cheeky and drag-queenish (striptease being a sort of drag act — 'performing the feminine,' as the gender-politics academics would have it). I think Jimmy Forrest's 'Night Train' was usually the second track for this one.

Then there's the black PVC outfits — there are a few different variations — bought from She & Me in South Kensington. Malcolm and Vivienne's SEX shop on the King's Road also sell the same stuff, but I get a working girl's discount at She & Me, so usually go there: thigh-high wetter-then-wet-look leggings or boots and matching full-arm gloves, a PVC basque or laced corset, and a kind of high-necked plastic bodysuit with straps at the crotch. And there's a whip, which someone has taught me how to crack. I know how to whip a cigarette out of a man's mouth, a trick that is always appreciated. The opening music for this one is Alex Harvey's 'Next,' segueing into Lou Reed's 'Walk on the Wild Side.'

Another routine is based on Liza Minelli in *Cabaret* (the film's been out for about five years now, and is still very popular). So this persona has a black felt bowler hat, and a striped gold-and-black waistcoat (from Biba, bought for a snip when the big store in the Derry and Tom's building on Kenny High Street closed down the year before) with matching gold lamé shorts. Underneath, a black net bodystocking and of course the classic Sally Bowles low-slung stockings and suspenders. I hide my long hair, wound up into the hat which gets removed with a flourish during the opening track — 'Mein Herr' from the film soundtrack. A brown wooden French café chair — you know the sort I mean, I say to the barman, I think they might even be called cabaret chairs — is essential, and most pubs have one somewhere in the building. I'm good with chairs. I'm taking jazz dance classes from a woman called Gina who has worked with Bob Fosse, so I've got all the classic *Cabaret* moves off to a T. I sometimes keep the whole routine a Fosse tribute, going from *Cabaret* into *Sweet Charity* with 'Big Spender.'

One of my favourite bookings is a Sunday lunchtime slot in Ilford where I'm on the same bill as a comedian and a wrestling tag team. Other pubs pair striptease with boxing. Although I'm here to make a living — not as an art project — my friendship with anthropologist and cultural commentator Ted Polhemus has given me a new way of looking at popular culture. Roland Barthes' *Mythologies* is on my bookshelf, and I like the bit in the 'World of Wrestling' essay that says that wrestling is based on contradiction: wrestling looks like a sport but is a spectacle of excess. Grandiloquence is a word that Barthes is very fond of. Striptease, he says, is also based on a contradiction: 'Woman is desexualised at the very moment when she is stripped naked.' He's right, you know. Striptease seems to be about nudity, but is actually about covering, exoticising, occluding the naked truth of the unadorned human body. Any of the girls who knows anything knows this: you never end naked. There must be shoes and/or stockings and/or gloves – or at the very least jewellery or hair bows. It's all about exoticism, eroticism and music hall, says Roland. Oh Lord, the semiotics of striptease! Quite naturally, I'm challenged a lot on my choice of job, and how it fits in with my feminist ideals, so it's handy having a bit of Barthes as a backup.

Punk — or whatever we call whatever is happening here in London in the mid-1970s — has brought with it a dismissal of trite leftism and hippiedom, and there's an interest in playing capitalism at its own game: hell yes, let's not wait for the revolution, let's take The Man for a ride, right now. And postmodern irony has entered the fray. I am not what you think I am, matey. In a truly postmodern nothing-is-absolute-all-is-relative way, I'm living a fractured double, perhaps triple, life. My days are spent as Dee-Dee or Lola, and by night I don another name, Max. It wasn't my choice: it was given to me by Andy Warren, who decided that I was going to be called Max, and I was going to play drums. Protestations that I didn't know how to, and didn't own a drum kit, fell on deaf ears. This is 1976 — knowing how to do something is hardly relevant or important; it's the urge to do it that matters. And I'm a Velvets fan too, so there's a noble precedent for female drummers with a one-syllable name beginning with M. Yeah, why not?

Often, when I'm travelling to and from 'work,' I dress down, saving the costumes for their onstage revelation. But the PVC, rubber and leather come in handy the rest of the time. Of course, dressed in a pink rubber miniskirt, with visible stocking-tops, I regularly get propositioned on the streets. Especially if anywhere near Piccadilly Circus. Men are surprised when I tell them I'm not for sale. Or at least, I'm only for sale on my own terms — but I don't say that. This ironic postmodern punk thing has brought with it a renewed interest in slumming it in Soho or down the Hackney Road. Down with sensible dungarees and worthy outdoor music festivals in muddy fields. Hurrah for inner-city dodgy-geezer / brassy-bird looks and pursuits. Winklepickers. Bleached-blond hair. Striptease. Wrestling. Boxing. Greyhound racing — I remember Jordan, or someone, saying we should all go greyhound racing. We embrace Len Deighton's London, Wolf Mankowitz's London, Diana Dors' London. This London, in all its trashy messy mid-Seventies decline and fall, has become our playground. Old man pubs with bevelled-glass mirrors and nicotine-yellow Anaglypta wallpaper. Expresso Bongo coffee bars with their 1950s formica and bakelite intact. Chinese restaurants with red-dragon decor and a late-night upstairs room full of Hong Kong gangsters playing pontoon. Who needs the tedium of the Socialist Workers Party when you can have DIY Situationism? Even a trip to the supermarket is exciting if you're dressed for it. *There's a punk in the supermarket.* We don't need politics, we are politics. We don't need art, we are art. We are the writing on your wall.

But back to the (bump and) grind. Some of the pubs on the circuit become firm favourites. I'll always take an offer on The Lord Nelson in Old Street, The Horns in Hackney Road, or the Arabian Arms on Cambridge Heath Road. I like the Arabian Arms a lot — the DJ Steve is very friendly and plays great funk and soul tracks, although I go off it a bit after I get bitten by the pub dog. I've been given the kitchen upstairs as a changing room (a notch up from the ladies' loos), but they've forgotten about the dog, who assumes I'm an intruder. There goes a perfectly good pair of retro ski pants. And I have to go to the hospital for a tetanus jab. The landlord gives me a £30 bonus — or is it compensation? — and sends me on my way. It doesn't occur to me to sue them.

The Arabian Arms also happens to be the local haunt of two new friends, Genesis P-Orridge and Cosey Fanni Tutti, who I met at the ICA, which is where I work part-time when I'm not plying my trade as a go-go dancer and stripper in the pubs of East London, or playing drums in a band that will never see the light of day, but which will give birth to both the Ants and the Monochrome Set.

I do all sorts of bits and bobs at the ICA. It's all pretty laid-back, and buzzing with artists of all sorts who are always happy to use an extra pair of hands putting up exhibitions and helping to organise events, and there is also ushering to be done and bars to be run. Sometimes I work for those other interesting new friends Ted Polhemus and Lynn Procter (who are a bit older than me, and hipper than hip — he has Andy Warhol hair and wears tight black jeans and a leather jacket; she's a bleached-blonde leopardskin-trousered remake of Marilyn Monroe) who curate an exhibition area in the bar and corridors. Ted also programmes talks and events — which include a *Fashion Forum* with Vivienne Westwood from SEX and the Swanky Modes girls, and an Ethnographic Film Festival which shows the Katy Oxo commercials as a full-length film, interspersed with thirty-second clips of Andy Warhol's *Empire* used as commercial breaks. Mike Laye and Keith Allen run the theatre, and I muck in there, assistant-stage managing and serving drinks. We use the space to put punk gigs on at night — no one is bothered, until there's a bit of a fuss about Shane Pogue 'biting' Mo-dette Jane's ear at a Clash gig.

The main exhibition space is pretty self-sufficient, but I'm sometimes brought in to give a helping hand mounting a big show. It's October 1976, and what's happening here and now is a show about to launch called *Prostitution*, by performance-art group COUM Transmissions. I'm introduced to Genesis and Cosey, the lead artists in the group, and they talk me through the show. Gen has shoulder-length hair parted on the side and held off his face with a turquoise plastic hair slide. Cosey is long-legged and gorgeous in Mary Quant black-and-white stripy tights. They are kind and friendly and enthusiastic, and we walk around together, making a last check on everything before the doors are opened for the press launch. Photos from Cosey's work as a model for porn mags — check. Used tampons in glass cases — all present and correct. As we walk, Gen talks non-stop — about the work in the exhibition, about Fluxus, and Burroughs, and Ballard, and the Velvet Underground. Cosey tells me about her work as a model and porn-movie star; I tell her about my work as a dancer and stripper. It's the start of a beautiful friendship — I go on to become Gen's muse and confidante and an Industrial Records artist, and eventually drummer in Psychic TV.

But that's all to come. For now, everything is in place and ready. Gen tells me that COUM Transmissions are going to self-destruct and reinvent themselves tonight as death-rock group Throbbing Gristle. We've now stopped before a stage area. I'm introduced to two other group members, Chris and Sleazy, who are fiddling with the musical equipment — great big bass bins and a bank of synthesisers, tape recorders, mixers, amplifiers and other machinery. There's a guitar that Cosey is going to play. She's not played one before. Gen is going to sing. He's not sure what yet.

The doors open, and in come the crowd, a posse of 'Hell's Angels, boys wearing nail varnish and girls dressed as whores,' as one newspaper puts it the next day. There's a short set from a band called LSD, featuring Gene October, Billy Idol and Tony James — later to become Chelsea, then (minus Gene) Generation X.

There is also a striptease show, featuring a girl called Shelley who works for the same agency as me. At the time, I did my best to keep my art/punk life and my burlesque work separate, so on this occasion I'm not strutting my stuff, I'm on the other side of the divide, sitting in the audience with a new friend — Mick Jones of the Clash. Mick thinks that we girls should get up and disrupt the strip show. I don't agree, but I don't say why.

The next day the newspapers have plenty to report: 'These People are the Wreckers of Civilisation,' screams one headline. 'This is the Art Connoisseur of Today,' sneers another, featuring a shot of Siouxsie Sioux and Steven Severin. Questions in the House of Commons. Outrage. Public money spent on strippers and obscene objects and this horrible, terrible death rock. The director of the ICA, Ted Little, and most of us smaller fish, who have anything to do with this outrageous exhibition, are sacked or encouraged to leave. The ICA gets its Arts Council money cut. No more porn shows on public money. No more late-night punk gigs.

Well, who needs art? It's back to the burlesque for me — far better paid, in any case. Genesis and Cosey turn up regularly at The Arabian Arms. Sometimes it's just Gen, and people sidle up to me and say, 'Is he your bloke? Does he mind you doing this?' 'Do you mind?' I ask Gen, who is always up for a little bit of role-play. No, not at all, he answers with wide-eyed wonder. I like it. Afterwards, we go back to their house (which also doubles as Throbbing Gristle HQ) in nearby Beck Road for a cup of tea and a chat. The door to the front room is plastered with pictures of female genitalia: 'Amazing how different they all are!' says Gen, as if he's talking about variations in flower species or something. But other than that, it's a pretty regular two-up, two-down house. Oh, other than the nursery, which is downstairs — but we don't go there.

A little while after this, Cosey tells me that she's looking for an outlet other than modelling for the porn mags to make some money. She asks me how the 'exotic dancing' business works. We talk it through, and I give her my agent's phone number. Opposite The Arabian Arms is a funny little dressmaking shop in an upstairs room, where two lovely old East End ladies make peephole bras, lurex G-strings and naughty Baby Doll nighties. I introduce Cosey to the ladies, and she gets some nice new knickers. She's booked to work one lunchtime alongside me at The Vauxhall Tavern, a lovely old vaudevillian pub in a battered part of South London. Of course, she is warmly welcomed by the crowd: everyone likes to see a nice new girl on the circuit.

Bob, the agent, is supposed to be coming down, but doesn't turn up — I've never actually met him, although sometimes a DJ says, 'Oh Bob was in earlier, did you see him?' He calls me after The Vauxhall Tavern gig to get the low-down on Cosey. She did really well, I say, they liked her a lot. So that's it — she's in. Bob's agency, Gemini, also handles a lot of party and event bookings, so has bands, DJs with sound systems and disco lights, and cabaret acts on his books. I'm playing in bands all of the time I'm working for him (which is from 1976 through to 1981) but he has no idea: I keep the two worlds completely apart. So my nom de drums, Max, is never mentioned. I try to avoid working at pubs such as The Greyhound in Fulham, or The Windsor Castle on Harrow Road, that are also music venues. Not that any band I've got anything to do with plays the pub rock circuit, but still.

1977 sees the odd-bod Ants/Monochrome Set hybrid dissolve. Two lead singers was never going to work — especially when the two are Bid and Stuart, who have completely different visions of what they want to do. I'm living with Andy Warren. 'Stay with me, Be My Wife, Share My life,' I say to him one day, so he does. Me, Bid and Andy are the Band With No Name, bashing out versions of 'He's Frank' and 'Flesh, Trash, Heat.' The quiet and unassuming Stuart (who comes and goes mysteriously) reappears after a break with a new look: black eyeliner, bare chest and a leather jacket. Andy and I bump into him in the newly-opened Roxy Club. Stuart phones me nightly to tell me that I need to persuade Andy to leave Bid and rejoin him (they had previously paired up in the B-Sides) in a new venture, which will be called the Ants. Like the Beatles, he says, except — the Ants. What do I think of the name 'Adam,' he asks. Like Adam Adamant, I say. Yeah, well… It's going to be all about Sex, he says. S.E.X. I can't imagine dear sweet Stuart as a sex symbol, but I humour him. Andy makes his decision, and the new band is born. Although I'm no longer working at the ICA, I'm still friends with the café staff, and I've reserved a 10 May slot at the ICA cafe for my band. Now that Adam has stolen Andy from Bid, I give them the slot. They're billed as the Shades, and havoc is duly caused and history written. But that's another story for another bedtime.

The bit that relates to the rest of this particular story is the sex bit. With the arrival of the Ants — or Adam and the Ants as they eventually became known — the sex worlds hinted at and played with by Malcolm and Vivienne and the crowd that circulate around their King's Road shop SEX get tackled head-on. *Ant Music for Sex People*. There's no ambivalence there. The previously secret worlds of fetish clothing, macintosh societies and bondage are bursting up and out from dingy cellars, braving the light of day. Soon, Hot Gossip will replace Pan's People, and the Torture Garden will become the nightclub to be seen in (preferably wearing little more than a dog collar and a few piercings) but we're not there yet — as Silver Jubilee year 1977 drags on, pulling the limping near-corpse of punk with it, *épater le bourgeois* is still possible. Punk gigs and clubs are awash with leather basques, rubber gimp masks and pierced nipples.

Is it all a dressing-up game, or is there some real sexual liberation going down? It feels real enough to me. Adam is certainly on a real-life mission; a quest to experience anything and everything on offer in the way of sexual experience of any sort. I tell people what I do for a living, and people are impressed and interested, not shocked or embarrassed. The sexual liberation promised in the 1960s seems to be actually happening — going on the busyness of the toilets at Louise's anyway. So many of the punk hangouts — like Louise's — are gay clubs, and there is a genuinely polymorphous perversity abounding. No one is at all bothered who is 'gay' or 'straight' or 'bisexual,' and in this post-Pill, pre-Aids bubble, anything goes.

And for the first time in rock history, the women hanging out around the bands are not groupies. They might (or might not) be sleeping with the boys, but they are also making sounds alongside them — or are being encouraged to do so. It's all a long way from the pre-punk days of encounters with dodgy DJs at the Radio 1 Club lunchtime sessions down at Lower Regent Street, or being propositioned by roadies when trying to get backstage to meet your glam-rock idols. There's a sense of equality, of parity.

It doesn't last of course — but then, nothing ever does. It's the moment that counts.

Eventually, Dee-Dee (or Lola or whoever she is) is retired. The industry is changing — the lavish, lusty world of burlesque is taking a back seat (for now) and the drab and soulless world of lap dancing is dawning. I find a new outlet: ballroom dancing. Teaching waltzes and rumbas sees me through the 1980s. I form a cabaret duet called Dorothy and Toto who dance deconstructed tangos and mambos, playing with gender identity. I even — sometimes — allow my dancing and drumming worlds to cross over: Dorothy and Toto support the Monochrome Set, and Bow Wow Wow on their New York opening of their American tour in 1982.

But all this is to come. Back in 1976, Lola is fluttering her feather fans and smoothing down her satin cheongsam. Dee-Dee is cracking her whip as Lou Reed sings his signature tune, undoing the crotch straps of her She & Me wet-look bodysuit to reveal, with postmodern irony, that her pubic hair has been shaved into a perfect heart shape and dyed a Crazy Colour punk pink. Modernity killed not only every night, but every lunchtime over a pint of Double Diamond in a City Road boozer.

10

A Letter to Jordan

by Richard Cabut

Jordan bounds into the RCA offices smiling and looking fighting fit. Small in stature, she compensates by exuding a nervous energy that dominates the room. She's dressed in a camouflage combat suit (original Vietnam I might add) and her hair has been chopped up into a severe 77 crop. We shake hands. Jordan is a hero.

Why? She has never really been in a band. Never starred in a smash film. Never actually stretched her talents on stage. She has dabbled in all these areas of media entertainment, and yet she is no dilettante.

What is it about her that, since the punk heyday of 1976, has demanded, if not adulation, then recognition and respect? Perhaps the answer is simply that Jordan has pushed her creative talents onto what she does best: being herself. For some people that is enough. She is a star. Her light will never be dimmed by a fickle public.

'To start a band would have been so obvious. So bland. Very early on Malcolm McLaren advised me to project and promote my own image and that is exactly what I have done.'

But more, much more. I tell you children, some day someone will make a film about Jordan's life...

I sent a letter on Monday
I sent a letter on Tuesday
...Oooh, I loved her
Send a letter to Jordan
— Adam and the Ants, 'Send A Letter To Jordan'

...A video slowly flickers into life. The scene is set on a train hurtling to London from the south coast. It is early 1976. A brash young lady sits with her legs crossed. She's wearing high-heeled black leather shoes, rubber stockings and very little else. A middle-aged businessman sitting opposite gives her a disparaging look. At the same time he gets *rather* excited and has to cover his lap with a newspaper. Jordan, the original pre-punk shocker, laughs. Hypocrite!

'I used to have so much trouble on that train to Seaford, where I used to live. People used to swear at me, abuse me, the lot. I wouldn't take any shit though and on one occasion I threw a tourist's camera out of the train window. He flipped! Eventually British Rail had to give me a First Class carriage to myself.'

Fast-forward... Later that day the same girl, abused, bemused and born into a world that she didn't create, stands outside *her* shop, SEX (later to become Seditionaries and World's End). In terms of style and culture, the most influential shop/meeting place ever.

I used to go down to the World's End
I used to go to that shop
I didn't like the clothes there
But I liked what she wore
I loved her
— Adam and the Ants, 'Send A Letter To Jordan'

Her hair has been swept up into long silver-and-blonde-coloured spikes. She's wearing a fluffy white mohair jumper, patent white boots and black leather belt. The camera has an eye for detail; Jordan is an original, or should I say an originator, an innovator.

A fashion report in *Honey* at the time reads, 'Go down to SEX, if not for the clothes then just to see the strange girl inside.' Punk Rock is just about to take off and Jordan, as much as the Sex Pistols, encapsulates the look and attitude: she sneers into the camera and spits in disgust.

Pause.

'I'd been dressing like that for ages so punk wasn't a new thing for me. My mother had found me uncontrollable since the age of seven, through choice I had absolutely *no* friends at school — the clothes were an expression of that chaos.

'Malcolm McLaren was always very interested in how people looked and I loved everything that SEX was about. Malcolm, Johnny Rotten and I were very close. Johnny always tells the story of how he went into SEX one day — I had on this T-shirt with a big rip right across the front and I'd put in a safety pin to cover it up. Johnny thought it was great and the safety pin thing started there and then.

'Johnny's like Frank Sinatra now. I saw him doing "Anarchy" on *The Tube* a few months ago, and it was really pathetic.'

Fast-forward. Through a blur of semi-realised images the film winds on to a heady night later in 1976. We are looking at a musical venue somewhere in London. The Sex Pistols are on stage, playing to what is a growing cult audience. The scene is full of tension, tinged with slices of manic wildness. Jordan, unable to control herself, suddenly jumps onto the stage. She dances along with the music. The sound and the fury. In a moment of sweet abandonment, Jordan's clothes literally fall apart (or so the camera would have you believe) leaving her naked from the waist up. Johnny Rotten ambles over and puts his arm round her shoulders.

Pause.

'76/77 was the most exciting period of my life — the adrenalin, the buzz, that is what it was all about for me. The Pistols used to really move me at that time. I just had to jump up and do things. On the other hand, the bands that came up afterwards were awful. I remember standing at the side of the stage and booing the Clash. Which is strange cos a couple of years later they became quite good. The Damned were the group that summed up everything that was wrong with punk.'

Fast-forward... to a scene that occurs even later, in the winter of 76. The camera pans round to a television studio in Manchester. Mr Smug himself, Tony Wilson, is introducing a band, 'And the next...' Before he can finish, the Pistols smash in to 'Anarchy in the UK,' and the man is stranded. It's little bits like this that made the Pistols great. Jordan wearing an 'Only Anarchists Are Pretty' shirt wanders, as if by chance, onto the set. A spur, a catalyst. Chairs are thrown about, general mayhem ensues. '*I want to beeee an-ar-chee.*'

Pause.

'That was all a set-up job. We planned it, like a lot of other things; the music business is still scared by the Pistols fiasco of three signings.

'Punk really died for me when the Pistols split up. It couldn't have gone on — it was like an orgasm, there for a few seconds and then... pfft. My prediction for the post-punk state of affairs was that Sid would become a huge star. We were close friends, and I was absolutely shocked when he died.'

Fast-forward... an eternity goes by, a fire has swept the land, purifying wherever its flames licked. Faster, faster. Round and around. Through a vortex the camera levels out and we're standing staring at the stage of the Nashville, a fairly small pub/club in West Kensington where a new punk group called Adam and the Ants are playing. Halfway through their chaotic set they launch into a piercing, repetitive riff; the sign for Jordan to leap up on stage and make her contribution to the Ants legend. Wearing her Venus leotard (her favourite SEX number) she sings '*New York coke joke.*' Sings? The noise is a wail mixed with a scream scrambled together to produce an inhuman choke/yell. In the future they will have special synthesisers whose sole function will be to reproduce that sound. The crowd go wild. And Jane Suck says, 'Do you know what Jordan *is* wearing these days? Soft woollies and tweed skirt. Oh yeah! Does Seditionaries sell handbags yet? No, no, no.' (Where are you when we need you Jane?) Adam has a guitar round his neck and joins in the choruses. Jordan jumps up and down. '*Andy Warhol — hero.*'

Pause.

'Adam used to send me love letters in the early days. I've still got them somewhere. He invited me down to a gig he was playing at the Man in the Moon in the King's Road. It was awful! The PA blew up and everything went wrong, but in Adam I saw something very special. I took Adam on the Pistols boat trip, where I tried hard to get arrested. I even spat in a policeman's face, but they weren't having any of it. Anyway, I got involved with the band: I nurtured and pushed them. I was a manager, and yet more than a manager. I finished with Adam for a while, when he insisted on signing to Decca. I thought it was the wrong move and I was proved right.

'The song I sang on stage with the Ants was *Lou*. It was great doing it, but then there was absolutely no pressure — doing it for a whole forty minutes is a different matter entirely.'

Onwards, ever onwards, the video is run fast-forward and stopped at a point only a few weeks later, in 1977. We are shown a film set where Jordan is talking to a middle-aged, balding man. He is Derek Jarman and the film they are making is *Jubilee*, a fantastic vision of a 'punk-rock' future, or 'no future' as the case may be. Totally over the top, totally wonderful. 'Pleased to meet you Mr G...g...Gintz.'

Jordan plays her part. Jarman gives her some loose instructions and the film camera rolls. Dressed in a ballerina's outfit, complete with tutu and pumps, she begins to dance elegantly if uncertainly around a raging bonfire. Heavy symbolism. Her statuesque figure cavorts around and around. A tall, thin hippy type wanders around throwing books onto the fire. Jordan pays no attention. Dance, dance, dance. This is perhaps the most bizarre scene from *Jubilee* as well as the most effective. Jordan whirls as the books are burnt. She doesn't lose her concentration once. Nerves I expect.

Pause.

'*Jubilee* pushed me to the limits, mentally and physically. I had to dance on points on concrete — no ballerina has to do that, they've got supple wooden floors. My toes bled and my legs were burned by the fire. We actually got arrested that day cos Derek insisted on using real guns and the police took us away. We tried to explain that the guns had no firing pins, but I don't think they even knew what they were. Derek Jarman is such a clever director though, he's got a knack of leaving certain mistakes in. The amount of lines that I fluffed... but I want to keep doing that, I want to keep it raw, I never want to learn all the tricks. I still to this day get fan mail from girls mostly who've just seen *Jubilee*. They say that I've made a big impression on them. After I was in *Jubilee* I was in a play in Edinburgh, and then in a couple of films that won awards in Spain, of all places. There's a strong possibility that I'll be in a West End play soon called *Gits*. I'm looking forward to that.'

Still onwards, fatly forwarded. Eons pass in a rapid eye movement. The times they have a changed, those who were first are now last. Oh God. And Jordan? Well, this is 1980 and the camera starts at Sloane Square and travels the length of the King's Road, finally stopping outside *that* shop. Now, the 'Clothes For Heroes' plaque and the metal-grid/black-glass front has been replaced by some rickety wooden steps and quaint curiosity-shop windows. Ours is the best effort so far to leave the 20th century? Indeed this is World's End.

Jordan is standing outside, her buckled foot on the step. Her brown hair cascades in curls from underneath a tricorne Napoleon hat. A girl called Annabelle is ushered past her into the shop. The time is again one of excitement, colour, change. Jordan is again at its nub, if not actually a main exponent. She is happy, we see her do a little jig-a-jig up the stairs and into the shop. We press the pause button.

'I worked in the shop until shortly after it changed to World's End. Not everybody can do a job that they enjoy and I loved it there, believed in the things that Malcolm and Viv were doing. Those two have split up now. I still see Malcolm, but not Viv. In fact, out of all my contemporaries and peers from 76, Malcolm is the one who's turned out the best. That pirate look was great — I'm like a snake though, I have to shed a skin every so often. At one time, I was going to get an Arts Council grant for being a living work of art. We discussed it, but it all fell through. I'm still going to get a £1,000 hairdo done, and no I can't tell you what it'll be.'

We switch on the video machine again, fast-forward it a little bit, not too far — ah, just there'll do. Adam and the Ants have, by a quirk of CBS, established themselves as the most popular group in England. The camera focuses on a typical living room, in a typical street, on a typical girl. It's Thursday evening, it's *Top of the Pops* on the TV and the daughter of the house (her name is Yvette, I think) is screaming because the Ants' new video is being shown. Adam, in his familiar Charge of the Light Brigade jacket is tapping a cane around blindly to the beat. His old mate Jordan dances to the side. And how. '*Ant-Mus-Ic.*' Press the pause please 'cause...

'I got involved with Adam after Malcolm walked off with his group to form Bow Wow Wow. Once more, I took care of their look and outlook. I was their advisor and sort of entrepreneur. Kevin Mooney, who's now my husband, and I left just after the show at the Palladium for Princess Margaret. I felt that Adam just wasn't giving one hundred percent anymore, and I can't work with people like that. He got the power that he was after, but he didn't even use it. He's not really enjoying what he's doing nowadays — he needs criticism, I need criticism, everyone needs criticism, and he's just not getting it from the eight-year-olds that he's playing to. We're still friends though, he sends me postcards every so often from New York or wherever.'

The video button is pressed, the clouds go by at the speed of an aeroplane, people walk around at the pace of speeding Keystone Cops (which incidentally they were). Slower... slower... the tape finally jumps to a sudden halt. Jordan and I find ourselves watching a video of ourselves watching a film of ourselves of a video of ourselves of STOP! The present.

Kevin Mooney is now in a group called Wide Boy Awake — 'a red hot dance band' who incorporate different styles of music and many levels of idea and ideal. They're the best. They are as indicative of, and distanced from, their times as were the Pistols and the Ants from theirs. By sheer quality. They are the best. Jordan is, very simply, at their core.

'The only reason that I'm not upset by the passing of 76/77 and the spirit that went with it is the existence of Wide Boy Awake. They hold the same excitement for me. They have that one hundred percent commitment. They believe. This group want to revert to a time when people *wanted* to go out and see groups and not just cos they were there, and the group want to promote a buzz, a *feeling*. My position within the band is the same as it was with the Ants on the two occasions, except intensified. I manage them and generally help to steer them. Kevin writes all the songs in my presence, which helps. RCA want me to do some vocals with the group, which I'd love to do. Kevin may write me a song. The group means everything to me, and I tell you, when we get the power we're going to *do* something with it.'

Jordan: always a natural rebel, both in medium and in message, with a flair for self-publicity — the limelight has always been hers. But instead of being content with the glow of infamy, she has turned her talent to concrete yet uncanny effect. Always a girl of action, a participator; her power is that of a modern-day Shaman. Hers is the ability to communicate with and stimulate the 'spirit.' The Sex Pistols (indirectly perhaps), Adam and the Ants and Wide Boy Awake (plus associated cultures) have all felt the lasting benefits.

Jordan wrinkles her nose into an irrepressible, infectious smile. Sips a lager and calms down after what has been a rush of commentary. It has been an impressive film, an impressive life. Jordan is a hero.

11

Punk's not Dead. It's in a Coma...

by Andy Blade

...I declared, my pint spilling everywhere, as I joined a group of people at the bar. The year was 1982, and I was speaking to, or rather, shouting at Wattie, the magnificently mohican-adorned singer with the Exploited, whom I'd just been introduced to by Carol Clerk, a *Melody Maker* journalist. I can't be certain, but I think we were at a Jesus & Mary Chain gig, somewhere near King's Cross — but to be honest, it could have been any Eighties indie group.

'Come on, you've got to meet Wattie, he'll be chuffed,' Carol had insisted. I'd long since moved on from Eater, and now had curly shoulder-length hair, looking like a cross between Marc Almond and — much to my disgust — B. A. Robertson. Wattie wouldn't have recognised me in a million years, but I knew who he was: with that hundred-foot mohican, how couldn't I? I admit I didn't know much about his band, other than having seen them on *Top of the Pops* recently, but I'd already dismissed them at that point, merely by virtue of being associated with the second coming of punk. It had very little to do with the first wave, which to me was the only wave that counted — that being the one that had changed my world.

Face to face with this Glaswegian giant, I most certainly wasn't trying to provoke or insult him. Nor was I being elitist, I just didn't (and don't) see the two movements as the same thing. However, I was far too pissed to consider either the complexities or protocol of the situation. I just thought the 'in-a-coma' comment was a funny thing to say. It was the first obvious thing that came into my head, the title of their debut album being

Punk's Not Dead. Wattie, however, wasn't laughing. To be fair, I don't think he'd even heard me speak. The bar area was so noisy, with people shouting their conversations over the top of the loud music, it was giving me a headache.

Ignoring my statement he looked at me for a second.

'Eater,' he eventually said, adding a hearty 'Fuck!,' no doubt to emphasise how excited he was. He then turned around, and continued talking to his mates. Personally, I don't even think he'd heard of Eater. His knowledge of punk rock quite probably stopped at the Sex Pistols, possibly even the fucking Dickies — and the latest *Daily Mail* exposé. I wasn't going to mention it, but as far as I was concerned, it was Wattie, and others like him, who had helped re-model the new wave, by isolating its uglier aesthetics, probably due to an overwhelming inability to understand or interpret the intelligent Situationism that led to the creation of the first wave, only a few short years before.

Truth was, punk had been in a coma since the autumn of 1977 — with no real chance of recovery. Whilst it might well have been having a very exciting near-death experience upon another realm, lying on its gurney, with a lick of dribble running down its jaw, it was clear that a priest would be called any second. It was soon to be deceased.

Now we all know that it's not good practice to abuse undernourished, post-war, teenage cultural revolutions, but somehow, this is what was happening, right under our noses, and so prematurely too. The build-up to punk's arrival turned out to have lasted longer than its eventual lifespan. Those bands and people from the original explosion of only a few short months before, who risked so much, and whose single-minded creativity had paved the way for it all to happen, watched, helpless, as its condition disintegrated.

In the end, despite the bonds of allegiance vociferously pronounced from every dingy venue in the land, punk — as far as the bulk of the media was concerned — was only ever about coat pegs upon which to hang the easily identifiable, the visual concept being the most obvious place to start: hello Wattie, Cockney Rejects, UK Subs, GBH, UK Decay, Dickies, Boomtown Rats, the Drones etc. Punk rock's intellectual, arty angle had been dispensed with, for the simple reason that arty intellectuals generally don't sell shitloads of records. Arty intellectualism does not go down too well in places like Wrexham, Luton, Milton Keynes, or North Wales — because the general public live in these shitty little places, and they don't get it. They need signposts, or they feel dizzy. All they were ever after was the easily identifiable, lest their brains begin to hurt.

12

Ever Fallen in Love?

by David Wilkinson

A few years ago, Liverpool's annual LGBT festival *Homotopia* featured an exhibition entitled 'England's Erotic Dream.' A selection of archival photographs interpreted through 'a queer gaze,' it was pleasingly described as an 'unapologetically homosexual exhibition on British punk.'

'England's Erotic Dream' did a good job of highlighting the undeniable queerness of early punk. This is something that remains depressingly under-played in most mainstream histories (Jon Savage's *England's Dreaming* is a welcome exception). The exhibition, though, was framed by interpretations that were more reflective of recent trends in academic thinking on sexuality than they were of the historical moment documented by the photographs. Punk approaches to sexual dissidence were celebrated as 'transgressive,' 'deviant' and 'parodic,' though not, interestingly, as liberating or egalitarian. Nor was there any mention of the disturbing crossover of same-sex passion with the far right in certain strains of punk, which was occasionally captured by the photographs on display.

The exhibition got me thinking about the influence of a certain strain of queer theory beyond the world of academia. I wondered if it would be possible to give a more historical account of early British punk's sexual politics, especially approaches to same-sex passion. In doing so, I also wanted to weigh up how punk might matter today to progressive struggles over sexuality, offering a less rose-tinted view of its transgressive impulses than that found in the work of writers like J. Jack Halberstam. What resources of hope might punk offer, and how might we learn from its missteps and dead ends, which, to be fair, are always easier to see in hindsight?

Not a very 'punk' approach, maybe, in its attempt at measured evaluation. Then again, punk and post-punk culture was constantly trying to take stock of its own runaway momentum. Through songs, fanzine editorials and running debates in the pages of the music press, the fractured counterculture spawned in 76 was persistently self-reflexive well into its 1980s afterlife. There was even a punk 'conference' at London's Conway Hall in 1981. Also, just as Matthew Worley has pointed out that punk resisted definition by political forces on the right or the left, so its attitudes to sexuality were complex and diverse, deserving of critical reflection.

Liberation, disillusion and 'terrorist chic'

In *England's Dreaming*, Jon Savage's still exemplary history of early British punk, it's made clear that the duo of Malcolm McLaren and Vivienne Westwood were the undoubted catalysts of punk in Britain. Their activities would therefore seem a good place to begin.

In the first half of the 1970s, McLaren and Westwood were part of the milieu identified by style journalist Peter York as 'Them.' Savage notes that the 'Them' were 'too young to benefit from the full sixties explosion but old enough, by 1976, to have established themselves as London's leading artistic/bohemian circle.' The 'Them' merged Pop Art's enthusiasm for pastiche, Americana and 'trash' with the ironic distancing of camp. Developing a proto-postmodernist style, which York dubbed 'Art Necro,' the 'Them's quick-change revivalism... became very big business around the turn of [the 1970s], when... people were looking for something *silly* to take their minds off depressing things.' Biba flounce and the kitsch designs of Mr Freedom (displayed on inflatable sex doll mannequins) were the order of the day. York's emphasis on the word 'silly' suggests the overall frivolity of 'Them.' This was a sensibility that served them well commercially, as an anxious embrace of hedonistic escapism took hold in response to the chaotic upheavals of the 1970s. In line with this, it was also a sensibility that, as York observed, remained 'apolitical' and 'jaded' with regard to 'odd sex.'

Politics and sex were the two pressure points upon which McLaren and Westwood leaned to effect a break with this scene, cannily tapping the mood of increasing polarisation as the decade progressed, economic crisis sharpened and dislocation set in. Savage notes, for example, that 'their interest in fifties clothes had nothing to do with fun or camp,' and believes that 'in their different ways, Westwood and McLaren were politicised: this gave them a *moral* purpose in their approach to clothes.'

But theirs was an idiosyncratic kind of politics, especially in relation to sexuality. McLaren and Westwood clearly had a nose for hypocrisy, recognising the mass-market incorporation of the 'sexual revolution' of the 1960s, and the 'real dynamics of desire... and repression' which were being 'fudged' by this 'window dressing.' Their response drew from a variety of sources. One was McLaren's bohemian background. From this came an understanding of sexuality as an irrational force capable of disrupting social norms once unanchored from the private sphere. Originating at least as early as the Romantics, this faith in overt sexuality as rebellion was resurgent once more in the counterculture of the 1960s through which McLaren had floated, haunting the clubs of Soho and embarking upon a string of unfin-ished art-school courses.

Thus the pair's shop was re-named SEX in 1975, and its stock began to include the kind of fetish wear usually only available by mail order, with the tongue-in-cheek slogan 'rubberwear for the office.' T-shirts attempted to go one further in the quest to shock. Designs included an image from a paedophile magazine and a picture of the mask worn by a serial rapist from Cambridge who was then still unconvicted and active. Similarly, the recycling of past subcultural styles (such as the associations of biker gear with 'sexuality, violence and death') may well have been driven less by the non-committal postmodern pastiche of 'Them' and more by the belief that 'bohemia is always yesterday.' As Elizabeth Wilson has noted, this nostalgic impulse for authentic resistance arises from the founding contradiction that continually reanimates the bohemian myth. In an industrialised and instrumentalist capitalist society, culture has long been invested in as a form of opposition. Its ever-increasing commodification, though, continually undermines such faith, leading successive generations to assume that the wave has long since crested and troughed; aesthetic radicalism seems always buried at some point in the past.

It's this contradiction, too, which produces the love-hate relationship between bohemia and the wider bourgeoisie of which it is often a class fraction. Sex, after all, sells. McLaren and Westwood's personalities are microcosmic metaphors on this score. Each combined elements of the bourgeois — their restless entrepreneurialism and Westwood's Calvinist work ethic — with the bohemian — McLaren's erratic lifestyle and their shared desire to shock. In an *NME* interview after their shop was raided by police, Westwood claimed, 'I'm trying to de-mystify these silly taboos... you don't make people think unless you upset them emotionally.'

For all such talk — and there was a lot of it from both of them — their conflicted stances meant that the designs they produced were often squarely within the terms of the conservative orthodoxies they provoked. Indeed, Savage shrewdly observes the uncanny parallel between Westwood's petit-bourgeois 'moral authority' and the ascendency of Margaret Thatcher, portraying the two women as 'mirror images of the same national archetype.'

McLaren and Westwood shared their understanding of sexuality with the new social movements that had sprung up and overlapped with the counterculture from the late 1960s. Elizabeth Wilson, a key participant in gay and women's liberation, even quotes the same entry from the diary of playwright Joe Orton to encapsulate this attitude as Savage does to explain the name of McLaren and Westwood's shop: 'Yes. Sex is the only way to infuriate them. Much more fucking and they'll be screaming hysterics in next to no time.' The conviction that sexuality could be harnessed for progressive political purposes marked the point at which the pair diverged from the liberation movements. The Gay Liberation Front in Britain, for instance, produced in its short lifetime a bewildering and still captivating array of theory and praxis which merged libertarian attitudes to sexuality with feminism, a critique of the nuclear family and a humanistic, often radical socialist collectivism. Not for nothing was the movement's paper named after the Beatles' 'Come Together.'

McLaren and Westwood had no such normative stance. On a visit to the shop in 1977, Westwood informed York that the clothing implied 'commitment,' to which he drily retorted 'commitment to *what* is less clear.' Commitment to transgression could well have been the response: rather than consciously alternative or oppositional values, the designs deliberately played on conservative understandings of unsanctioned sexuality as perverse, sordid and violent in order to provoke a reaction. And although the pair had broken with 'Them,' a residual affectlessness carried over from that milieu in the particular tactics selected in order to shock. Reviewing a confrontational early Sex Pistols gig at the loft party of 'Them' artist Andrew Logan in February 1976, Nick Kent evoked the 'air of heavy-duty ennui,' feeling that the SEX crowd's 'aesthetic gang warfare' was as 'sexless and desperate' as the clique it opposed.

Westwood and McLaren's approach exemplified a mood that York was onto, tracing it back through pop-cultural flirtations with terrorist, sado-masochist and fascist imagery earlier in the 1970s. Interestingly, York also referred to the thesis of US academic Michael Selzer, who named this mood 'terrorist chic' and characterised it as 'a fascinated approval of violence' that 'apotheosises meaninglessness.'

Via a series of case studies that included punk and gay sadomasochist clubs, Selzer argued that one root of 'terrorist chic' was the desire of 1960s counterculturalists for transgressive new experiences. After a time, and in a less idealistic moment, such impulses had taken increasingly extreme and amoral forms in their attempts to achieve novel kinds of sensuous stimulation. Importantly, however, even these forms struggled to connect within the alienating environment of consumer society, often resulting in cynical detachment and nihilism. Selzer's judgement of the phenomenon was conservative, but his analysis had a degree of accuracy. Savage notes that the 'overt sexuality' of SEX designs actually 'became an abstraction of sex,' referring to a 'distinctly unsettling' shirt that featured a photograph of a pair of breasts at chest height. Attributing a polemical intent to the designs, Savage views them as a comment on 'industrialised sex districts like Soho, where, by the mid-1970s, the great promises of liberation had been honed down into a series of stock postures.'

'Ello Joe'

It's hard to say what McLaren and Westwood viewed as the alternative to the repressive incitement of sexuality they seemed to scorn and parody: a provocation of sexual awareness and desire which, as David Alderson has noted, commodifies, fetishises and alienates sexuality in the pursuit of profit. What's clear is that it was within the approach to sexuality that I've so far sketched that McLaren and Westwood understood same-sex passion. Thus clothing designs might feature the 'fervid lesbian fantasies' of Scottish writer Alexander Trocchi, whose work bridged 1950s bohemia and 1960s counterculture.

One of the most well-known SEX designs, meanwhile, brought together transgression, affectlessness and intimations of violence: two men in cowboy outfits, minus the trousers, face each other outside a dancehall. One is grabbing the other by the lapels and their penises are almost touching. As Savage observes, their genitals are at the same height as one cowboy's pistol in its holster. The caption reads: 'Ello Joe, been anywhere lately? Nah, its [sic] all played aht Bill, gettin to [sic] straight.' Through its explicit depiction of two semi-naked men, the image aimed to shock. Simultaneously, there is a hint of 'terrorist chic' in the forceful gesture, the elision of pistol and penis and the debt to gay pornographic artist Tom of Finland, whose illustrations featured eroticised images of Nazis. Yet the image also conveys a jaded artifice, an affectless absence of connection, in the cowboys' weariness with the scene, the fact that they are actually Cockneys dressed up as cowboys and the small but all-important gap between cocks.

Given this portrayal of same-sex passion as alienated, perverse and violent, it's unsurprising that McLaren and Westwood were prone to possibly ironic homophobic gestures that were calculated to shock in their contempt of even reformist demands for respect, understanding and openness. Westwood's response to her belief that Derek Jarman's film *Jubilee* had misrepresented punk was to produce an 'open letter' to the director on both sides of a T-shirt. It claimed that the film's costumes had 'something to do with a gay (which you are) boy's love of dressing up... ("does he have a cock between his legs or doesn't he" kinda thing)' and compared *Jubilee* to 'watching a gay boy jerk off through the titillation of his masochistic tremblings. You pointed your nose in the right direction then you wanked.' McLaren, meanwhile, played the predatory homosexual stereotype for comic effect in the Sex Pistols film *The Great Rock 'n' Roll Swindle*.

The pair's attitudes transferred to their protégés too: at a Pistols gig in Texas, John Lydon wore the cowboys T-shirt whilst Sid Vicious heckled the crowd by shouting, 'You cowboys are all a bunch of fucking faggots!' Jordan, the imperious and startlingly dressed shop assistant at Sex, had played the character of Amyl Nitrate in *Jubilee*. Interviewed by Julie Burchill for the *NME*, Jordan discussed Jarman's milieu and her attitude to gay subculture. She claimed to have 'hated' Jarman's film *Sebastiane*, saying 'it was full of prancing, whining queens.' A diatribe against '*Gay News* readers and all that lot' followed: 'they're so precious... so *weak*... the ones who don't need to mention it I don't dislike.'

The SEX crowd's antics were inseparable from the moment of late-1970s Britain, conjuring their wider impact out of a volatile set of circumstances. As resentful sensibilities began to surface in response to economic crisis, they were amplified and given reactionary shape by a newly vociferous tabloid media. The progressive advances of the 1960s and early 1970s were homogenised and demonised by the ascendant New Right as a corrupting, destabilising 'permissiveness.'

Same-sex relations were key here: even before the downfall of Liberal Party leader Jeremy Thorpe and Mary Whitehouse's successful legal campaign against *Gay News*, the 1975 documentary *Johnny Go Home*, which implicitly associated homosexuality with paedophilia, provoked a media furore which engulfed Alan Jones, a young gay shop assistant at SEX. Arrested by plain-clothes policemen for wearing the cowboys T-shirt in public, Jones was prosecuted and the arrest reported on the front page of *The Guardian*. In a dress rehearsal for the Bill Grundy TV incident that catapulted the Pistols to fame a year later, McLaren and Westwood achieved the publicity they sought. McLaren's response to Jones' arrest betrayed a wary self-interest when it came to the consequences of shock tactics: Jones claims that McLaren promised 'a really good lawyer... What happened? Fuck all.'

The Bromley Contingent

Despite all this, the presence of queer imagery in McLaren and Westwood's designs was undoubtedly a central factor in the coalescence of what *Melody Maker* journalist Caroline Coon dubbed 'the Bromley Contingent.' The original nucleus of punk subculture, this collection of largely teenage sexual dissidents from scattered outer-London suburbs seized on punk as a classic metropolitan escape route — irrespective of Westwood and McLaren's commitment or otherwise to gay rights.

Punk also offered a new form of belonging for a fresh generation of sexual dissidents at a moment of conservative backlash. The initial impetus and publicity of gay liberation had declined, while its countercultural links had weakened as reformist identity politics came to predominate over the radical concerns of the movement's early years. The Bromley Contingent, it should be noted, set the precedent for the frequent regional germination of punk subculture on the gay scene. In Manchester, punks congregated in The Ranch, the basement of a club belonging to drag-queen entertainer Frank Foo Foo Lammar, a boxer and son of an Ancoats rag-and-bone man. Jayne Casey of Big in Japan recalls that 'in Liverpool you went to gay clubs like the Bear's Paw,' and Marc Almond, later of Soft Cell, noted the crossover during his punk years at Leeds Polytechnic. Even in far-flung Norwich, punks adopted gay club The Jacquard.

Importantly, the Bromley Contingent's introduction of the Sex Pistols to the gay scene influenced the early portrayal of punk in the weekly music press, a powerful media mouthpiece when it came to defining and representing punk. A camp gossip column in the *NME* written under the pseudonym 'Velda' reported John Lydon's attendance at London gay club The Sombrero and his involvement in preventing a robbery: 'such a *plucky* act, don't you think?' It also featured an interview with Jordan in which she claimed obliquely of Lydon: 'He doesn't have actual girlfriends.' Though the music press would later air the macho and sometimes blatantly homophobic turn of certain punk bands (Jean-Jacques Burnel of the Stranglers commented disdainfully of his peers, 'There are a lot of ponces involved, and a lot of poofters, and a lot of posers who have never dirtied their hands'), early articles like the 'Velda' column may well have been influential on the fostering of connections between punk and gay subculture.

There was an affinity, though, between the Bromley Contingent and the activities of McLaren and Westwood. The pair had drawn inspiration for their designs from the grassroots innovations of those young people, including the Bromley Contingent, who frequented the King's Road, pioneering new styles of their own. The predominantly middle-class background of the Bromley Contingent, too, meant that there was often a residually bohemian attitude to same-sex passion. Bertie Marshall, who renamed himself Berlin aged sixteen in 1976, opined of a homophobic assault he suffered that 'it wasn't queer bashing, it was freak bashing.'

Prior to punk, the Contingent had been fans of the art-school glam associated with 'Them,' including Roxy Music and David Bowie. Savage noted in 1980 that the model of same-sex passion Bowie had introduced into British pop slotted into the broader images of decline in his 1970s output, chiming with the break-up of postwar consensus: 'The puritan hangover still bit; homosexuality had to be perceived as part of some greater decadence... if it's all ending, anything goes.' There was a shared fascination amongst the group for the film *Cabaret*, and Marshall mythologises the Contingent's early days by comparing them with Christopher Isherwood's *Goodbye to Berlin*. As in McLaren and Westwood's designs, then, same-sex passion was part of a broader transgressive sensibility that relied on conservative ideology for its effect. There was a comparable attraction to publicity too, bound to the same New Right dynamic: members of the Bromley Contingent appeared on the front page of the

Daily Mail on 19 October 1976 under the headline 'These People Are the Wreckers of Civilisation,' after they attended the opening of performance-art group COUM Transmissions' 'Prostitution' exhibition at the ICA (COUM would later become the post-punk industrial act Throbbing Gristle). The exhibition included framed pages taken from pornographic magazines and used tampons, and the scandal it provoked led to the Arts Council withdrawing support for COUM.

'Terrorist chic' was also present. There may well be some creativity with the truth in Marshall's memoir *Berlin Bromley* — a kind of mythologising bohemian performance of everyday life. However, its overall depiction of Marshall's milieu and experiences seems largely plausible, and often adds up with the recollections of others. There's a gleeful element of teenage rebellion in the anecdotes recounted, such as the occasion when Susan Ballion, later Siouxsie Sioux, posed as a dominatrix and Marshall as a dog on a lead, causing havoc in a fashionable Bromley wine bar by refusing to leave until a bowl of water was provided. Yet the power relations played out here hinted at a darker undertow, as various members of the Contingent including Marshall became romantically involved at a young age with a life of prostitution and drug abuse. Marshall also experienced a string of exploitative relationships and encounters, the most extreme of which led to him being raped.

The affectless distance present in Westwood and McLaren's clothing designs appeared at first glance to have been dramatically closed by the Bromley Contingent. Savage claims that 'the women and men that Vivienne collected acted out their wildest fantasies… they became part of the Sex Pistols and gave punk its Warholian edge.' There was something unnerving about the character of these fantasies, however. Though there was nothing sexless about experiences such as Marshall's, a callous and amoral affectlessness nevertheless continued to permeate them. It frequently spilled over into other kinds of relations too. Marshall, for instance, claims that after seeing Pier Paolo Pasolini's film *Salo*, he shat in the grocery cupboard of neighbours described as 'a crip and his God-fearing Aussie nurse' who'd attempted to report Marshall and his flatmate to the police for prostitution.

Musically, this sensibility was clearly detectable in Siouxsie and the Banshees' 'Carcass,' a highlight of the band's debut LP *The Scream*. The song depicts a protagonist who, in his desire for 'raw love,' butchers his objects of desire and hangs them in 'cold storage.' Its chorus ('be a carcass... be limblessly in love') neatly encapsulates the transgressive violence and alienation that characterised many of the Bromley Contingent's socio-sexual relations, including instances of same-sex passion. Meanwhile, the song's black humour — in a reference to the food company Heinz, the victim is referred to as the '58th variety' — generates an affectless distancing. Paul Morley's generally positive account of *The Scream* nevertheless fretted that 'there is a twisted passion but no compassion.'

Like McLaren and Westwood's approach to sexuality, the Bromley Contingent's framing of same-sex passion had implications that went beyond their milieu. In the late 1970s, support for the far-right National Front burgeoned amidst racist media scapegoating for the economic and social dislocation of Britain. It was in this context that same-sex passion was being lived in transgressive and often compassionless ways. It's interesting that Marshall's response to Pasolini's *Salo* was not to share in the film's critique of the links between fascism and libertinism, but to allegedly shit in the cornflakes of someone he held in contempt. And so Marshall's memoir romanticises, more than any other of his encounters, his relationship with Martin, a nineteen-year-old 'bloke' who had been in a youth detention centre, passed through the Navy and was a member of the National Front. For Marshall, Martin was 'pure Jean Genet.' Marshall was not alone in this flirtatious referencing of the historical crossover of fascism and same-sex passion. Other members of the Bromley Contingent repeatedly wore swastika armbands at Louise's with the aim of provoking the DJ, a Jewish lesbian.

'I Like Boys'

The broader punk scene, however, auto-critiqued such leanings almost immediately, sensing the danger involved. Jon Savage's 1976 *London's Outrage* fanzine featured cut-ups from Freudian Marxist Wilhelm Reich's *The Mass Psychology of Fascism* and worried that 'the English have always been great ones for emotional and physical S&M — now we are as weak as so many kittens, nationally, the bully-boy sex-power of Nazism/fascism is very attractive.'

That same year, Rock Against Racism was set up partly in response to Bromley Contingent hero David Bowie's claim that Britain might benefit from a fascist leader. By 1978, it had become one of the key infrastructural supports in the regional spread of punk. Especially during 1978 and 1979, RAR's influence shaped the political character of punk and post-punk. RAR's concerns tended to extend beyond racism to encompass issues of gender and sexuality, reflecting the cumulative effect of the new social movements on the left. Telford's *Guttersnipe* fanzine, facilitated by local RAR activists via a local youth club, featured an interview with a lesbian aimed at furthering understanding amongst its largely teenage readership. Its earnest title was 'In This Issue We Talk To A Lesbian About Her Homosexual Life.' RAR's official fanzine *Temporary Hoarding* promoted gay protest singer Tom Robinson and included fascist persecution of gay people in its nightmare scenario of a Britain ruled by the NF: 'If we're gay we're locked away... sexual orthodoxy, patriotic ditties on the radio, mashed potato for tea.'

In Manchester, punk's second city, punk forms of same-sex passion took on a very different character from those of the SEX milieu and the Bromley Contingent even before the increase in momentum of RAR. In part this was due to Pete Shelley of the

Buzzcocks, the unassuming godfathers of Manchester's punk scene. Shelley was born in the Lancashire mining and cotton town of Leigh, where Coal Board clerk Alan Horsfall had established the North Western Committee for Homosexual Law Reform (later the Campaign for Homosexual Equality) in 1964. Shelley himself had been involved with gay and women's liberation whilst studying at Bolton Institute of Technology in the mid-1970s. He gave an interview with *Gay News* in 1977 and openly discussed his bisexuality in the music press. Echoing the emphasis of liberation politics on pride, he wore a badge that declared 'I Like Boys' for the Buzzcocks' first *Top of the Pops* appearance the following year. The early scepticism of gay liberation regarding clear-cut sexual identity, and the desire of its more radical elements to 'change the sexuality of everyone, not just homosexuals,' in the words of activist Michael Brown, may well have played a part in Shelley's repeated emphasis that the lyrics of Buzzcocks songs were deliberately non-gender-specific in an attempt to maximise their potential for empathetic response.

Shelley's fanzine, *Plaything*, was concerned with 'personal politics,' one of the hallmarks of gay liberation and of the libertarian left in general. It argued that punk or 'new wave' was 'not just about music' but 'a challenge to consider everything you do, think or feel... the way you react to the people around you. The ways that you love them, fuck them, hate them, slate them.' A stained archival copy features a cheeky photocopied image of a topless Bay City Rollers on the reverse of this declaration. Manchester's key post-punk fanzine *City Fun*, meanwhile, was run from the office of the New Hormones record label set up by Buzzcocks' manager Richard Boon. It featured adverts for Manchester Gay Centre and national advice line Friend. Edited by the teenage *enfant terrible* couple Liz Naylor and Cath Carroll, *City Fun* displayed the influence of gay liberation's irreverent countercultural style and Shelley's witty and heartfelt interrogations of desire and romance in articles such as 'The Joys of Oppression — By Mouth Or By Rectum.'

Despite this distinctively Mancunian take on punk and same-sex passion, and the success of RAR and related movements such as Rock Against Sexism in claiming the movement as broadly progressive for a time, the far-right flirtations first explored by the Bromley Contingent persisted and developed far more literally amidst the diverse fall-out from punk. By the early 1980s a consciously fascist sub-genre of punk had crystallised, which had direct links to the National Front and was led by Blackpool band Skrewdriver. It later transpired that the band's roadie Nicky Crane, a skinhead with a series of convictions for racist violence, had been leading a double life on London's gay scene and working as a doorman for a sadomasochist club.

Conclusion

Transgression, then, is not automatically progressive. Rather than celebrating it as such, it is worth reflecting briefly on what else sexual dissidents might learn from punk. This is not a capitulation to the myth of bohemian yesterdays, a belief that only the countercultural moments of the past have anything to teach us. Rather it's an acceptance of the open-ended legacy of punk and an attempt to engage with its politically contested history — especially in the context of the fortieth anniversary 'Punk London' celebrations currently being coordinated by the office of Conservative mayor Boris Johnson.

Short of space to engage in this way, I'll end with a single example. Nowadays, transgressively exaggerated sexual-power dynamics are all over gay smartphone app Grindr, with relentless peer pressure to define as a 'top' or a 'bottom.' Many profiles specify preferences by race (white people are rarely, if ever, excluded) and an affectless ennui predominates: 'no agenda,' 'nothing serious' and 'not interested in...' are all common phrases. Despite huge advances in LGBTQ rights since the 1970s, such a situation is broadly reflective of continuing inequalities (around race, for instance, and the expectation of unequal roles), not to mention the alienation and isolation still experienced by many in a persistently heterosexist society. It's no coincidence, after all, that suicide rates, self-harm and mental-health issues are all disproportionately higher amongst LGBTQ people.

It's difficult to see how this situation might be illuminated much by that sexual sensibility within punk that dwelt romantically and sometimes nihilistically on transgression, violence and alienation, however darkly alluring and culturally significant it may be. Instead, we might look to the collectivist and inclusive connections made between punk, queer subcultures and populist movements like RAR for inspiration in the fostering of comparable affective links in the present. The continued focus on some form of transformative sexual liberation in certain quarters of punk, inherited from an earlier countercultural utopianism, offers a similar glimmer of possibility now that notions of sexual freedom are almost uniformly colonised by the market. Like the Buzzcocks, I'm still nostalgic 'for an age yet to come.'

13

For Your Unpleasure

by Mark Fisher

It is well known that the Banshees were formed as a result of the future Siouxsie and Severin meeting at a Roxy show in 1974. So, unlike the Birthday Party, who were famously disgusted when they arrived in London to find it dominated by new-romantic poseur-pop, the Banshees belonged to an art-pop lineage which had a relationship to music that was neither ironically distant nor direct. For all their inventiveness, for all the damage they wreaked upon rock form, the Birthday Party remained Romantics, desperate to restore an expressive and expressionistic force to rock; a quest which led them back to the satanic heartland of the blues. By contrast with this carnal heat, the early Banshees affected a deliberate — and deliberated — coldness and artificiality.

Siouxsie came from the art-rock capital of England — that zone of South London in which both David Bowie (Beckenham) and Japan (Catford, Beckenham) grew up. Although Siouxsie was involved with punk from the very beginning, and although all of the major punk figures (even Sid Vicious) were inspired by Roxy, the Banshees were one of the first punk groups to openly acknowledge a debt to glam. Glam has a special affinity with the English suburbs; its ostentatious anti-conventionality was negatively inspired by the eccentric conformism of manicured lawns and quietly-tended psychosis Siouxsie sang of on 'Suburban Relapse.' But glam had been the preserve of male desire: what would its drag look like when worn by a woman? This was a particularly fascinating inversion when we consider that Siouxsie's most significant resource was not the serial-identity sexual ambivalence of Bowie but the staging of male desire in Roxy Music. She may have hung out with 'Bowie boys,' but Siouxsie seemed to borrow much more from the lustrous PVC blackness of *For Your Pleasure* than from anything in the Thin White Duke's wardrobe. *For Your Pleasure* songs like 'Beauty Queen' and 'Editions of You' were self-diagnoses of a male malady, a specular desire that fixates on female objects that it knows can never satisfy it. Although she 'makes his starry eyes shiver,' Ferry knows 'it never would work out.' This is the logic of Lacanian desire, which Alenka Zupancic explains as follows:

> The... interval or gap introduced by desire is always the imaginary other, Lacan's petit objet a, whereas the Real (Other) of desire remains unattainable. The Real of desire is jouissance — that 'inhuman partner' (as Lacan calls it) that desire aims at beyond its object, and that must remain inaccessible.

Roxy's 'In Every Dream Home a Heartache' is about an attempt, simultaneously disenchanted-cynical and desire-delirious, to resolve this deadlock. It is as if Ferry has recognised, with Lacan, that phallic desire is fundamentally masturbatory. Since, that is to say, a fantasmatic screen prevents any sexual relation so that his desire is always for an 'inhuman partner,' Ferry might as well have a partner that is literally inhuman: a blow-up doll. This scenario has many precursors: most famously perhaps Hoffman's short story 'The Sandman' (one of the main preoccupations of Freud's essay on 'The Uncanny' of course), but also Villiers de L'Isle-Adam's lesser known but actually more chilling master-piece of Decadent SF, *The Future Eve*, and its descendant, Ira Levin's *Stepford Wives*.

If the traditional problem for the male in pop culture has been dealing with a desire for the unattainable, then the comple-mentary difficulty for the female has been to come to terms with *not* being what the male wants. The Object knows that what she has does not correspond with what the subject lacks.

Remember that the original sense of glamour — bewitchment — alludes to the power of the auto-objectified over the subject. 'If God is masculine, idols are always feminine,' Baudrillard writes in *Seduction* (1995), and Siouxsie differed from previous pop icons in that she was neither a male artist 'feminized' into iconhood by fan adoration, nor a female marionette manipulated by male Svengalis, nor a female heroically struggling to assert a marginalised subjectivity. On the contrary, Siouxsie's perversity was to make an art of her own objectification. As Simon Reynolds and Joy Press put it in *The Sex Revolts*, Siouxsie's 'aspiration [was] towards a glacial exteriority of the objet d'art' evinced through 'a shunning of the moist, pulsing fecundity of organic life.' This denial of interiority — unlike Lydia Lunch, Siouxsie is not interested in 'spilling her guts,' in a confessional wallowing in the goo and viscera of a damaged interiority — corresponds to a staged refusal to be 'a warm, compassionate, understanding fellow-creature' (Žižek). Like Grace Jones, another singer who made an art of her own objectification, Siouxsie didn't demand R.E.S.P.E.C.T. from her bachelor suitors (with the implied promise of a healthy relationship based on mutual regard) but subordination, supplication.

In *Rip It Up and Start Again*, Simon Reynolds says that the early Banshees were 'sexy in the way that Ballard's *Crash* was sexy,' and Ballard's abstract fiction-theory is as palpable and vast a presence in the Banshees as it is in other post-punk bands. (It's telling that the turn from the angular dryness of the Banshees' early sound to the humid lushness of their later phase should have been legitimated by Severin's reading of *The Unlimited Dream Company*.) But what the Banshees drew (out) from Ballard was the equivalence of the semiotic, the psychotic, the erotic and the savage. With psychoanalysis (and Ballard is nothing if not a committed reader of Freud), Ballard recognised that there is no 'biological' sexuality waiting beneath the 'alienated layers' of civilisation. Ballard's compulsively repeated theme of reversion to savagery does not present a return to a non-symbolised bucolic Nature, but a fall back into an intensely semioticised and ritualised symbolic space. Eroticism is made possible — not merely mediated — by signs and technical apparatus, such that the body, signs and machines become interchangeable.

14

1977

by Richard Cabut

In the summer of 1977, I am seventeen — perfect.

I don't work. Although I washed cars for a week once when my mate Steve went on holiday. The boss said they'd be cleaner if he'd pissed on them. Fuck off, baldy.

I speed a bit — little brown packets tucked in zip pockets — and do other stuff, too. Inspired by the Ramones and Mark P, I try sniffing glue, but it doesn't work for me. I open the tin, take a tentative little snifflet of Cow Gum and am surprised when nothing happens — little do I realise that you have to tip the stuff in a plastic bag and stick it over your head for five minutes before you can satisfactorily fall flat on your face, off your napper. They should print clear, precise instructions in the punk zines for God's sake. I also occasionally indulge in over-the-counter decongestants. One tablet per day is the recommended dose. So I take eight and get a buzz. Wait. If I feel a mild hit on eight then, well, what if I take thirty? I'll feel really good, right? I vomit for a whole day and feel like shit for the next three. But this doesn't stop me from going through the whole process all over again a few weeks later. And so on. Seventeen...

Mostly I dream of escape. I live in small-town, working/lower-middle-class suburbia. Dunstable, Bedfordshire. Thirty miles from the capital. Here, kids leave school and go on the track, the production line, at the local factory, Vauxhall Motors. If you get some qualifications you can join the civil service. Meanwhile, Trevor and Nancy have been going out with each other since third form and watch telly round each other's house every night, not saying a word. I don't know what I want, but I know I don't want any of that shit ever.

Instead, I'm in love with punk rock. I'm in love with picking up momentum and hurling myself forward somewhere. Anywhere. Rip up the pieces and see where they land. I am suburban-punk Everykid in pins and zips, with a splattering of Jackson Pollock and a little Seditionaries — getting chased down the King's Road, after bunking the train down to the Smoke, by (strangely) American rednecks rather than Teddy Boys, although that does happen too (the Rasta at the antiques market, Troy his name is, hands out cut-throat razors to harassed punks). And wraparound shades worn after dark so that everything is but murk, which might explain a heavy snogging session that turns out to be same-sex — rolling about on the stage while the Damned are playing. Divine decadence, I like to think.

I write my first fanzine, *Corrugated Boredom* (which later becomes *Kick*), pondering pretentiously on Dada and Surrealism, and penning bad poetry. Hey, luckily I still have some around. Here's one: 'You live in a coffin / You can't move / You're buried alive / You've done it to yourself / What can you do? / Before, you wanted life / Now you just want existence' — which I actually read out live. You get the picture.

I also bash away on an old four-string acoustic guitar and write crappy, clichéd songs. I remember one: 'Blades for flowers / drainpipes for jeans / Hippies are dead / and they'll never return / 67 reversed has destroyed that dream.' It's actually written the year before, in the summer of 76, after seeing Dr Feelgood (mid-set, Captain Sensible crept up behind Lee Brilleaux and gave him a mighty two-handed shove into the audience. What a wag). But is obviously inspired by the Pistols — whose gig at the Leighton Buzzard Bossard Hall is unfortunately banned when I turn up to see them.

Meanwhile, in my bedroom there's *Sniffin' Glue and Other Self-Defence Habits* (July 77), some Aleister Crowley, a bit of Sartre, *48 Thrills* (bought off Adrian at a Clash gig), Sandy Roberton's *White*

Stuff (from Compendium in Camden) and John Peel, of course. And tons of records — I love the smell of fresh new punk vinyl, as well as the slightly different scent of Jamaican imports (pressed on old recycled vinyl, because of cheapness rather than eco awareness) — all of it a shining, odorous promise of unexpected imaginings. It smells of the future. Can't wait till 78? Definitely. The intensity of sitting in a loud room in a silent town, full of electricity. Floating above circumstances. Soaring...

...and flicking V-signs during the Jubilee itself, while nicking Union flags from wherever they can be found (everywhere), and invariably hanging out in the Ladies' (à la the Roxy Club) — although this has repercussions. But local reaction is bemusement rather than hatred. There's only a handful of punks in town; no threat. There's also a certain amount of crossover anyway. Skiz, who was there at the Clash Rainbow gig, is still into football aggro: at Luton v Fulham, he fights it out with a Londoner, who is also a punk. A weird feeling, says Skiz, who shouts: 'He's got a knife!' — and even a nearby copper starts putting the boot in on the Fulham fan. And everyone is still into funk, too: the California Ballroom is Dunstable's equivalent of the Lacy Lady or Global Village. Since 75 or so, hip kids had been travelling from miles around (even from London) for the plastic sandals and pegs scene there. It was all quite retro — Forties swing fashions — until punk.

The real hatred around my way comes early in the following year, in 1978. That's when all the rough kids from the surrounding 'orrible London-overspill estates get into punk for a couple of months or so. On the way to another Clash gig, on 25 January, Steve and I join a big group of new punks, maybe thirty or forty strong, walking along the main road. A police car stops us, and everyone waits his or her turn to be searched. The kid in front of me surreptitiously pulls out a gun, a real revolver that he's nicked from a party, apparently, and passes it back through the group to a girl who sticks it in her handbag, crosses the road and walks away. I should have done the same. The gig itself is a bloodbath. Different estates slug it out with each other — Lewsey Farm v Stopsley — people stagger around with axe wounds, blood everywhere, the Wild West. A support band called the Lou's gets killed, the Sex Pistols' minder English wanders around with a knife. I'm backstage and the Clash are worried: they're popping Mogadons (a downer). I'm worried, too — that I'll get stuck forever in all this bollocks. I know it's time to move. Which I do — to London. And, as it's obligatory to say in pieces like this, I'm still moving.

15

Sexy Eiffel Towers

by Andrew Gallix

I love you Eiffel Tower, you've got something I admire,
I love you Eiffel Tower, falling legs around your spire.
— Bow Wow Wow, 'Sexy Eiffel Towers,' *Your Cassette Pet*, 1980

When I look at the city of Paris I long to wrap my legs around it.
— Anne Carson, 'Short Talk on Hedonism,' *Short Talks*, 1992

The opening of the *Jeunes Gens Módernes* exhibition at the Galerie du Jour, in 2008, offered a whole generation a sense of closure. Quite literally, in the case of the hundreds of people who, unable to get in, transformed rue Quincampoix into an impromptu al fresco carnival — a gathering of the tribes. Once-dodgy skinheads rubbed shoulders with effete dandies under the eyes of mohicaned whippersnappers, who could have been (and indeed often were) their offspring. At times, it felt a bit like having a chinwag with a grizzled Dorian Gray in front of his youthful likeness. Most of the faces on the Parisian punk and post-punk scenes were out in force, simultaneously plastered on the walls of the labyrinthine gallery and getting plastered in the cobbled courtyard. Weather-beaten but unbowed. Still high from a thousand and one nights at Le Gibus, Palace or Rose Bonbon. Happy to have lived to tell the tale.

The 'Jeunes Gens Módernes' ('Módern Young Things') tag first cropped up in an issue of *Actuel* in February 1980. It referred specifically to a small coterie of rarefied hipsters epitomised by Jacno, the former Stinky Toys guitarist who was fast becoming a synth-pop Erik Satie. Despite being a media in-joke, this label

had the merit of pinpointing the existence of a typically French
(and largely Parisian) take on new wave, for want of a better
term. The scene revolved around nightclubs with the strictest of
door policies, as well as bands like Artefact, Taxi Girl, Marquis de
Sade, Modern Guy or Suicide Romeo (whose 'Möderne Romance'
surely aspired to manifesto status). The reference to this
phenomenon, as curator Jean-François Sanz was eager to explain,
was simply an 'excuse' to gauge the far wider cultural fallout
from the 1977 explosion. The moniker was thus given a more
comprehensive definition to include most aspects of Gallic post-
punk culture between 1978 and 1983. Like Spain's La Movida or
New York's No Wave (partly inspired by French ZE Records co-
founder Michel Esteban), this was indeed far more than just a
musical movement. It was a fully-fledged cultural revolution,
bent — sometimes outrageously so — on redefining *fin-de-siècle*
modernity.

'Modern' (or 'novö' to use Yves Adrien's coinage, with its
trademark umlaut, which had not yet been completely annexed
by the heavy-metal fraternity) was a ubiquitous watchword in
the wake of punk's Year Zero. With hindsight, however, it is quite
obvious that this scene bore all the hallmarks of postmodernism
— from its recycling of the major 20th-century avant-gardes to its
space-age retrofuturism. Philippe Morillon, one of the
emblematic artists of that era, argues that 'it is at the very point
when things disappear' — the very notion of modernity in this
instance — 'that we cling on to them.' He belongs to a generation
that jettisoned the traditional highbrow/lowbrow dichotomy to
the extent of shunning museums altogether. Newspapers, T-
shirts or record sleeves were the Bazooka collective's media of
choice; the Musulmans Fumants exhibited their works in nightclubs, while the Frères Ripoulin turned to billboards. As for
Morillon, he worked for advertising agencies.

The exhibition's achronological *bric-à-brac* organisation was in
keeping with the eclectic spirit of the Jeunes Gens Mödernes

themselves. Paintings, badges, films, fanzines, photographs, installations and videos were all showcased in deliberately haphazard-fashion: this, after all, was the first truly multimedia movement. A totemic synthesizer, an old-school keyboard and a couple of guitars propped up against diminutive amps took pride of place at the centre of the main room. Cigarette butts — perhaps a subtle nod to Jacno, whose name derived from the inventor of the Gauloises logo — were studiously littered around the pretend stage for added authenticity. This installation of sorts embodied the ghost of gigs past, but also drew attention to the deafening sound of silence. Visiting agnès b's gallery was not dissimilar to attending a concert wearing earplugs, or watching television on mute — and, frankly, it was all the better for it. With a few notable exceptions, French punk was derivative and, more to the point, devoid of any real social resonance. Singing about anarchy in front of a handful of socialites and junkies on loan from the neighbouring gay clubs was unlikely to threaten the status quo. This is probably why the extraordinary creative energies unleashed in New York and London were channelled, most effectively, into the edgiest fringes of the French art world.

Imagine Jamie Reid stealing the Sex Pistols' thunder, Malcolm Garrett upstaging Buzzcocks, or Peter Saville being more influential than Joy Division: this is pretty much what happened in France, at the end of the Seventies, with a groundbreaking art collective. Its founders met at art school — the prestigious, albeit rather stuffy, Beaux-Arts de Paris — in 1973. Bazooka Production saw the light of day a couple of years later, in 1975. The group was thus ahead of the curve, summoning a spirit that was already recognisably punk at a time when the subculture was still yet to emerge. Its nucleus was composed of Kiki Picasso (Christian Chapiron), Loulou Picasso (Jean-Louis Dupré), Olivia Clavel, Lulu Larsen (Philippe-Guy Renault), T5 (Philippe Bailly) and Bernard Vidal (Jean Rouzaud, who would be expelled in 1978, played a more peripheral role).

Bazooka was always more than the sum of its parts, each member's distinctive style contributing to a common goal: the production of an ongoing *Gesamtkunstwerk*. The collective dimension of their endeavour challenged the myth of individual genius, already mocked by Kiki and Loulou's iconoclastic *noms de pinceau*. (Kiki was sued by Pablo's heirs in 1989 and forbidden from using the master's name: for a while he signed his works 'ex-Picasso.') One of Bazooka's most reproduced pieces is a doctored picture of an aged, bedridden Matisse, painting on the wall of his room, in Nice, with a brush attached to a long pole. Underneath, an innocent-looking little girl, holding a teddy bear on her lap, outstares the viewer while applying abstracted brush-strokes to a sheet of paper. Possibly of their own accord, the slapdash splashes take on the shape of a malevolent black skull. 'Grandad is called modern art,' reads the caption, 'but I'll do better than him.' Another striking piece from the same year — 1978 — shows a hyperrealist toddler, giddy with glee, smearing his paint-splattered hands round a scrap of paper. Driven by the velocity of the swirls he is producing, geometric shapes fly in the air, like a Kandinsky spinning out of control. It never fails to remind me of Carr addressing Tzara in Tom Stoppard's *Travesties*:

> *When I was at school, on certain afternoons we all had to do what was called Labour — weeding, sweeping, sawing logs for the boiler-room, that sort of thing; but if you had a chit from Matron you were let off to spend the afternoon messing about in the Art Room. Labour or Art. And you've got a chit for life?*

This, I suspect, is how these guerrilla artists saw themselves: unruly kids running amok in the nursery of modern art — with a chit *for life.*

Bazooka's group ethos placed them squarely in the avant-garde tradition: 'All hail the graphic arts dictatorship,' trumpeted one of their most infamous slogans, reflecting a marked penchant for Suprematism (Lissitzky), Constructivism (Rodchenko) and totalitarian propaganda. They also functioned like a rock band, of course, wielding Rotring pens and paintbrushes in lieu of guitars. Their communal modus operandi was even carried into their living arrangements. Most of the members dwelt poetically, sharing a series of large Parisian apartments which were part Warholian Factory, part Bauhaus-style powerhouse. Fuelled by drugs, they worked night and day while musicians drifted in and out. Once described as the Parisian Edie Sedgwick, Dominique Fury embodied the restless creative spirit of this milieu. After leaving L.U.V. — a shadowy all-girl punk band — she moved in with the rest of the gang, having been attracted by the 'sheer intensity of their production,' and soon found herself embroiled in a convoluted *ménage à trois* with two Bazookas of either gender (Olivia Clavel and Loulou Picasso). There is a stunning picture showing her flanked by Kenny Morris and John McKay of Siouxsie and the Banshees sporting T-shirts she had just produced. Speed and acid led to Bazooka's Stakhanovist output, ranging from countless record sleeves to the opening credits of TV programmes via an issue of *NME*. The switch to heroin soon slowed them down, heralding the group's demise in 1980.

If Bazooka are remembered in Britain for designing the cover of Elvis Costello's *Armed Forces* (1979), they first shot to infamy during the summer of 1977 when they were invited to (dis)grace the pages of *Libération*. The self-styled 'graphic commando' mounted a series of nocturnal art attacks, over a six-month period, adding increasingly provocative artwork, slogans and comments on every inch of space available. Sometimes they even went as far as doctoring the content of articles or changing the layout. This was usually done at the eleventh hour — just before the daily paper went to press — so that nobody could foil their subversive plans. Environmentalists, who embodied the hippy lifestyle, were obvious targets (*vide* Métal Urbain's 'E202'). An anti-nuclear militant who had just been killed during a demonstration, thereby achieving instant martyrdom in the eyes of the paper's core constituency, was branded a 'dead tosser' by Kiki Picasso. The following year, Loulou Picasso would celebrate the *Amoco Cadiz* oil spill, off the coast of Brittany, with images and texts ('Smother my body in petrol') that seemed to anticipate Tom McCarthy's *Satin Island* (2015). Bazooka were a Burroughsian virus — the poison in the media machine. They squatted *Libération*, acting as infiltrators and agents provocateurs. For the first time, the counterculture was countered from within, outflanked by a new generation who were testing its pious certainties and tolerance to breaking point. The aim was to wind up the leftist 'war veterans' of May 1968 and their hippy fellow-travellers who still made up the bulk of *Libé*'s journalists and readership. In this they succeeded only too well. Lawsuits were filed and tempers flared. On one occasion, Olivia Clavel was slapped by a female photographer whose work she had sabotaged; Kiki Picasso and Loulou Picasso were both beaten up for their provocative flirtations with fascist iconography. Tensions ran so high that the editor, Serge July, eventually gave Bazooka their own separate monthly magazine to avoid a full-blown rebellion among his staff. 'Society is destroying my work — I will destroy society': the headline that prefaced their last intervention in the daily sounded like a mission statement.

Six issues were published, in 1978, before the magazine folded due to exhaustion and flagging sales. Yet *Un regard moderne* was arguably Bazooka's finest hour. As its title indicates, it offered a modern outlook on current affairs through what could be termed art journalism. Each month the collective would select a number of news stories which were then subjected to various forms of artistic treatment. The starting point was not so much an event as its representation: a photograph. Reality was always already mediated. This reflected a kind of bunker mentality: like terrorists holed up in their hideout, Bazooka seemed to view the outside world exclusively through the media. Olivia Clavel (who often signed her works Olivia Télé Clavel) invented an autobiographical comic-strip character with a TV screen strapped to its head. Belonging to the first generation to have been brought up in front of the box, as commentators were prompt to point out at the time, they were indeed the bastard progeny of Marshall McLuhan and Guy Debord. The rise of a media-saturated dystopia was one of the most common punk tropes: off the top of my head, I can think of the Lurkers' 'Mass Media Believer,' the Jam's 'News of the World,' the Boomtown Rats' 'Don't Believe What You Read,' the UK Subs' 'T.V. Blues' and the Germs' 'Media Blitz,' plus of course band names like the Adverts, Television or Alternative TV... Bazooka, however, went beyond such clichés. By offering a quasi-instant artistic response to the flow of information, they seem to have anticipated the rise of twenty-four-hour news channels — CNN was launched in 1980 — but their interventions slowed that flow down as though they felt that all these fleeting images needed attending to. Their work often has an oneiric, almost serene and possibly opiate-induced quality, despite the focus on natural catastrophes, surgical operations and violence. The brief sentences, phrases and slogans accompanying the visuals often read like news wires abridged by Félix Fénéon. Perhaps Bazooka burned out not through trying to keep up with the news, but due to the intense attention they focused on it.

In many ways Bazooka provided a blueprint for the post-punk art collectives that followed in their wake. The Musulmans Fumants (a reference to Chester Himes), co-founded in 1980 by Tristam Dequatremare (former lead singer with Guilty Razors), preferred to exhibit their works in nightclubs rather than traditional galleries. They were instrumental in reviving figurative painting and launching the international careers of Robert Combas and Hervé Di Rosa who spearheaded the successful Figuration Libre movement (1981). The Frères Ripoulin (1984) were the Musulmans Fumants' partners in aesthetic crimes. They included Nina Childress, who graduated from art-punk band

Lucrate Milk, as well as Claude Closky and Pierre Huyghe, who went on to find fame and fortune. Jean Faucheur, their theoretician, believed that the streets were the new art schools at a time when graffiti art had hardly reared its head. The Ripoulins were 'affichistes': they painted their works on posters which were then pasted on strategically-placed advertising hoardings. All these groups were linked to Basquiat, Haring and the whole Lower East Side scene across the Atlantic, but they were also the forefathers of the current street-art movement.

Lulu Larsen died in August 2016.

16

The End of Music

by Dave and Stuart Wise

An interesting historical document written by the core members of King Mob; a pre-post-punk (1978) response from the group which helped to inspire Malcolm McLaren/the movement in the first place. Its critical, anti-punk stance was understood to be in itself punk.

Fossilized representatives of capital tried to silence punk. Who are they? Various formations of the State apparatus — the British Broadcasting Corporation/the Greater London Council, local councils in the provinces and Parliament where MPs like Marcus Lipton said, apropos of 'God Save The Queen,' if pop music is going to destroy our established institutions, then it ought to be destroyed first. In truth punk was against certain fuddy-duddy attitudes embodied in some institutions though accepting others that are rooted in capital. Who else tried to silence punk? Well, various distribution outlets in influential private hands, the International Buyers Association (IBA)/the chain store of WHSmith and some venue ballrooms.

While the state is necessary for business, it is generally so for Dept I — the production of the means of production (heavy machinery etc.). Exceptions of course are giant monopolies like British Leyland, Rolls Royce etc., which fall into the category of Dept II — the production of the means of consumption. Often, however, state functionaries are at loggerheads with some tendencies which they regarded as distasteful in the arena of consumer capital. Punk and pornography are two examples. In spite of the hysteria which spills over into the media, it is still an internecine conflict between bourgeois archaisms and those modernizing representatives of capital who are more daring in terms of marketing lurid possibilities.

An appearance to the contrary, the state is always fighting a losing battle. As Marx said, in a different context (that of the industrial bourgeoisie against feudalism), 'profit is a born dissenter' and punk is profit. Zombies in the UK state apparatus finally have to recognise the real interests of an important fraction of capital even if it is marketing the disintegration of moral values. As Al Clarke, press officer for Virgin Records, said on 9 November 1977, with reference to *Never Mind the Bollocks, Here's the Sex Pistols*, 'The LP was released 11 days ago. It brought in £250,000 before it was even released and went straight to no 1 in the charts.'

Punk was initially suppressed through a moral force present in the UK state apparatus. No law in Parliament was needed after the moral outrage of some mainly Labour party MPs who ensured through their diatribe that the English puritan consensus was respected. This morality was faithfully driven home by intermediary bodies of the state hypocritically using safety regulations to ban punk concerts in local council halls, virtually ensuring that insurance companies no longer financially cover concerts in private halls. But what a loud silence, as punk music got a wider and wider audience and the more the thumbscrews were turned the more the cash registers jingled. The UK state, once able to enforce bans on music it regarded as popularly subversive (cf. the fate of calypso and festivals in the Caribbean prior to 1850), was made a mockery of. Now, in spite of real threats, the state lost because music has become more capitalized since the early phases of industrial capitalism. With the unprecedented development of the production of the means of consumption after the second inter-imperialist world war, the state cannot maintain any effective ban on a musical style which is capitalized by private companies. Only if a state has full control over marketing and distribution outlets can pop music be silenced. In Czechoslovakia, where the state has far greater control over pop music than in the West, the pop group the Plastic People has been silenced through the cover of a smear campaign suggesting that pop musicians are against communist society (e.g. potential fascists etc.).

Punk rock has been promoted by small entrepreneurial record companies like Stiff Records, Anchor, Beserkley, Polydor. These are companies in a kind of semi-competition with the big monopolies like EMI (Electric & Musical Industries Ltd), CBS, (Columbia Broadcasting System), WEA (Warner Bros/Electra Records/Atlantic Records), who tend to handle the record distribution of the smaller companies through superior servicing outlets (cf. the arrangement between United Artists and Island Records). Thus competition is more in terms of hip image promotion with the small record companies winning hands down because they have their ear to the ground unlike the cumbersome, bureaucratic ways of the large companies. As companies, they seem more liberal and hip, but when the going gets tough the tough get going. Biba was a trendy clothes boutique catering for 1960s swinging London. Once class conflict erupted in the early 1970s in the UK and the fall of sterling had made 'the right little, tight little island' the troublesome sick man of Europe, Biba for safety's sake moved to the calmer situation of Brazil where fascism guaranteed profits. However they end up, the point is that small capital is generally the innovator but the big companies don't remain outside of the mad scramble for long. CBS quickly signed up the Clash and United Artists signed up the Stranglers and Buzzcocks. EMI, in chagrin after their cold feet and the aborted contract with the Sex Pistols, promoted the Tom Robinson Band — of all the new-wave bands the most obviously leftish — supporting George Ince (a gangland guy framed for a murder he did not commit), gays and blacks.

Punk managers want to modify the superstar system but they can only do so in terms of the spectacle itself. Some of their more sophisticated apologists confront the problem of the Spectacle but in a very half-hearted way. After all, their jobs would be at stake if they went any further. Rock wordsmith Charles Shaar Murray said in *New Musical Express*, 9 July 1977: 'We have a new kind of rock star now, and like all other new kinds of stars it arose out of an attempt to break down the star system.' He goes on to note what the star system does to those caught in its 'veritable Pandora's box' and it's the predictable, frightening conclusion (but without analysing the essential compulsion which drives individuals to become stars): 'So its not surprising that people get pissed off with stars, except it was exceptional naivety to believe that those folks who hit the Stardom Jackpot wouldn't get affected by it' [sic].

Then the big comedown.

Radio, television, movies, rock and roll, politics and sport alike all create stars by their very natural stardom is implicit and unavoidable. To talk of destroying the star system is completely and utterly utopian. (Murray, ibid)

On the contrary, what is demonstrated is Charles Shaar Murray's utopian-cum-social-democratic perspective because he does not recognise the spectacle as an historical category, which will be superseded by a communist mode of production. Like all previous modes of production, the society of the spectacle exists as an historical finite and there's nothing eternal about its existence.

The spectacle is in flux and because capitalist society has become direr, its image reflects this misery and questioning. Thus, the new superstars must somehow be ordinary people: Elvis Costello, for instance, isn't allowed by Stiff Records' managers to have a fan club as it would look like an earlier era of rock 'n' roll. Nor would it fit in with the contemporary superstar populism of dole queue artists. Because of these glaring contradictions manifested in the spectacle effect — in the programmed marketing of an image schizophrenia — punk/new wave is literally forced into being more dishonest than any other previous rock 'n' roll epoch. They must be poverty-stricken but necessarily rich. They ride in Rolls Royces and wear bin liners. If the new stardom is too obviously into conspicuous consumption they'll lose the support of a no longer marginally affluent social base in comparison to the 1960s. Already, the recuperated fallout from 1968 had made its impact before the dawn of punk. Chris Jagger informed big brother and his radical chic partner, Bianca (famous daughter of Nicaraguan Latifundista/Paris barricade fighter and new friend of Princess Margaret, Rhoddy Llewellyn) of the subversive use of graffiti in 68. Mick Jagger (in admiration) then hired down-and-outs to promote his new record, *It's Only Rock 'n Roll*. With the birth of record company graffiti, many musical con stars followed, *I Fought the Law/Whatever Happened to Slade* etc. Punk promotion followed on from this tendency but with a DIY kit. Punk musicians had to be more sacrificial and do their own street-wall graffiti promotions. They were forced into being the living embodiment of image rebellion. Thus Joe Strummer ended up in a Kentish Town magistrate's court for spraying 'The Clash' on a wall in Camden Town.

Why was punk/new wave greeted with such hysteria? Indeed, the UK state reared itself up in a frenzied religio-secularized frothing at the mouth at the excesses of a licentious and amoral capitalism over which it pretends to preside. What greeted punk was not a critique of its pro-capitalist role but a quintessentially English moral outrage which unites in uneasy alliance state functionaries, managers of record companies, hip musicologists, journalists and ex-revolutionaries gone respectable. Although the American record companies (CBS and WEA) were for the Sex Pistols, their local English managers were not, obviously realizing they would offend the morality of the English state. In spite of the fact that the major record companies are international corporations, they nevertheless have to take into account national ideologies.

Punk gave aspects of capital an illusory radicalism again. Small record retailers were unsuccessfully prosecuted by the state for exhibiting *Never Mind the Bollocks* in shop windows. Dusty laws were brought out of the Statute Book: the 1889 Indecent Advertisement Act, and in Notting Hill and Marble Arch managers of record shops (owned by Virgin) were charged and cleared with contravening the indecent advertisement section of the 1824 Vagrancy Act. Victorian morality? It points to the state's antediluvian character as a moral if not as an economic force in the era of state capitalism. However, with the disintegration of values, the state must insist on the antediluvian to make the fabric of bourgeois society appear intact, as it must also act economically to maintain many an archaism.

State capitalism has moved into the arena of culture. Once various arts companies can no longer survive economically through the aid of trusts, private donations and charities, the state then becomes the most important benefactor. Artistic forms that are entering into a social and historical demise (opera/theatre etc.) have then a preservation order taken out on them by the state, artificially arresting their decline (Sadler's Wells, Royal Court Theatre, Glynbourne etc.). These artistic events must be maintained in the major metropolitan centres if not in the provinces. If the state adhered to its logic (always somewhat ideological anyway), laissez-faire capitalism would have allowed them to die an artistic death but the state, confronted with the decay of bourgeois — and even pre-bourgeois — aesthetics, has a moral necessity to maintain their existence and the semblance of a higher aesthetic order. The state and state capitalism generally and ineffectually opposes changes in the mode of artistic production (e.g. the opposition to rock 'n' roll). Moreover, the state must try and enforce the separation between high and low art but has great difficulty in so doing.

Consequently, private capital is credited with the image of rebellion in the arts because it operates as a subversive force against more traditionally bourgeois attitudes. It is this tendency that holds the attention of youth (Elvis Presley, pirate radio stations and now new wave or reggae). Absolutely contrary to the leftist faith in state capitalism, culturally it is private capital which is the progressive force, as it records more accurately the bankruptcy and potential of supercession at the heart of the last phase of bourgeois society. It is therefore not surprising that leftist parties like the Communist party and the Trotskyists with a large theatrical/artistic membership support culturally archaic statist tendencies.

The modern state oscillates between acknowledging the revolt of artistic forms encompassing the 20th century and suppressing them. Is it possible that a highly developed modern state may abandon outmoded art forms and emphasize modernist ones? We will have to wait and see. As it stands, entrepreneurial capital will more readily acknowledge the void at the centre of modern survival if it is good for business. Perhaps a paradigm may be drawn from Yves Klein selling 'the void' of a pocket of air — drawn with his finger — at $300 a throw.

The state subsidizes avant-garde experiments but rather more in the period of capitalist expansion than in the present period of economic crisis. Only those states with a greater economic power (West Germany, America and Japan) can still, with something like aplomb, finance the nothing exhibition (see Kassel 1976 and the construction of expensive earth works funded from the proceeds of taxation). But precisely because these exhibits are not directly profit-making and largely act as a drain on that part of accumulated surplus value deposited in the coffers of the state, the fury expressed over such events is more successful in preventing follow-ups than journalistic diatribes against a profit-making punk rock like Genesis P-Orridge and Cosey Fanni Tutti's *Prostitution* exhibition at the ICA (the Institute of Contemporary

Arts). The ensuing campaign in the media and Parliament was effective in curbing the funding of such future ventures by that state aesthetic body, the Arts Council. Here, media persecution worked in suppressing avant-garde events, whereas for private capital, scurrilous persecution of avant-garde commodities generally acts as incitement to surplus value realization.

17

Banned From the Roxy

by Penny Rimbaud

January 2016

I wrote 'Banned from the Roxy' in late 1977 as a contribution to Gee Vaucher's adventurously radical newspaper, *International Anthem*. At the time of writing, Crass were an all-male band and frankly, on rereading the article almost forty years later, it shows. Eve, Joy and Gee weren't to join the band until early 78, bringing with them no small amount of moderation to our otherwise boyish, bad behaviour.

I was Crass's drummer, lacking any of the skills normally associated with the playing of drums, but so what? Apart from Pete, our bassist, none of us could make any reasonable claim to be musicians, preferring as we did to depend on attitude and a fair dose of chutzpah. The Roxy gig described in the article was the third gig that Crass had ever played, and whatever audience we had was most certainly not there because of us. At our previous gig in a small London park, we'd been turned off by an angry local resident who'd informed us that we were lowering the tone of the neighbourhood, which at the time seemed quite an achievement. As yet we had made no studio recordings, although we had played a desperately disorderly set for a London-based pirate radio station which, we liked to think, put us a step above the rest. All in all, we were heading nowhere, but all in all, we didn't care a toss.

In returning to this article after all these years, I was amused and appalled in equal measure by the mixture of heady idealism and downright naivety. Crass later became known and much respected as hard-line anarchists with a deep sense of purpose which, within reason, is fair comment. Over our seven years on the road, there's no question that we became increasingly serious and focused, but in our early days we no more understood what we were doing than did those who were unwittingly exposed to us. It was perhaps core to our thinking that we were all in this together — band and audience — but at this early stage it seemed worrisome that our audiences didn't appear to agree. Nonetheless, despite our eventual rise to becoming leaders of a movement, which was, of course, never our intention, we stuck to our guns by promoting the DIY ethic and chanting the credo 'there is no authority but yourself.' But still we remained leaders.

Beyond checking the spelling and punctuation, and despite the discomfort I feel with some of the opinions expressed, I have made very few major edits to the original text. But why, I now ask myself, were we so unpleasant with each other? I dearly loved everyone in the band, so what's all the bad-mouthing about? Although it might not seem a good enough justification to say that it was punk to behave like that, I can see now, in our desperate attempts to redefine ourselves, that it probably is: we were attempting to create a new future by trashing the past and, until that job was done, maybe there was no other way forward for us.

So, this is as was, with a few warts removed. If nothing else, I'm certainly a more experienced writer now than I was then, so I could easily have rewritten the original from beginning to end, but ultimately I felt that to do so would have been to de-authenticate it. What changes I have made are more to do with presentation than they are with subject matter, which I can only hope isn't reflected in the greater story of my life. To finish, I have to admit to having been somewhat taken aback by the excessive number of 'fucks,' 'fuckers,' 'fuckings' and the odd 'cunt' that appear throughout the text, but I guess I left them intact because that's how it was at the time, and if it wasn't, well, so fucking what?

Banned from the Roxy — October 1977

And then I alter the inflection. The trees beyond the window are somehow bleached, but is this mist, faded memory or silver fish caught in the sun's contemptuous rays? The net flies and he stands there, clasping the body of a mutilated woman.

'Where are the women? Why this masculine battlefield? Always seen before, tormented. Mary, Lisa, Joy. Sisters, where are you?'

He speaks to me through the glass. I can hear nothing. I see only the grasping wretchedness of his clumsy inactivity. He has broken her limb by limb. He raises his voice, louder, then louder through the shiny blanket of the windowpane.

'Your mother,' he cries, 'your mother.'

He tosses the corpse into the sighing arms of tansy and mallow, angelica and rose.

'Where are the women?'

Ah, rose, what flesh gripped now in your sharpened claws? She is so dead, so very dead. What death shared now in those oh so very red petals? So dead, so very dead. What perfume is this? What but sorrow? What but that of her flesh, the scent of death, rich now in the idle mists of dawn?

Across my black uniform, a flash of light makes an uneasy journey. The dull, matt-black cotton is punctuated with safety pins, dog chains and other chrome ephemera: a punk plaything, a death of surface. She is gone, long gone. No light upon this drab exterior, only the hopping body of the cat flea adds movement to this moment of repose: deadly rest.

Rest? What rest? Debate? What debate? There is no rest, no debate, yet I have rested these last several days, questioning again and again my newly adopted stance, doubting every part of me that drives towards what it seems could be an early destruction. But why be destroyed by self-passion? Why tumble battled, bruised and beaten through self-desire? No debate here, just nothing. Nothing, the only available vision in a blind reality.

Nothing, the only immediate answer to give in an unquestioning world. But I know, I know, I know, it's there that the perfume describes a distant past, a past that is not mine.

'Come on, you fuckers, I know we're a pile of shit, but I also know that you're a pile of shit as well, so why can't we be shit together?'

I plead with the numbheads. They stare back at me. I guess they know I'm not mad, just juiced out, a lush, a wino, a bum for this temptress night. I expose myself to them, strip naked, stand exhilarated, neither antagonistic nor shamed. In any case, what's shame? Shame is the corpse in the herb garden, lying there like bluing patchwork. I haven't had the heart to move it. Maybe that isn't shame.

Fifth columnist, resistance fighter, counterculturist, self-confrontationist, because I am me. Maybe first out of bed, me, last out of bed, yawning, limbs akimbo, taut, tricky tightness. I, me, jerks across the beer-soaked floor, sliding across and over the black edge of self-containment. Breaking down, down, down to break up insidious social controls that have veiled my savage perception for far too long, inhibited my instant intuition and Buddha's erection alike: just a limp plaything. I like to think that rock 'n' roll isn't just background muzak, no, I like to think it's the soundtrack at the forefront of revolution. Sometimes I just like to think. That's what it is, I know it. Presley might have greased his shaft, but that doesn't mean it slid up my arse. Rock 'n' roll isn't just entertainment, it's a battle, a kickback against tired old history books, a punch in the face of grey prophets who would have us all believe that our life is a death. Oh, whorish cross, what pains you like to carry. Of course, of course, he died, they died, we die. Of course, of course, deathly dead the dead ones.

For the last few months of 1976 and first few of 1977, the Roxy club, black hole in the sodden London streets, drain-sucker for the painted sewer rats, played host to a phenomenon. Out from the hippy coffins of Haight Ashbury, out from the rural copses where anarchy had hidden its face these last few years, out again onto the streets came a new voice of hope; the cry of futures that had been buried in the narcotic fuck-ups of the Sixties. Yes, punk came out to air its dirty wings, rising like a phoenix from the stagnant mire that was the Beatles' death-pickings in Central Park, the Beach Boys' sperm on Malibu Beach and the Stones' apologies from the back seat of a limo. But now the next generation, the Pistols, the Damned, the Clash, the Stranglers, the Jam, were talking 'bout their generation, the now generation, their new generation: new sounds, new vocabulary, oh we're so pretty vacant. And yes, the little old Roxy bounced to the new energy, bounced and bounced, not really noticing that its lead players were tiptoeing their way up the stairs and over the road to Tin Pan Alley where music pimps seduced with back-handers and city gents pricked up their dollar-ringing ears, or is that eared up their dollar-ringing pricks? Either way, within but a few months, the new generation had been bought out by the capitalist counter-revolutionaries: killed with cash. From being a movement of potential radical social change, punk became the biggest media bonanza since hippy, little more than a burnt out memory of what it might have been. For now it was cleaned up, souped up and fucked up: just another crappy stereo prick-tease, just another cheap product for the consumer's head. Suck, suck, he hangs his dick. Suck, suck, it's just a media trick.

Waves of alcohol-induced nausea drift through my skull. The PA speakers blast out discordant noise, jarring my every nerve. I feel myself falling into an abyss, down, down, wrenching, wretched and wrecked, but then, driven by a force greater than mine, I rise again, out of the blue, supported by desire, crutched by desolation, frail but determined. I'll bloody well show 'em.

'One, two, three, floor,' mumbles Steve Ignorant, Crass's formerly belligerent vocalist, fucking up something rotten as his usually angry tirade slops from his drooling jaws like so much tinned soup turned vomit: Campbell's? Heinz? The variety is in the imagination, at least would be if there were one. His angular freneticism and angst-ridden howls are being lost in a narcotic haze. He's good and proper fucked up on grass: time warps, hallucinatory trembles, paranoia. Too much friggin' weed. He mounts another stumbling attempt to articulate a song loaded with social attack, but with a skull bursting with turn-on, drop-out and never-mind-the-bollox, he really doesn't stand a chance. Talk about contradiction or, come to think about it, don't talk about contradiction. Do they owe us a living? Fucked if I know.

I fight with an intense desire to get up and walk off stage and out the door, but I'm held back by my by now blistering drunk-enness, glued to my drum kit with sticky booze or boozy sticks or, fucking hell, what a mess. I take it out on the skins, wham, bang, banga, bang, bang: such passive victims to my rage. Ignorant turns around to land me a sneer.

'Too fucking fast,' he barks, 'too fast by fucking far.'

'Fuck you, Ignorant,' I hiss back, 'am I too fast or are you too fucking slow? Which? Do you really know, you shithead? The dream's fucking over, right?'

In its infinite ability to adapt and consume, the mainstream has taken punk on board as a musical genre and, with the aid of cynically contrived poncy packaging, has been able to totally ignore the real social issues from which it largely originated. The socio-political aspects of punk have been consumed by the greed of marketplace vampires. Too eagerly and all too soon, the new young revolutionaries have accepted the party line of play as you earn: the greenback volley with a dead red under the bed.

And yes, the Beatles are dead, the Beach Boys are dead, the Stones always were. Dylan is dead, Bowie is dead, and so now are the velvet zippies. There was a time when a torn sweatshirt was some kind of a political statement, not a fashion fad. Who'd have guessed that the catwalks would one day adopt the style and sell it as a line, but they have and they do. Punk has become radical chic, encouraged by a coterie of simpering superstars who bought the ticket, but never really boarded the train. Yes, they talk of revolution, but it's from the back seat of a limo, and all the while some tired old ex-con changes gear and sees to it that the wheels are kept turning. It's an offer that no one can refuse, at least not yet. Yes, they talk of revolution from the safety of the stage, protected by security guards protecting their newfound wealth and the securities that it accrues: the armour of armoured minds. Well then, by my reckoning, they climbed onto my shoulders to gain those heady heights and right now I'm moving clear away: wham, bang, thank you ma'am, see what I mean?

And the limos run on cash and the cash flows and record sales grow. And the Clash are bored with the USA, and Johnny's getting pissed and destroys with wordy platitudes alluding to revolution. And comfortable liberal clichés resound across the pinewood furnishings of the American dream, Bacardi and dissent, shaken not stirred, and no one really gives a toss or cares a fuck. Not one of those Bacardi bullshitters would show their face at the Roxy, even if the Roxy is now a tame commercial rip-off where tired old ex-blues bands pump out sanitised versions of what they think punk might once have been: fucking poseurs. So just what kind of revolution is this? It seems that almost everyone's living off the brief glory of what appeared to be a radical cultural uprising and imagining that the battle's over; and now they're waiting for something else to happen, waiting for orders from above. So, the generals might have retreated behind the lines, but like it or not there's still an army out here, small maybe, but ready and able. Rotten and Strummer had their balls sliced off up the knacker's yard of Tin Pan Alley, so they won't be back, and neither will any of the rest of the superstar elite, they're all too busy stuffing safety pins up their arses and hanging about for a slice of the meat. No, this time around it's up to us, you and me, together.

With about as much energy as a sick sloth, Ignorant has fumbled his way through our first song. He's desperately hanging onto the mike stand as if it were a crutch. Help me, I'm falling: a Long John Silver without a parrot to squawk. He leers at the bemused audience, sneering.

'Right? Right?'

But it isn't right and wasn't right, and he knows it. The shiny metal of the stand seems to bend beneath the onslaught of the herbal infusion of his halitosis. He coughs, partly out of embarrassment, partly as it's something to do, blows his nose on the ragged sleeve of his sweat-soaked shirt and, for all I care, lets out a rank fart.

The guitars had been desperately flat, my drumming had been hopelessly out of time with anything, including myself, so on all fronts the whole song had been a total cock-up. The Roxy audience, who at the best of times are not disposed to overt shows of generosity, treat our presence with a solemn silence, but what do they want? Muzak, or even, heaven forbid, music? Yes? No? Maybe? Fuck 'em, they'll have to learn some time. Punk isn't about music, it's a way of life, a way of thought. Punk isn't a fashion, it's a way of being, it's anarchy in the UK, USA, wherever, and that isn't tuned guitars and pretty lyrics any more than it's limos at the stage door of the Roxy or CBGBs. Oh, you Monroes, how you line the corridors to the morgue. If the first wave of punksters became Concorde anarchists under the ownership of some wanked-out economic system, it's down to us, the second wave, to fight a hard battle. This time around it'll be against an army wearing the same uniform.

By now I'm wondering whether we really look and sound as bad as we feel. I can't work out whether to throw up the last slug of crappy Chinese wine or to get another one down me before it's too late. Ignorant quite simply doesn't look possible. He's waving around like a wind-blown feather, supported by one feeble arm wrapped around the mike stand, and then, crash, the whole lot collapses into a heap on the floor. Very slowly, and muttering blasphemies under his breath, he climbs back onto his feet, his eyes aflame, his body a desperate parody of a freshly skinned dog. He lets out a fetid burp. Andy, who might normally be expected to pump out wildly aggressive rhythms on his guitar whilst gyrating as if under supernatural forces, has fallen against one of the PA speakers and seems to be doing a bad imperson-ation of Elvis' last public appearance, dead in Memphis. Maybe I'm talking values here, bourgeois standards and all that nonsense. And yes, I know there shouldn't have to be values and standards except your own, but this evening I feel that my standards are being stretched to the limit. What we play is always shit, very fast, very plain, very heavy shit, but this isn't even shit. It's sloppy, messy, dirty crap and, deep beneath the alcohol, far beyond the wavering social me who's on display here, something says 'no,' and that's the ultimate freedom, yes? The right to say no.

Ignorant decides to exercise his rights. He decides that he doesn't want to do the next song. He feels it's too fast or, put another way, he can't crack through the dope. Well, tough shit because this is meant to be a band, and that's supposed to mean some sort of shared responsibility, even if in our case it's a pretty frail one.

'For fuck's sake, Ignorant, fucking get on with it.'

'Piss off, Rimbaud.'

Halfway through the next number, I realise that he's decided after all to do the song he'd said he didn't want to do. I try to slow down, speed up, it all seems much the same to me, and either way I make a right cock-up of it, totally blow it. I don't seem to recognise a thing, don't know what we're doing, don't remember what we've done. Where the hell am I? Major Tom? Here we go again. The ultimate freedom, the NASA negative.

If the music business, the record labels, the club owners, the press and the public think they've got us tamed, wow, have I got news for them. I might not get invited to their next celebrity gathering, but I do categorically know that I've got it fairly right and they've got it all terribly wrong, so they can stuff their fucking pineapples on a stick. If you suck cock too hard there's a good chance you'll get piss, and that's exactly what seems to be happening. So they bought up the pedigrees forgetting that pedigrees suffer from inbreeding; all fucked-up heads and weak legs. Yes, one by one they bought out the punk elite and neatly pressed their products onto vinyl and stuffed their heads into money bags: pinball wizards without a wand.

Punk, at least as it was seen from the streets, was a statement: make your own, do it yourself. Own band. Own words. Own sound. Own attitude. Own future. Own life. The pundits who say that punk was an extension of pub rock or the New York Dolls, Iggy Pop or some such shit have totally missed the point. How come they can't see beyond their own narrow history of events? Don't they understand that sometimes things can develop pretty much independent of the illusory past to which they haplessly cling for survival. The blues wasn't music, it was a people's search for dignity and respect, and punk is very much the same in its quest for personal liberty and social change, so try putting that in your piggy bank.

CBGBs charges bands for the use of their sound system while the bands get bugger all for the privilege of doing so. The Roxy has made it a condition that all gigs are recorded so that they can put out a 'Live at the Roxy' album, but will the bands be paid for their troubles? I rather doubt it. So who's conning who? Ah yes, the fat cats will sit all smug behind their cocktail bars drinking a toast to future prosperity while another generation of hopefuls either joins them or gets burnt out on its own idealism. Wealth is a ghetto that sucks. Who shares what? It's all a pile of shit and there's folk out here that know it. It's been a while now, the real colours are flying and they're no more red and black than they're red, white and blue. If the first wave has failed, maybe the second wave will succeed. The first wavers' vision was fucked by the first banknote dangled in their faces, and it wasn't a roll and it wasn't a line. No, it isn't narcotics that kill creativity, it's greed for cash: dollars, dimes, pounds and pence. Oh yes, they talk of the system being the oppressor, well what fucking system are they a part of? Leadbelly sung from the jailhouse, so who ate his dinner? Van Gogh painted in the madhouse, so who ate his dinner? Bird was propped on a trashcan and told to play, so who ate his dinner? Genet wrote on bog paper. Kerouac died behind a bottle. The fat cats just love it, love it. They simply fucking love it: cash or cruci-fixion, either way they'll get you.

After the first two numbers, the alcohol of three litres of good French wine and one of bad Chinese has fractured my skull. My head's bursting from blasts of mind-buggering noise, hotting up something rotten, fermenting on the various layers of uncaring intoxicants. All the same, I'm somehow or other connecting with some of the band along a sinewy thread which, if it weren't for the grass that continues to stifle both Ignorant and Andy, might normally have led to some sort of an energetic outcome. But no, we're in the temperate zone and the capsule just isn't moving. Our life-force has drifted away leaving not a trace. An escapee caged bird burns its wings on the gas ring. Enola Gay rights herself as the payload is released: crash, to put it mildly. I try to collect the fragments, but they slide away from me quick as snakes in a pit. Kyoto rivers flow beneath our feet. Passing bells toll forgetfulness. I lumber and lurch up to the microphone. It takes a week, and then I push Ignorant aside.

'Come on, you fuckers, I know we're a pile of shit, but I also know that you're a pile of shit as well, so why can't we be shit together?'

I as good as crawl back to the drum kit, clamber onto my stool and heave into it with the best I can muster, but the sweet Chinese red is cramping my arms and locking my legs, so my best is seriously crap. The response is pathetically, if predictably, low. It's a no comma death zone negative nowhere black shirt bummer. Ignorant impotently floats by like a drowned goldfish.

'Do it, you fucker, do it,' I shout.

'Piss off,' he ripostes.

That's right, isn't it? We are, aren't we? Being? Knowing? That's our right, isn't it? Rich now in the idle mists of dawn. Yeah, fuck off.

Three hours ago I'd found Ignorant and Andy hanging out in a friend's squat demolishing their third massive joint, and I'd known that the gig was going to be a tough one. Andy was totally psyched. Earlier, he'd been terrorising innocent commuters at bus stops, tired souls simply waiting for the hearse home. I didn't like that. It's a narrow line between confrontation and abuse, and there's no doubt that bad dope and bad alcohol can push it all the wrong way. I knew that Andy had seriously overloaded, but that didn't make me feel any the better about it or him. Surely we should have some sense of responsibility towards others? I accept that it was bad timing, but I'd taken up the issue with Andy because in a few hours' time we'd be on stage, supposedly as a united force. Crass? My arse.

'You don't need to frighten people, they have their own pain and they don't need you adding to it.'

'Look here, you fucker,' he responded, waving a fist in my face, 'you play your game, and I'll fucking play mine, right?'

But for me it wasn't right. By then I'd downed two bottles of wine and most of my inhibition, fear and hopeless self-consciousness had been eroded, but that didn't make me want to frighten people. The media could do that all too well, portraying punk as some sort of pathological illness, making us into scape-goats, which made it all the more important for us not to conform to their misconceptions. We're not the hooligans in this scenario, no, they are. They set it all up while we're just the blotting paper for their bile. I probably wouldn't like the sort of world that those people at the bus stops represent, but it's their world and it'll remain their world until something better is on offer. So, rather than frightening them, I'd like to help them see that there are other choices beyond the rigid structures that they accept as reality. There is more, always more, and in my own paradoxical way I'm gently searching out a route to it.

Punk attitude and its broad adoption of anarchist ideas has been totally discredited by a press hostile to change, indeed, dismissing our demands for peace, they declared all-out war against us. Equally, the British Establishment, being the political, industrial, military complex that it is, has a particularly insidious way of protecting itself against dissent; it's called 'free speech.' In reality, this simply means that the ruling class extend an illusion of liberal openness to us, the proletariat, trusting that we'll be conned into thinking we've got a voice. But what is it that most people do with that voice? They shut the fuck up and look after number one. So, we get it from all sides, from the politicians and the wealthy corporations to the press and then, most sad of all, from ourselves, the people.

The much reported battles between punks and Teddy Boys in central London, in which the press were at pains to create a new mods and rockers drama, are a graphic example of the manipulations of the media and the methods used to discredit alternative lifestyles. The greater truth in all this was that the Teds were attacking punks willy-nilly, yet it was the punks who took the rap as the perpetrators of violence. When members of the extreme right attacked Johnny Rotten, the press gleefully joined in, effectively legitimising the resultant wave of 'punk bashings.' Punk isn't concerned with violence, it's sick and tired of it, sick and tired of a society that's so obsessed with it, but now, ironically, it's become tarred with it. Meanwhile, the real barbarians are out on the streets of Belfast, wearing the Queen's colours and killing in her name and, if we're silly enough to vote, ours.

'No, it bloody well isn't right,' I yell, pointing an accusatory finger in Andy's face, 'people have got their own life and you should respect them for that. You demand freedom for yourself, well, shouldn't we learn to give it to others too? People are frightened, they don't want to hear about change, don't want to be told by some crazed punk that it isn't working. They can see it for themselves. You're just conforming to the media's idea of what punk's all about, just playing a part in their fucking charade.'

'You cunt,' Andy isn't amused and doesn't hold back on letting me know. 'You fucking cunt. Call yourself a punk, do you? Do you? Give him some dope, someone, for fuck's sake, give him some fucking dope, and don't you tell me what to fucking do, right? Right?'

That's the ultimate freedom, right? The right to say no, yes? I feel moderation creeping through my veins, doubt coursing through my body. A sad dusk. The windows are becoming misty. I sink back into an armchair, despondency and another bottle of wine. Andy and Ignorant fight it out over a pack of cigarettes on the sofa and smash up a pile of records with their flailing boots: Sex Pistols, Patti Smith, Clash, Television, Blondie, Buzzcocks, Joni Mitchell. Joni Mitchell? Now then, I care about her, but I guess now's not the time to say so, but sometimes that gentle voice is such a comforting balm, soft against the abrasive textures of my new-found punk lifestyle.

Pete arrives to get the band together for a soundcheck at the Roxy. He looks us over with an air of haughty disgust. I tell him I'm not coming until I feel right. He looks me over with complete contempt. I feel angry for all the wrong reasons, confused by the diversity, concerned that maybe punks are the muggers in the street. I don't want to be the fall guy. It can all fade away so quickly. One moment I know, just know, I feel clean, feel that this is the way through those years of shit, those layers of faux niceties that left me feeling so barren. Then, because of fear written on a face, because someone backs off or rushes forward too fast, I collapse in doubt, painful, devouring doubt, always falling back to somewhere I came from, yet knowing that I've never been anywhere.

I feel fucked. The wine is numbing whatever sense I might've had left. The rest of the band have staggered off for the sound-check. It's raining, pissing down, and I don't want to get wet, don't want to go out onto the street. I hate the flashing neon reflected in the raindrops, hate the damp wind blowing down the alleyways of tower blocks, hate the swish of tyres on wet roads and the puddle-splash of passing taxicabs. I hate the sense of insecurity, hate the loneliness. Maybe I'd like a limo and a fur coat, a chic rooftop studio and a swimming pool, or maybe I'd like to be just plain bloody ordinary, whatever that is.

I stay at the squat and talk with Martin, one of its residents who's just got back home to discover the carnage. We talk of social unrest, race riots, fascism, totalitarianism, over and over and over again; you name it. Martin has recently been to Lewisham, a suburb of London where the National Front were staging a march. Lewisham has a large black community, and it was inevitable that they would object to a rally being allowed in their neighbourhood. The police were there in force to protect the marchers from possible attack. Martin was there to give support to the black community and their sympathisers. He suffered from a not-so-mild beating from the police for shouting insults at the marchers. Apparently, however, it was okay for the National Front to chant their foul-mouthed racist abuse because it was, after all, an officially sanctioned gathering. Yes, that's right, a fascist march in Britain, in 1977, protected by the state, right? Yup, just another example of the glorious concept of free speech. Yup, that's democracy, that wonderful British democracy we hear so much about, right? Well, Martin is still badly bruised by the right to free speech, so who's protecting who from what?

For the same highly dubious reasons already referred to, the press has also made efforts to label punk as being rightist in its politics, but whereas the message might sometimes be nasty, it certainly isn't Nazi. When it is nasty, it's nasty for good reason, nasty because a society that offers little more than unemployment and homelessness to its underprivileged is in itself pretty nasty. It's all reflection; ugly faces in cracked mirrors. Contrary to what hysterical reportage would have us believe, the punk movement is in general strongly anti-racist, indeed, much of the spark that fired punk came from black counterculture. On the other hand, the National Front has exploited the righteous discontent of the underprivileged to become the fourth biggest political party in the UK. However, like its mindless brother, the dinosaur, it will not survive, and this is because radicals from both black and white communities are joining hands to fight back, and where radicals step today, the general public follows next week: something to do with fools and angels, isn't it? Well, it seems they got that wrong too.

Another major source of inspiration for punk was the race riots of 1976 that broke out during the Notting Hill Carnival. It was there that blacks, intimidated by a massive police turnout, made known a sense of unrest that had been smouldering beneath the surface for years. The complaints voiced by angry blacks of oppression, lack of housing, lack of jobs, lack of education and health facilities, lack, lack, lack, found a mirror in the consciousness of white radicals and working-class youth alike: reflections, right? There ain't no future, right? So, reggae was an expression of black ideals and aspirations which at the time had no white counterpart, but then, from the darkness of white urban ghettoes, a voice rang out: I'm shit, I'm shit. S, h, i, t. I'm punk, I'm punk. P, u, n, k. But for all that, there still isn't a future. Just after the punk baby learnt to walk, the capitalist counter-revolutionaries stole the ground from beneath its feet, and there's no going back on it, at least not by that route. But as I saw it, punk was never so much about music as it was attitude. It was a cry of dissatisfaction, a scream of despair, a tormented voice challenging a demented society, so maybe it could yet find a way forward.

After twenty-five minutes of our torturous noise, anger, slur and fucked-up confusion, the Roxy management decide to switch us off. So now then, who's eating whose dinner? Well, the serpent just bit its own tail and I'm hovering right up above ready to swoop. This time the phoenix is coming down fast. From here on in, punk is a voice of revolt whose music is incidental to the message, and the message is 'do it,' and if you don't like it, fuck off. So then, after twenty-five minutes of torturous noise we get switched off and reggae blasts across the apology for a dance-floor. It seems to me that the blacks got it spot on at Notting Hill, but if the disc jockey at the Roxy thinks he's going to drown out my anguish with theirs, he's got it wrong. In this instance, two rights make a wrong. This is my riot. I haven't done yet. For all the booze, I'm not yet spent. I know it, I know, I just fucking know, and if some smarmy gangster points a gold-ringed finger at his fake gold-plate Rolex to tell me I've got to row in on his pleasure boat, boy, have I got news for him? I don't recall having had a number emblazoned on my side.

'Come in number forty-nine, your time is up.'

'Up it, mate, fucking right up it.'

He can piss off out of it. This is my time, my place, ain't it? Well, ain't it?

Britain is suffering the effects of severe recession, an economic slump which means the poor will get poorer while the rich get richer. It's always been the same old story, but this time around a larger number of the poor know it.

Released from the restraints of our set songs, I lob into a fast tribal rhythm that I'd first heard on a Joni Mitchell album. The rest of the band have climbed down from the stage, but on hearing the drums come alive again, they clamber back up. Phil, our lead guitarist, argues with one of the sound engineers who won't switch us back on. Never one to take no for an answer, he then lays into one of the PA speakers with his elbow and almost instantly we get back our sound, albeit at half volume and barely audible beneath the disco which still pumps out reggae.

Back Britain? Fuck Britain. Too many times have the working population been told to tighten their belts and make an effort for their country. But what is this country of theirs? Effectively, it's the sum of centuries of cynical, cruel, bungling governance, a cock-up, a hypocritical, complacent and dangerous con. Governments rule and governments kill, right? Ireland, right? Vietnam, right? On and on and on, and don't look back just now. Democracy is a lie. What we've got is two-party totalitarianism, so, whoever wins, the picture stays exactly the same: God, Queen and Country, and never mind the people. Tomorrow we eat better. Today we wait. Who ate my dinner? The begging bowl is a form of crucifix. Who's hanging where? Tomorrow never comes.

It doesn't matter if they can't hear us, it just doesn't matter. Who the fuck cares? They can see us, can't they? It doesn't matter a shit if the sound is crap because this is a battlefield and battle-fields never sound too pleasant. I begin to shout and scream, demanding attention, looking around for receptive faces in the audience, someone who might understand what it is we're trying to do. This is my moment, our moment, and no grease-arsed manager is going to stop me or us.

At last, the people on the streets are finding a voice. It's taken a jobless, homeless, futureless reality to make the message clear, and right now it's becoming clearer and clearer. Governments aren't there to care for the people; let them eat shit. It's a cash-led democracy, so fuck the poor. Jobs? What jobs? If there are jobs, they're mindless, monotonous and soul-destroying. The factory floor is a mental morgue. Homes? What homes? If there are homes, they're twenty floors up where the industrial pollution kills faster than the rising damp. Rotten was right, there is no future in England's green and pleasant, at least not one that any government is about to offer.

Slowly, bit by bit, little bubbles of response burst out on the dancefloor. A number of people have moved up to the stage, raising their fists into the sweaty, noisy air. It's a show of solidarity; the walls are crumbling. For as long as we're able, we build up as much energy as we can, and then, at last, the walls come tumbling down. The group of fist-wavers swells, bigger and bigger. We've broken through, broken out. This moment is ours, ours alone, theirs, theirs alone, we're breaking through together, and we know it.

Ultimately, it's up to us, the ordinary people, the common folk and our common sense, to make our own lives for ourselves. It took the only revolution Britain has ever known to create democracy, but all too soon it fell into the hands of the same old ruling elites. It was inevitable because democracy is a system, and systems enslave those who they claim to serve. Not Marx, nor Mao, Carter, Callaghan, Thatcher, Stalin or Hitler nor even Buddha or Christ: no one. Just you, just me, just common people with their common sense and, yes, their common decency, right?

I'm done for, wiped out. I fall from my drum stool onto the sodden carpet of the stage, crawling about like I'm in the trenches. But we've done it, yes, done it, and it was enough, enough to unlock some of those crazy mind games and let in some clear light. The air certainly isn't fresh, but for this glorious moment it feels so pure. For the rest of the evening, the Roxy hosts a near riot. Beer cans cartwheel through sprays of alcohol, bodies bounce and leap, surfing the waves of a joy released. Wild dancers dance the dance of life, dragging body on body down to the filthy beer-swilled floor to roll in parodies of our fathers' violence. Touch on touch, parodies of the awful coldness that ripped us from our mothers' bodies into the blue fluorescent light of heartless futures where we heave away at the adopted umbilical and share this moment of birth. Phew. But beware, the reality surgeon is always near, scalpel in hand, nearer, nearer, but this time around he's beaten off by the pulsing body of bodies. The violence is a parody and, when it's over, we nurse our bruises and share our stories. But where are the women?

The system trains its men to be heroes that they might willingly die in the mud of the trenches, while women are to be delicate flowers to be fucked, abused, raped and ruined. So is it any wonder that women play it with caution while men exploit the ugliness they've been led to believe is manhood? Is it any wonder the dancefloor is primarily a male domain?

She stands awkwardly peering into the space where the men perform their sexual rites. Then, suddenly, she leaps to the centre of the dancefloor, her arms held high, here to dance the dance of life all alone in the sexual ocean at high tide. She is alone because she did not wait to be asked, did not wait to be told, courageously defying all ideas of abuse, rape and ruin. And now she jumps up on stage and snatches the microphone from its stand.

'Where are the women? Who's afraid of what? Why this a male battlefield? Is it they alone who can love and laugh? Why the torment? Marion, Rachel, Anne, where are you? Sarah, Jane, Sally, where are you?'

But what is it that so holds us back from cutting through these lines? What power holds us to our defined roles in this soap opera we're told is life? What do we really have to lose in breaking all the rules, defying conformity?

'Mary, Lisa, Joy. Sisters, where are you?'

Yes, another set of false values to be questioned, another layer of conditioning to peel away. We are all responsible one to the other, and it's our responsibility to realise it. The audience are the people and the people are the voice that no entertainer can silence. The people want what no band can offer: self. The people are the people and the people are the voice that no politician can silence. The people want what no government can offer: self. The people want self, the right to self, the self that springs from something much deeper than anything that anyone can give them. The people want the self that is life, life lifeing life, unparalleled and free, life beyond definition, the real no future of a now that is safe to exist in, the unquestionable right of the individual, the raising point of hope. And, yes, we can do it ourselves and we will do it ourselves because deep down we know that we can. In those clammy hours at the Roxy, something of those true selves was exposed; no fear, no shame, no false dignity, no future. We all died together, empty, dissolute, and from there we began at last to live.

The fear created by the media and the censorship of radio and TV has led to the silencing of the more radical and political voices of punk. Those who are still able to play in the few clubs prepared to promote punk, swing more and more towards the safe option between pop and punk, ironically named 'new wave.' Being a mutant, new wave is a deadhead, a drifting snowflake on a summer's day cashing in on the publicity surrounding punk, but reflecting none of its more radical ideas. It is nothing but a continuation of accepted commercial practices, with no philosophy but to suck: new wave, no wave. To step outside prescribed standards of dress and attitude requires a degree of conviction. Not all punks are extroverts, in fact the majority of those who I know are quite the reverse. To publicly sport outfits which are guaranteed to attract derision, if not open attack, is more than an idle game. No, it's the same desire to confront the new which draws the space traveller from the capsule; a new self, a new planet, and this is what in their own way a lot of punks feel. No process can be final. The future's never clear because we haven't come to it yet, and that's because the future is forever tomorrow. In six years it will be 1984, how's that?

Outside on the wet London pavement, we air our discontent. It's one o'clock and London town is closing down, closing down, and this is 1977. We vow that the next time we play the Roxy, it'll be free. Why should we, the audience and performers, pay to keep each other's company? We daub graffiti on the Roxy door to let them know we're still here, alive and ready to ruck 'n' roll, but it's cold and wet, and we're tired, so we all drift off on our different ways home, saying our goodbyes.

'Is it real?'

'What?'

'Are you real?'

'Don't know. Does it matter?'

'Guess not, but is it alright really?'

'Guess not.'

'Bye now.'

And no, it wasn't alright. For four days after the gig, I laid in bed covered in bruises and crippled with doubt. In some crazy demonstration of trust and hope, I'd as good as burnt myself out. Now, ten days later, I still feel weak, and in a couple of days' time we're off to do it all over again, not at the Roxy, we've been banned from there, but somewhere else, some other dive where we'll ask for more than we'll be given; more of self, more of other.

'Come on, you fuckers. Come on, come on, break out, life isn't a fucking prison cell.'

We'll demand a greater energy of ourselves and others, search out a clearer vision. We're learning, learning to fight and learning what to fight for, because we're not happy with what's on offer and we're not happy with what we offer ourselves. We didn't get paid at the Roxy because we broke one of their speakers, but hey, let's do a retake on that. We didn't get paid at the Roxy because they switched us off, right? So let's start putting the horse back before the cart. There is no future, at least there isn't one for as long as we allow them to get away with eating our dinner. Cash or crucifixion? Oh yes, I can buy a future from the Roxy management, or take a stroll down Tin Pan Alley in search of a pimp to have me fucked, but I guess I'd rather do it my way. And, yes, I could lick arse with the crook who elbowed me for working so hard to make his grubby little club seem less like a cemetery, but this time round it's time to kick arse. I don't know whether it's possible, but I dream of taking it all away from those gangsters, conmen and business-world shysters. They stole it all from us in the first place, so now it's time to claim it back, right? And if that's not possible, if that's not the future, then I'll opt for the only real future that I've ever been truly able to trust; myself, the feel of myself, the sense of myself; me, I, the grip of ice upon a leaf, the desolation, the joy, the disillusionment, the certainty, the laughter and the sorrow. This is the landscape to which I awake. I'll take that if I have to, and I'll love it and cherish it.

They're selling solid gold safety-pin earrings in fashionable London jewellers. Who bought Dean's crashed limo? I'll wake to my own sweat. Did Monroe leave the light on? I'm determined that the next move will be mine. They wheel the bodies from the morgue. Memories? Yes, I have some; the sighing arms of tansy and mallow, angelica and rose. They are turned, turned away before they form. It's all so fast.

I reach away from the solace I have sought for self, burn away the passages so neatly cut in the psychic jungle. I sit, a simple idiot before you. I ask that you do not let me die alone on the pavement, for my death is yours also. We are so very deeply bound, you and I, each a part of the other. Can you destroy this moment? We are, and that, surely, is enough? And with that in mind...

18

Learning to Fight

Tony Drayton talks to Richard Cabut

Tony Drayton (aka Tony D) chats to Richard Cabut, annotating the influential 'Pet Puppies in Theory and Practice' article from the second issue of Kill Your Pet Puppy. *The original piece appears in italics.*

Ripped & Torn was one of the first punk fanzines, and lasted from 1976 until 1979, when I fled England to travel around Europe for a while. I started *Kill Your Pet Puppy*, my next fanzine, on my return to the UK later in 79. Joly McFie, who ran Better Badges from the Portobello Road, offered to print any new venture I might have in mind for no fee. The deal was: he would give me a thousand copies, and print as many as he wanted for himself — only Joly knows how many copies *Kill Your Pet Puppy* sold in the end — I shifted my own thousand copies very quickly.

The tone of the new fanzine was a reflection of my environment at that time. My friends and I, subsequently dubbed the Puppy Collective, had been kicked out of various squats, a couple of churches, fire stations and hospitals, including St Monica's in Kilburn. We had nowhere to live. We had nothing. We — my sister Val, an Australian guy called Brett, and a couple of others, were walking around, just to see what we could find. On Sherriff Road in West Hampstead, we saw a young guy in red patent leather trousers walking into a house and reappearing at a second-floor window. We waved at each other, and he came down to let us in. The red-trouser guy turned out to be Kevin Mooney, who later joined Adam and the Ants, and who lived at what was a housing association house in Sherriff Road with Adam's wife, Eve. The first-floor flat was empty, and we quickly squatted it.

This squat was totally different from the ones I'd lived in before, which at least had somewhere to wash and electricity. Here, there were no such luxuries. No power. No water. No toilet — we used the nearby Railway Hotel pub, where the Moonlight Club was situated, for our needs. But it was home to nine of us — sometimes more — in one room. But at least we had somewhere to sleep. We felt we'd achieved something of a victory against the odds.

This was the impetus for *Kill Your Pet Puppy* — the rejection of possessions and the idea of any kind of security. The name meant: get rid of responsibilities, anything that ties you down; get rid of your past, reject domesticity, keep on moving, start afresh, walk forward, never look back, leave your family behind. Nowadays, of course, I would preach: kids, look after your mother and father!

From the proceeds of a brief leafleting job, I bought a typewriter and the first issue was published in January 1980. It covered the burning topics of the time: Crass, Ants and Tuinal, the drug that plagued punk. It sold out straight away.

The second issue, which Joly asked me for in February 1980, would feature no bands I decided. Instead, I was concerned about the condition of punk itself. The media had declared that punk was dead. But all I could see around me were punks. So, for *Kill Your Pet Puppy* 2, I wrote two biggish 'state of the nation' pieces: 'Apocalypse Now,' and the more successful Sid Vicious March article. It starts with me lying in bed with a blonde girl in the Sherriff Road squat...

Pet Puppies in Theory and Practice
'Steal your future back and live it out for yourself,' the boy mumbled, tossing slightly in the bed, he began to wake up...

'Steal your future...' was a quote from some anarchist or, more likely, Situationist text. There was also, of course, the famous anti-consumerist Situ graffiti, 'You can't buy happiness. Steal it.' I had recently come across a lot of such graffiti on my travels in Paris, where old 1968 favourites like 'Under The Paving Stones Lies The Beach' had been freshened up by the French punks — there were a few big punk squats in Paris at the time.

Another big influence was the small pamphlet *Spectacular Times*, a series produced by the late Larry Law in the Seventies and Eighties. They were funny and simple beginner's guides to Situationism. Easy to digest, great for dipping into in the toilet. One particular issue was devoted to vegetarianism and posited that if you're not a vegetarian, you're just a revolutionary between meals. Bang! That summed it up, and the next day I became a vegetarian.

I had first come across anarchist and Situationist theory at the Rough Trade squat in Frestonia, where I lived when I first came to London in 1977. There was an older guy there called Pete, who had an extraordinary library of alternative literature, including all the Situ texts. Pete also owned a complete collection of *Oz* magazines, the design of which informed *KYPP*'s seeping colour look. It was that idea of experimentation and taking chances.

The name *Kill Your Pet Puppy* itself had Situationist connotations, of course — although I had originally wanted to call it 'Fuck Your Mother,' which came from the text on a Seditionaries T-shirt. But that charming title received a thumbs down from the *KYPP* focus group, and after Andy Palmer of Crass had also given it the thumbs down, I settled on *Kill Your Pet Puppy*.

I wake up tired, trying to remember the rapidly fading remnants of my tortured dream about radical anarchy.

Radical anarchy at that point meant feeding and housing people. The practical side of punk rock. Not gigs and badges. Living in Frestonia had had a profound effect on me. This was an area of

Ladbroke Grove/Notting Hill that had been left to rot by the council and squatted by hippies — who famously declared independence from the UK. Actor David Rappaport was the Foreign Minister, while playwright Heathcote Williams served as Ambassador to Great Britain.

Punks didn't get it together as far as squatting was concerned until a little later. I was at the Adam and the Ants gig at the Roundhouse in 1978, after which dozens of punks, and one rockabilly — Toby the Rebel, who had a Confederate flag dyed into his hair — walked from Camden to the West End, opening squats on the way. We ended up on the Charing Cross Road, where we opened a whole block of punk squats — where the 'eat what you like' buffet is now — kicking in door after door. This was the beginning of mass punk squatting in London. It was necessary: there were loads of punks in need of somewhere to stay, pouring off the ferries from Europe, and train stations from up north.

The underlying ethos for me was the anarchy that McLaren promoted along with the Pistols. There was no separation. Anarchy meant living for yourself — with no authority. Obviously, squatting was part of that or, at least, what I call creative squatting, which created an environment for anarchists, bands, writers, artists — lively people with a passion for punk — to run wild in. The other side of punk squatting was found at places like King's Cross or Campbell Buildings in SE1, full of people into bad drugs, living in complete squalor, in need of others to tell them what to do, and at the mercy of roving gangs of skinheads who would rape and beat at will because there was no resistance. By 1980, punk squatting had become so widespread that there was a real distinction between those punks who squatted and those who still lived with mum and dad. The latter were looked down on. Squatting became a badge of pride: I'm better than you, I'm more punk than you. I didn't like this attitude; it wasn't exactly anarchist. In fact, you could call it rather bourgeois. There were some punks who did both, squatting during the week and going home to their parents at the weekend to get their washing done and have a decent meal. Like that film, *Dogs in Space*, in which the main character, a hardcore punk, does exactly that.

We, the Puppy Collective, had a lucky break. At Sherriff Road, Kevin Mooney and Eve moved out and we took over their housing association flat. Then the co-op rehoused us, at minimal rent. So, luckily, we missed out on the frequent skinhead raids on the punk squats.

Battle plans conceived, but only fragments remembered, I realise that today is the Sid Vicious March. I have to make plans for today. I still haven't moved or opened my eyes — when I do I see the blonde figure beside me is still motionless. What time is it? I go back to sleep.

What's the fucking point of marching for Sid anyway — I never thought anything he did was so important, except maybe smashing Nick Kent's head open, throwing Kent's glorification and fascination with violence in his face.

Kent was enamoured with the glamour of violence: destruction and self-destruction. You only have to read his *Rolling Stone* pieces. Drug-fuelled mayhem was his bag. And Sid certainly gave him that. Kent was into that biker lifestyle — leather and giving out lumps. I remember his review of the Ants at the Marquee in which he said the Ants were dressed in leather but were only posers, meaning they weren't proper biker types. I actually saw him at that gig, looking miserable on his own at the back. I was going to ask him what he thought of the band, and I wish I had now, I may have been able to cheer him up and talk him round a little.

It would make more sense to celebrate the first Sex Pistols gig or the release of Anarchy.

I didn't see the early Pistols gigs, but I saw Sid's debut with the band at the Screen on the Green. I'd moved down to London from Glasgow in February or March of 1977, and the gig was in April. I knew about it because of connections at Rough Trade. It was on after that evening's film had finished. We had to wait in the pub across the road until about eleven-thirty pm, and hung around on the Green itself until about twelve o'clock when the doors opened. Actually, hanging around in the pub beforehand was as interesting as the gig itself. It was fantastic to see people in the flesh who I had only heard or read about before. Ollie Wisdom, with the question mark shaved in his head, stands out in the memory for some reason. At that time the streets weren't exactly paved with extreme people from the edges, despite what you might read now. I was talking to people from Rough Trade like Geoff Travis, music journalist Sandy Robertson and his mate Alex Ferguson, who went on to be in ATV. In the cinema, we shuffled into the rows — you couldn't mingle or chat. I was quite near the front, six or seven rows back. They showed a film, *Sex Pistols No 1*, about the band, and the Slits played, but they were disappointing.

There was some waiting, and when it happened it happened. John, who had just dyed his hair black, walked down one aisle and, at the same time, Sid came down the other. I can't remember whether Steve and Paul were playing while they walked down or whether there was silence, but there were some gasps of amazement from the crowd.

The band was phenomenal. It was something to celebrate. It was a vindication of everything I had done up to that point, leaving Glasgow, my home and family. I knew 'Anarchy' and 'I Wanna Be Me,' but I didn't know any other songs. It's incredible to think it was the first time I heard these songs. 'Did You No Wrong' really stuck out. That one really got people pogoing.

Later, Howard Wall of the Lurkers, who was an earlier follower, told me that this song was special. It was for them. The real fans.

I recently went to an anniversary event celebrating the first Pistols gig at Saint Martin's. It's important to remember these things. And it was an event. Like the Sid Vicious March.

And besides I can think of far better ways to commemorate than marching from Sloane Square to Hyde Park or wherever — but I'm going to go anyway because at least it's an EVENT, maybe there'll be some good atmosphere and unity (I'll probably get beaten up, arrested, or both).

Remember 'Brighton' and the Jock McDonald football match. Remember the 'meetings' in Hyde Park about a year ago? And yet I still manage to raise some optimism, well wouldn't you?

Jock McDonald was one of those chancers on the fringes of punk who wanted to be Malcolm McLaren. Lots of people wanted to be Malcolm McLaren — Jake Riviera, Terry Razor, who managed Theatre of Hate, and so on. Jock, though, had links to gangster, criminal society — like Kevin St John, who ran the Roxy after Andy Czezowski. Jock, who was in the 4" Be 2" s, traded on his association with Johnny Rotten, and took in a lot of gullible young punks. He sold bootleg tapes and held court in Beaufort Market on the King's Road. Jock came up with a variety of schemes designed to boost his own standing in the punk world — a thousand-a-side punks v skins football match on Brighton beach (I went to this, but didn't make it onto the beach), a rematch or two in Hyde Park, and an Ants gig at the Rainbow — all of them were dismal failures, as was Jock himself.

My room is a total shambles, I lay in bed surveying everything, trying to decide whether to finish off my sulphate supplies before I go, or if I should even get out of bed — the blonde girl's gone to wash her hair and various people wander in and around — vaguely I try and work out who stayed the night in Puppy Mansions before I realise I'd better get up or forever stay in bed.

I used the word 'sulphate' but what I meant was 'blues.' I took sulphate more in the *Ripped & Torn* days, but by this time I had moved on to pills. I first came across speed in Frestonia, where I was shown how to chop it out, roll a note — all of that ritual is enough to get you high anyway — followed by the blinding pain in your nose as you snort it! Then the disgusting taste in the back of the throat as the drug goes down. After a while you start to long for that foulness — crave the foulness! — because the door has opened: the speed is starting to work.

I was heavily into uppers in 1977. I tried cocaine, but it was just like bad speed. At the Frestonia squat, I started taking blues, chipping in with housemates to buy £100 worth of them at a time — quite an amount in those days. Life consisted of crazy binges and huge comedowns. Blues were perfect for punk of course: easy to take, cheap, no need to spend money on beer, which slowed you down anyway. Speed made it all work. The Lurkers and 999 at the Red Cow in 77 — that period was all about blues. I usually bought them on the Portobello Road from the regular dealers who were a bit hippie, a bit glam: leather jackets and messy hair, that kind of street New York Dolls look. Everyone was taking speed, including everyone at our house. I remember the manager of a First Division punk group knocking on the door desperate for speed. I felt sorry for him and gave him the last of our supply. This didn't go down too well with my fuming house-mates. Next day, I was sent off again, cash in hand, for more drugs.

Everyone seems to be cynically enthused about the March I discover, as I make the rounds of the house trying to find a brush — vive le [sic] revolution and I feel fucking awful. I've gone beyond the states that can be cured or at least, temporarily numbed with sulphate —

anything speedy or energising I take now will transform in PARANOIA, and that I don't need. Not today.

Cynical enthusiasm was the punk attitude. Or, at least, the London punk attitude. Everyone I knew was cynically enthused, meaning that we were into things deeply, but still maintained a sneer. Like at the Pistols' Screen on the Green gig, when Johnny walked down to the stage, people weren't saying, 'There's Johnny! Great!' They were saying, 'There's fucking Johnny in his pop star rags.' The inference was: he's going to let us down in the end. Cynical enthusiasm meant revelling in the scene while harbouring the belief that it was bound to go wrong. It wasn't a sense of cool. Cool isn't cool because if you're cool then you don't show you're cool — that means you'd be acting cool, which is uncool! People would say that about the Puppy Collective: 'Oh, we saw you at such and such a gig, and wanted to talk to you, but you were too cool.' But we were never cool, we were always bickering.

The other prevalent punk attitude, at least by the time of writing this piece, was cynical apathy rather than cynical enthusiasm. There was a thin line between the two, and it was difficult sometimes to drag people out to gigs or events such as this Vicious March. Of course, drug comedowns played their part in all of this. Such psychic states also produced paranoia — a punk feeling if there ever was one. We were moving targets, and within our rights to feel paranoid. Again, after a while you would crave that paranoia: it became a drug or high in itself; a spark. It was good to be on the edge.

Last night I went to see the Swell Maps and Pink Military. Not because I really wanted to see either, but I feel it's important to get out to gigs – keep in touch. It was sold out when we (me and Iggy/Grant) got there but after a hassle we got in because a Swell Map knew the name 'Tony D'.

The Swell Maps had a song called 'Ripped & Torn,' and that's why guitarist, the late Nikki Sudden, let us in. I wrote about the Swell Maps gig because I wanted to show people that we didn't just go to see Sid Vicious-type bands. I wanted people to think: *this* is KYPP, *this* is punk. And the fact that this gig had sold out showed just how far punk had spread. Some people called it post-punk, but that was just a media invention. I never understood the term — not now, not then, not in the future. Post-punk was a media phrase used by people who didn't go to gigs. A way for them to distance themselves from what was happening; a refusal to accept that there was a continuation and that punk hadn't died. Most of this audience had Crass or the Ants on the backs of their leather jackets. The best music press writers had been the likes of Charles Shaar Murray, who wrote about music from a sociological standpoint. Music writing became very boring when Paul Morley and Ian Penman started writing from an intellectual position.

I didn't enjoy it, even though I sold 36 copies of 'Pet Puppy', but at least I knew there was a party on in the squat in my road to look forward to when we got back. I didn't stay long there although that was where the blonde came from, and I returned there on Saturday morning to rouse them for the March.

Thirty-six copies... a fairly good night. I spent my time at gigs wandering around with a plastic bag full of fanzines. I wasn't alone. There were many of us fanzine writers selling our wares. Most of them would try to barter and swap with me. If I was in the mood I'd agree, if not I'd be snotty about it. After all, this was KYPP! I guess I got karmic comeback when, at a Hyde Park Free Cannabis Festival, I picked up my bag and when I got home found it was someone else's, and full of sanitary towels. I used to give issues away to the famous people. Outside the Music Machine, I gave a copy of *Ripped & Torn* 14 to Nico — it featured a poster of her. She signed a copy for me with: 'To the beautiful boy who reminds me of Brian Jones.' My favourite Rolling Stone.

When Puppy Mansions had woken up and got itself sorted out there were six of us, four guys and two girls, ready to go — from the squat I collected four participants, three girls and a guy. Today's Puppy Collective.

A ten strong 'Puppy Collective' marching boldly for Sid Vicious? No, ten people marching for their right not to care. Ten people, along with other groups of tens, fours, threes, other individuals who care enough to march for their right to not care — their right to live fast, their right to be ABLE to live fast IF THEY WANT TO. We want the choice even if we don't use it, that's why we're going to Sloane Square.

I wanted to make it clear: we are punks, but we don't care in the least about Sid. At that time, February 1980, I was aware that Sid was wrong. He wasn't a good punk figurehead. That swastika T-shirt of his was a disaster for punk. In Paris, for instance, punks were completely enamoured with the Nazi imagery that Sid had helped to popularise. I have a lot of respect for Malcolm McLaren, but I couldn't imagine what he was playing at. Imagine if Sid had been dressed up with an anarchy symbol, it would have been phenomenal. Instead, Sid had a big influence on the slobbering-mess wing of punk, as well as on the Oi! punks, who came later, and who were really skinheads dressed in punk clothing.

Not because some poxy junkie died trying to live up to someone else's myth, but because we want that chance of creating our own myth, our own future. I'm not sure how and I'm not sure why but there HAS to be a way to create a future where things aren't just 'alright' and where we don't have to put up with 99% of our lives being wasted waiting for things we KNOW are only going to be second or third best, where we don't have to be afraid to walk the street just because social failures attempt to 'get their own back' on a society that rejected them by beating up and robbing anything identifiable as a separate group or tribe.

We, the Puppy Collective, step beyond prescribed decent standards of dress, attitude, and behaviour. We, as punks as part of a mass punk consciousness that was shown to be still alive and inspired even today, ESPECIALLY TODAY, publicly wear outfits guaranteed to attract derision and abuse, if not open attack, not as an idle game. It is because we have a conviction that can never be destroyed by any number of abusive or physical attacks, a desire to confront people's standards. To confront and violate their conceptions of decency, to make null and void their false judgements of right and wrong.

A desire to confront MYSELF, to draw from myself a new self. Because it's there.

By the time we get to the King's Road it's half past two and we hear many distorted versions and stories of what we missed.

There's punks wandering around in every direction, disorganised and colourful — but there's an atmosphere you could cut with a knife, and it's not the sort of atmosphere I want to get disorganised and colourful in.

Too many skins — organised and GREY — I often wonder how scared inside you have to get, how bitter and full of hate for everything you have to get before you're driven to such brutally ugly extremes.

The biggest enemy of a skinhead is COMPASSION, and love, and yes, understanding, but especially COMPASSION. It so negates and empties every value they feel necessary to flaunt that they have to violently crush, ruin, destroy and wipe out any trace of it especially if that trace happens to involve other people doing and enjoying everything they can't, or are too scared to try. Like being yourself, and letting other people be themselves, understanding WHY other people need to be different from you. Like anarchy.

I had first come across groups of skinheads in 1979 while squatting in Old Street, where the British Movement HQ was also based. We saw more and more of them arriving at the Underground station every day. I saw it first-hand, and it was hugely worrying. At the beginning there was no trouble, we walked past each other and nodded. My sister Val asked one of them why he was a BM skinhead, and he told her they gave away free badges! They weren't the sharpest of sticks.

Then, starting with Crass events of that year, gigs suddenly turned into battlegrounds. It was clearly organised by the British Movement and National Front leadership to spread terror on the streets. Suddenly you had skin gangs turning up at gigs, and attacking punk squats, beating and raping. Some individual skins were on our side and tried to stop the violence. But it was impossible. Out-of-town gangs started coming in, and there was bloodshed all the time. Some punks caused trouble for themselves — the Ants crew travelled around the country fighting the locals. Those people then thought all punks were like that and the violent cycle was perpetuated. There was almost daily intimidation. Skins hung around outside the Music Machine and Marquee extorting money out of punks, patting down small seventeen year olds and taking what they found. The bouncers watched and did nothing — they had that skinhead mentality themselves and beat punks up too. The Sid Vicious March started badly when skins came up onto the top floor of the bus, and worked their way along robbing all the punks. It was disgusting and it was war.

Peaceful anarchists say, 'Teach them love, let them have a chance to feel compassionate.' The Pet Puppy Survival Guide says the only lessons skinheads collectively can understand are hard, brutal ones, like a small anonymous militia seeking out their leaders (the ones who use the others by politically organising them for the leaders' own gain) and killing them. And making fucking sure the under-

lings know exactly why there's dead skins lining the streets.

I mean it's fucking war already, when we (the Puppy Collective) left the King's Road and went straight to Hyde Park (but the diagonally opposite end from Speakers Corner) we walked right into a confrontation, one side blinded in organised hatred, and one side a loose collection of individual conviction.

That killing idea was extreme and came only from one particular Puppy, whose name I won't mention. The notion was diluted to simply driving around South East London, abusing any skins we came across before quickly driving off. I wouldn't be here now if the van had broken down. Another idea was to put adverts in the music paper, purportedly from girls asking for personal pictures of skinheads. We would then publish them in *KYPP* and dish out humiliation. This too was abandoned — if we had done it, it would have been the very last issue!

As we walked along the Serpentine Lake to reach the bridge that led onto the Speakers Corner side of the park we became aware of a gathering of skins watching us. We'd swollen to about 20 (half male and half female) spread about thirty yards apart, there was about 20-25 of them, all male. There was about a minute to decide whether to stand or run.

As I had been at the back of our group I moved up through, sussing out the attitude. Most weren't aware of any impending doom, and I'd just reached the front of our parade when one or two skins started moving forward with intent.

By this time we were almost at the bridge (or at least the front end was) and they were coming in from out right with the bridge an obvious escape route on our left, leading into the open park. The front skins started running, leading a massed attack and I take off over the bridge, with others following and in front.

They managed to get one punk on the ground, but they stop and walk off in the opposite direction from us almost immediately.

They seem to have been interested in a massed charge rather than a fight (perhaps the odds weren't one sided enough, after all it was only two of them to every male punk) — but it's hard to tell.

It was the surprise element that fucked us, but we were ready for any further attacks as we crossed the remainder of the park. Within minutes of us regrouping and marching off though, we'd separated into another shambling stretched out line of spikey hair and leather — but maybe that's why 'PUNK' is so creative (at times), this stubbornness to avoid the security of organisation. The sterility of orderliness.

I'd read about the skins attacking hippies in the Sixties, and I was on the side of the hippies. I hated skinhead conformity and brutality. I was sad to see it happening all over again. But it showed that punk was important enough for these thugs to appear and try to destroy it. It was, as I described, an organised grey mass against a bunch of sporadic, colourful, lively people. But being individuals we were easy targets. The world isn't meant to be full of thugs and targets — it shouldn't have happened like that.

The skins would attack each other as well. I remember watching from the entrance of the Roundhouse as gangs of skins fought a turf war — the Harrow Skins versus the Highbury Skins, or whatever. They turned on themselves. That always happens in these sorts of organisations — they attack each other until one guy is left standing. A bear pit.

My paranoia was pushing out fever-pitched thoughts and speculations but the rest of the day was an anti-climax.

At Speakers Corner — nothing. We were three steps behind the 'real' march all the way thru Oxford Circus, Carnaby Street, Piccadilly Circus and Leicester Square.

All we found and met were straggling bunches telling us where they'd last seen The March vanish into the distance. With people drifting off like flies and newcomers drifting along we met all the massed police wagons and police hostility that burst into aggression at Piccadilly Circus (just as we seemed to be creating a frail unity amongst the straggling punks following us) when they moved in and really split us apart.

Two grabbed and questioned and searched me (whilst a member of the Puppy Collective was stashing his drugs into a hole in the wall three feet away). I told them I was on my way home, in a voice that screamed Defeat, Depression and an Apathetic Acceptance of both. Which was how I felt at the time (if I had any feelings left apart from stark, paralyzing paranoia) at half past four in the pouring rain with two police holding my arms and my feet aching from all the pointless walking.

Needless to say, the police didn't like punks. Any meeting between the two involved pain. Usually it came in the form of everyday harassment — questioning and searches. There was always one stupid incident after another. At the Nashville before an Ants gig, one tough Scottish copper was going to come down hard on me for having the audacity to wear a kilt, until I spoke up with a Glaswegian lilt. On special occasions, such as demos, there would be physical brutality involved.

At an anti-nuclear event at Hyde Park in the early Eighties, with a turnout of some fifty thousand people, everyone — the left-wingers and the police — hated us anarchists. We were an easy target and became the focus of a large-scale baton charge. There is a famous photograph of a seemingly oblivious couple kissing during the Poll Tax Riot while the police cause havoc around them, but that couple wasn't the first to do this. As the police attacked us at Hyde Park there was nowhere to run and nowhere to hide, so I instinctively grabbed a girl who I knew and started snogging deeply. It was a conscious tactic, and it worked — the police swarmed around, but left us alone. After all it would have been rude to assault a kissing couple.

'Are you alright?' No, I'm not alright, it can't be alright, it's not alright if you have to spend a day defending your faith, carrying your banner only to have THEM try to crucify you on it. When you allow yourself some HOPE that you're going to gain some ground only to finish up with your back to the wall defending your already hard-fought for space, with clouds of disillusionment poisoning the very conviction you're using as a weapon.

But we're learning still. I'm learning to fight and why it's okay to fight for peace, and the most important lesson of all is that you can talk and talk. Write and write, think and think, but unless you physically back it up when you're challenged, unless you physically show you believe in your theory you're just a hypocritical waste of time to yourself and others.

'I'm learning to fight and why it's okay to fight for peace' was aimed at Penny Rimbaud. In *Kill Your Pet Puppy* 1 we had included a negative response to his pacifist Crass manifesto. I had just received his reply while writing this piece.

Crass revitalised the anarchist current in the UK, but when the skinhead movement started growing, their pacifism became out of step with the street. Crass asserted that left-wing and right-wing were all the same. Well actually, no, they weren't. I didn't encounter any left-wingers robbing me at the Tube station, and the Socialist Workers Party weren't attacking and raping punks in their squats. But the right-wing skins were. Crass saw it as an abstract, theoretical problem, but we had to actually live with it. Crass weren't up to the changes on the street — and soon encountered criticism for hiding in their Essex commune. At this time, Boy George and the new romantics were saying dress up your life, mod-style — peacock around. Crass were saying destroy your life and start again. I believed in starting again, but I knew, having gone forward, we had to fight for punk or lose it. I had no intention of losing it. I believed in punk.

19

Unheard Melodies

by Andrew Gallix

'As a rock critic, when you reach a certain age, you begin to wonder if all the mental and emotional energy you've invested in this music was such a shrewd move,' wrote Simon Reynolds in the introduction to *Rip It Up and Start Again*. More recently, he wondered if 'searching for utopia through music' had not been 'a mistake' (*Totally Wired*). To ascribe such doubts to impending middle age alone would be to forget that there *was* a time when music seemed a matter of life and death; when days were whiled away listening to records and poring over album covers in some ill-defined but all-important quest. Instead of producing plays or paintings, the best and brightest were busy perfecting two-note solos on replica Starways from Woolies. Rock 'n' roll was central to contemporary culture: it was where it was at.

Needless to say, no band could ever totally live up to such high expectations. Malcolm McLaren shrewdly ensured that the Sex Pistols made precious few live appearances in order to enhance their mystique. The band's early landmark performances often took place in offbeat venues — Andrew Logan's decadent Butler's Wharf studio, a Brewer Street strip-joint, or an Islington art-house cinema — far from the grubby pub-rock circuit. These were events — happenings — rather than mere concerts. Music critic Jonh Ingham witnessed how McLaren set about creating an audience for the band before contriving to prevent these fans from seeing them: 'Malcolm made the Pistols invisible. The kids are there, and you can't have the Pistols. I guess it worked, but it was a dumb thing to do, making the band Olympian' (Jon Savage, *The England's Dreaming Tapes*). Spandau Ballet, described by

David Johnson as a 'rumour band,' would use a similar trick at the beginning of their career by playing invite-only performances: 'They staged secret "tease dates", never "gigs", at clubs and venues calculated to annoy the rockists, such as the Blitz, an art-house cinema, or a warship on the Thames. The audience got in only by looking good — which applied to critics, too' (*The Observer*, 4 October 2009). Keats (Morrissey notwithstanding) was right: heard melodies are sweet, but those unheard are sweeter. After all, bands are necessarily approximations of the dreams that conjured them up. Some — like the Libertines, whose Arcadian rhetoric was frequently far more exciting than their songs — are condemned to remain pale reflections of their Platonic ideals. By the same token, a record is always a compromise, whereas an unreleased (preferably unrecorded and strictly fictitious) record remains pure potentiality. The La's famously spent two years recording and re-recording their debut album without ever achieving the desired effect. In the final analysis, music can never compete with the silence it comes from and returns to — the silence inhabited by phantom bands.

We are not talking dead silence here, but rather something akin to the background noise during a performance of 4′33″ or the tinnitus burned onto the mind's ear by imaginary songs overheard through the static in between radio stations. A living silence, perhaps. One thinks of Theodor Adorno limning fictitious twelve-tone compositions for Thomas Mann as though they were, as he put it, 'descriptions of real pieces of music.' According to the great critic George Steiner, 'A book unwritten is more than a void.' The same could be said of songs unrecorded or unperformed: they actually exist, virtually, in some Borgesian iPod of Babel. Phantom bands themselves are not complete figments of the imagination either: to qualify, they must have some kind of shadowy existence, leave some kind of (lipstick) trace.

The Chris Gray Band never existed beyond a few graffiti

marks around Victoria Coach Station in the early Seventies, but the idea of forming 'a totally unpleasant pop group' designed to subvert show business from within would obviously be a major influence on the Pistols project. The eponymous Chris Gray was a one-time member of the English section of the Situationist International (expelled in 1967) and the author of the seminal *Leaving the 20th Century* anthology (1974) which popularised Situationist ideas in Britain. Like Malcolm McLaren and Jamie Reid, he had been involved with political pranksters King Mob.

The London SS — whose short lifespan was one long audition bringing together most of the major players on the future London punk scene — is probably the most influential group to have neither released a record nor played a single gig. Legend has it that a demo tape exists somewhere, but Mick Jones and Tony James have vowed, in true phantom-band style, never to release it.

The Flowers of Romance (Sid Vicious, Viv Albertine, and Keith Levene) gave an interview to a fanzine although they had never graced the stage (and would never do so). The Castrators, whom Vivien Goldman wrote a sensational piece about for the *News of the World*, never played a single gig either. The Moors Murderers (Chrissie Hynde and Steve Strange) were also talked about in the press without ever really doing anything much.

Synthpunk pioneers the Screamers were once described by Jello Biafra as 'the best unrecorded band in the history of rock 'n' roll.' Typically, their first photoshoot appeared in a magazine when they were yet to play live. At a later stage, they were approached to release a record sleeve containing no record — an art stunt which never materialised, but would have been a fitting metaphor for this textbook phantom outfit from Los Angeles. It was also in keeping with what Tomata du Plenty, their outrageous singer, told Jon Savage: 'I think advertising is more exciting than the product most of the time.' The Screamers' uncompromising music — all synthesiser, keyboard, drums, screamed vocals and not a guitar in sight — was unlikely to get heavy rotation, but delusions of grandeur probably explain why the big-time eluded them. A prime example was their decision to turn down a tour with Devo. There were also rumours that Brian Eno wanted to produce them, but the band felt that their histrionic live performance could not possibly be captured on vinyl. Instead, they envisaged a video-only release, which would have been commercial suicide pre-MTV.

Fronted by Julian Cope, the Nova Mob from Liverpool were a purely conceptual group dedicated to never playing a single note of music. Instead, they would hang around cafes discussing imaginary songs — a practice they referred to as 'rehearsing.' Definitely one for the Borgesian iPod. Of course, they eventually went and spoilt it all by playing a disastrous headline gig at Eric's, following which they did the honourable thing and disbanded.

I can see three reasons why phantom bands flourished in the punk years. The first is that punk, for many of us, embodied all our dreams and aspirations: it was a materialisation of the Absolute. The second is that many punks had never picked up an instrument. The third is that punk music was often read about — and into — before being heard. Brian Young (Rudi) encountered the New York Dolls in *Melody Maker*: 'Without even hearing them, I knew this was the band for me.' Vic Godard (Subway Sect) found out about the American scene through Andy Warhol's *Interview* magazine: 'We used to get that and look to see what was going on in New York. And we'd read reviews of Television, Talking Heads, the Ramones, and we had a rough idea of what they looked like without having a clue what they sounded like.' Viv Albertine (The Slits) bought *Horses* at HMV Records on Oxford Street (where she bumped into Mick Jones, who was there for the same reason) on the strength of a short review and a picture of the cover: 'I half dread it in case the music doesn't live up to the promise of that bold cover' (it did). John O'Neill (The

Undertones) says that he 'cannot emphasise how important the *NME* was from 1974 to 1977' as it was 'impossible to hear these groups' in Ireland at the time. His brother, Damian, recalls the excitement caused by Neil Spencer's first live review of the Sex Pistols: 'We hadn't heard anything by them.' It was the very same review that would lead Howard Devoto, Pete Shelley, TV Smith and many others to go and see the band.: 'Immediately I was a fan, I wanted to see this band. I was loading so much imagery into this name' (John Ingham). In a way, the Pistols started off as a phantom band and ended up as one (through a mixture of necessity and design).

'It's like being in love with a woman you've never had,' says Dominique Fury, trying to account for the enduring fascination exerted by the group in which she briefly played guitar four decades ago: 'The relationship hasn't been consummated.' She smiles. A ray of sunshine has crept into her artist's studio near Belleville. Through the open window, I can glimpse the pink apple blossom in the middle of the dappled courtyard. All is quiet. All is still. *When I say I'm in love, you best believe I'm in love L-U-V.* For me, the most phantomatic of phantom bands has always been L.U.V., an elusive and largely illusive all-girl punk combo from Paris. I remember reading tantalising news snippets about them in the music or mainstream press at regular intervals. A quote here, a namecheck there. Just enough to whet my appetite. And then — nothing. A tale told by an idiot, full of silence and fury, signifying nothing. Nostalgia for a band yet to come.

Only one picture of the complete line-up was ever published (in the long-defunct *Matin de Paris*). Granted, it is worth a thousand words, but the fact that there seem to be no others speaks volumes about the fragility of L.U.V.'s collective identity. It is also rather paradoxical given that style was all the substance they had. From left to right you can see Aphrodisia Flamingo (the rebel), Dominique Fury (the femme fatale), Liliane Vittori (the cerebral rock chick) and Edwige Belmore (the It girl). Wearing matching sunglasses, Aphrodisia and Dominique — the terrible twins who formed the nucleus of the group — stand very close to each other as if they are an item. Aphrodisia stares the world down, her full mouth a smouldering moue of utter contempt — Bardot gone badass. Dominique, in terrorist-chic mode, adopts a far more glamorous, almost provocative pose. Liliane, for her part, seems to be fading into the background, a faraway look on her anguished features. Edwige towers above her like some Teutonic titan, sporting a Billy Idol hairdo and the blank expression of a Galeries Lafayette mannequin.

L.U.V. was the brainchild of Aphrodisia Flamingo (Laurence 'Lula' Grumbach) who, having mixed with the likes of Nico, Lou Reed and Patti Smith in New York City, returned to Paris determined to launch a girl group of the punk persuasion. One night, down at the Gibus (France's answer to CBGB or the Roxy), she caught sight of Dominique Fury (née Jeantet). It was L.U.V. at first sight: 'I just made a beeline for her because I instantly knew I wanted her in the band.' The fiery, long-haired brunette and the glacial, short-haired blonde were attracted to each other like polar opposites. Dominique speaks repeatedly of a 'magnetic relationship': 'There was chemistry between us — something magical that was more than the mere sum of its parts.' Both came from very wealthy, but troubled, backgrounds. Aphrodisia lost her father when she was only eleven. Fury never really found hers, which may explain her penchant for collective experiences. He was a shadowy character: a spy with multiple identities, who was involved in a plot to assassinate Hitler and had been a member of a far-right terrorist group before the war. (Fury's godfather was another protean figure, future President François Mitterrand.) Before punk, Dominique was a revolutionary heiress who made donations to the Black Panthers and bankrolled a couple of utopian communities that she describes as 'a quest for something beautifully wild.' Once the opium fumes of the communal dream had dissipated, she embarked on an equally eventful American road trip (almost meeting her fate near the Mexican border) and was soon drawn towards punk's 'dark and romantic aesthetics' — which brings us back to the Gibus circa early 1977.

The band's name is obviously a reference to the New York Dolls' 'Looking For a Kiss,' but according to Laurence Grumbach it also stands for 'Ladies United Violently' or 'Lipstick Used Viciously.' Laurence's nom de punk was chosen because she was born on 9 August which is St Amour's day in the French calendar (hence Aphrodisia) and because she was fond of the Flamin' Groovies (Flamingo). Apparently, it had nothing to do with John Waters' 1972 film, *Pink Flamingos*. Dominique Jeantet reinvented herself as Fury in homage to Faulkner and the Plymouth Fury automobile. She once owned a guitar with 'Fury' inscribed on it.

Although L.U.V. revolved mainly around these two soulmates, the most famous member at the time was in fact Edwige — a striking bisexual amazon who was already a face on the local clubbing scene and would soon be crowned *la reine des punks*. For fifteen minutes, Paris was at her feet: she ran the door at the hippest joint this side of Studio 54 (Le Palace), was photographed with Warhol for the cover of *Façade* magazine, formed an electronic duo called Mathématiques Modernes, posed for Helmut Newton and allegedly had a string of affairs with the likes of Grace Jones, Madonna and Sade ('The Sweetest Taboo' is rumoured to be about her). Given her stature, Edwige seemed destined to bang the drums for L.U.V. As Fury puts it, 'The group was primarily an image — a work of art — so it was great to have this iconic figure.'

This conception of the band as tableau vivant or performance art was (and indeed remains) at odds with some of the other members' more conventional aspirations. 'Aphrodisia gave me the opportunity to create something,' says Fury, but that something was not rock 'n' roll. When L.U.V. petered out, she joined Bazooka, an art collective (where she famously found herself embroiled in a convoluted *ménage à trois* with two artists of either gender) rather than another band. But Liliane, the bassist (who was also a talented photographer working for the music press) simply could not understand why Dominique showed no interest in musical proficiency, insisting on teaching her how to master — mistress? — her instrument. Fury reckons 'she just wasn't mad enough.' 'She simply didn't get it,' concurs Aphrodisia. Whenever journalists or A&R people attended rehearsals, they drafted in Hermann Schwartz — Métal Urbain's axeman — who would play concealed behind a curtain while Fury struck guitar-heroine poses. Schwartz also acted as L.U.V.'s Pygmalion, introducing the girls to the Shangri-Las, for instance.

L.U.V. covered two songs: Nico & the Velvet Underground's 'Femme Fatale' and the Troggs' 'Wild Thing.' Dominique Fury showed me some lyrics, both in French and English, that she had written for the band, but it was unclear whether she had ever shared them with the other members. Some are reminiscent of X-Ray Spex in that they describe a dystopian consumer society. Others stood out because of their violent imagery: 'We'll take the handle and you'll take the blade.' Aphrodisia, who is currently writing her autobiography, sees L.U.V. as a missed opportunity: 'We never wrote a single song. We wanted to, but were probably too stoned.' She explains that rehearsals were constantly interrupted because someone always needed to score. She talks about major label interest. She remembers how *Rock & Folk*, the top French music magazine, would beg them to play a gig that they could cover in their next issue...

Some of us are still waiting for that next issue.

Come, let us dance to the spirit ditties of no tone.

Dominique Fury is a successful artist. Laurence Grumbach and Edwige Belmore have both passed away since this interview was conducted in 2009.

20

Punk Movies

by Nicholas Rombes

1.

She doesn't believe...

There are films that are about punk. And there are movies that are punk not in their content, but in the conditions of their creation. And there are movies that are both *about* punk and perform punk aesthetics in the mode of their production.

Filmmaker Richard Baylor has said that:

> *I have always been interested in films, but never really thought about making my own until I was exposed to the work of Richard Kern, Nick Zedd, Lydia Lunch, and other Cinema of Transgression filmmakers. What captured my interest was their approach to the media. It was very much 'punk film'. The emphasis was on the content and the expression, not on the technical skills and budgets.*

Like the term 'punk' itself, 'punk films' is a contested term. One of the earliest critical appraisals of punk films was J. Hoberman's 1979 *Village Voice* essay 'No Wavelength: The Para-Punk Underground,' which set out some ideas that were developed in greater detail in the seminal book he co-authored with Jonathan Rosenbaum, *Midnight Movies*. In the section 'Punk,' Hoberman writes that 'seen strictly as a youth movement, punk was a kind of perverse, high-speed relay of the counterculture, complete with its own music, press, entrepreneurs, fellow travellers (including more than a few ex-hippies) and, ultimately, movies.' Doberman discusses key films, such as Derek Jarman's *Jubilee*

(1978), which he deems 'the first narrative feature to deal with punk.'

He also discusses super-eight filmmakers Eric Mitchell, Beth and Scott B, James Nares and Vivienne Dick, whose works are closely linked to local art-punk, no-wave bands, films that 'began to parallel the music's energy, iconography, and avowed anyone-can-do-it aesthetic.' Finally, Hoberman mentions *Rock 'n' Roll High School* (1979), starring the Ramones. And, although he doesn't discuss it in his chapter on punk, Hoberman might just as easily have included David Lynch's *Eraserhead* (1977), which in its own strange way creates a time-warped punk universe slowed down to a crawl. One could imagine the nearly inarticulate ('stoopid') Henry, with his wild hair and skinny tie, bursting to life on the stage at CBGBs.

2.

She doesn't believe it was poison...

In truth punk — and punk movies specifically — was a constellation of previously articulated movements and artistic strategies. In cinema, for instance, there are the British 'kitchen-sink realism' films of the 1960s, notably Ken Loach's *Poor Cow* (1967), the French new wave, and, in the States, the films of John Cassavetes, all of which shared, in various and diverse ways, a DIY aesthetic. The most compelling punk dramas — such as Amos Poe's *The Foreigner* (1978) and Beth and Scott B's *Vortex* (1982) — harness the implied anarchy of the punk scene and shape it into a whole that barely coheres, showing its seams. However, unlike punk music, graphic design and fashion, punk literature and cinema remain canonical outliers, having never really formed bodies of work sustained and distinct enough to be immediately recognizable. This is due, in part, to the fact that film and literature have long and rich legacies of outsider or 'underground' movements, so it's difficult to tease out elements (other than obvious subject matter, i.e. films *about* the punk scene) that are 'punk' in their conception. Whereas the sound and style of punk music broke clearly with previous trends of progressive, arena-rock and Sixties psychedelic music, punk movies seem to have stronger continuity with previous *auteur* directors and movements. Was not someone like Godard a punk filmmaker, a good decade before there was punk? Shooting on the fly, stealing shots, improvisation, non-professional actors, allowing mistakes to remain in the film, alienation from the audience: these French new wave elements are punk elements too, just as they are elements of the early Dogme 95 films, and many other lesser-known but no less important international cinema movements.

From another angle, punk cinema wasn't cinema at all, but television. Public-access television in the US emerged in the early 1970s, a product of progressive thinking by certain members of the Federal Communications Commission (FCC) and resulted in the ability for anyone to make locally produced content at very low cost. A federal mandate in 1972 stipulated that cable systems in the top hundred markets provide at least three public access channels. The result was a wild-west panoply of types and varieties of shows, some serious and some anarchic and absurd and highly self-aware, a sensibility which would bleed into two landmark TV shows which, in their early seasons, would absorb the aesthetics and energy of public-access television: *Saturday Night Live*, debuting in October 1975 as *NBC's Saturday Night*, and *The David Letterman Show*, which began as a morning show in June 1980. A punk-era forerunner to this was *TV Party*, a public-access show out of Manhattan that debuted in September 1978. The brainchild of Glenn O'Brien — who served as the first editor at *Interview* beginning in 1971 — the show featured Blondie, Jean-Michel Basquiat, the Fleshtones and many other musicians and artists from the New York scene. Many of the show's episodes were directed by Amos Poe, who brought his punk-cinema sensibility to the intense feeling of controlled anarchy that characterized the show.

Malcolm Garrett, the graphic designer for Buzzcocks, Magazine, Red Crayola and others, has said that, in designing Buzzcocks' singles, 'I was also very keen to include technical information, such as catalogue numbers and the text that is normally consigned to the small print on the back of a record. I always worked with that material to include it as a feature of the design.'

The ambiguity of punk at the time that it was becoming self-aware as 'punk' during the 1975-1977 years, and the swirling terms with unstable meanings that characterized the forces of marketing and naming by record companies and promoters: new wave, punk, no wave, anarcho-punk, post-punk. In the U.S., 1976 was the Bicentennial. A boy in rural northwest Ohio, eleven years old, having lost his younger sister to a brain tumour the previous year. Her pigtails, her Indian braids, her dark Greek blood, her bare feet, her death leaving an infinite void, a B-L-A-N-K, in his life that no Church could fill (that would come later) and that filled and drained and filled and drained and filled and drained and filled and drained...

3.

She doesn't believe it was poison... that Donnie slipped into their drinks that night.

The first thing he told her was that he was a hunted man, though he never acted scared until the very end. She came to know — everyone did — that he was in the band to save himself from something, some 'terrible terrible' as he once said. Worse than guns, even. Than hot bullets tearing through flesh. But Donnie talked so often in apocalyptic language that after a while it didn't mean anything. Bullets were too abstract to scare them. They were all on their way to being fired or kicked out of school. The campus was falling apart under the weight of bad ideas.

The Outpost was an old schoolhouse (so they said) converted to a tavern not far from her apartment at the edge of campus. It was some fevered Hieronymous Bosch hallucination of hell: the blood-red décor, the enormous ink-black shadows from life-sized carved-wood sculptures of naked men and women in fight scenes; the long, warped mirror behind the bar that cast back a wavy, distorted reflection of the place. She'd sit at a small table in the corner and make her way through a few pitchers of cheap beer as the house band — Donnie Desperate — tore through their first set like lightning, and then slowed down for their second set —their 'midnight' set — into some kind of trance-like waltz of distorted feedback and crackling guitar. Donnie writhed on the stage like a worm stuck with a pin.

That's when she became, for a brief time, the lyricist for the band.

She with her sharp black bangs.

This was her job. For three months, she spent her nights in the back of a bar, working on songs, writing lyrics and then breaking them down and then putting them back together again. She was paid for this, mostly in drinks, but also in cash. $5.00 per song. She spent the money on more drinks and baked rolls from the bakery next door.

'I'm a hunted man,' Donnie said to her, shaking from fear or delirium. 'Will you write the words to my songs?' That's how it began. From a distance his face looked clawed-at, but up close you could see right through him, like one of those deep-sea fish from miles down. They called him Dead Donnie, but he could have been Donnie Transparent. His skin was so tight on him it threatened to split apart at any second.

It was one of those desperate decisions that turn out to be good. Somebody told him she was a writer who had published some poems. He never even asked her her name. It was easy for her to say yes. She'd sit at the table in the corner as the band played, penning lyrics about drowned lovers, bloody revenge, head-on car wrecks, hopelessness, ghosts, destruction, mutilation, total war, power. She'd always try to write the songs from the point of view of the 'bad' person, to give voice to his or her perspective, to create a space in the song where the worst parts of human nature could roam free. For instance, 'Blood Brothers' told the tale — in the sparest of terms — of Brother A, whose affair with Brother B's beautiful wife is not at all the secret that he thinks it is. In fact, Brother B lives with the knowledge of the affair. At a banquet for his cheating wife's birthday, Brother B drugs them both and scoops out their eyes with spoons before hanging himself. Another song, 'Three Bullets For Four People,' tells the story of an ingenious hit man who is sent to murder a family of four. When he discovers he only has three bullets for the job, he — shall we say — makes good use of bullet number three, concocting an elaborate, cruel method to kill two people with one bullet.

One night, Donnie's band played her songs like it was the end of the world, desperate, speed-of-light addresses to the nothingness of the cosmos that all ended in various forms of bloodshed. He took the stage like a Revelations-man, like some creature that had been sent here to imitate a human, drenched in sweat, wielding the microphone like it was a weapon, hurling abuse at the crowd. The band thundered through song after song, like an earthquake, like uniform noise. 'It's fucking something, these songs,' Donnie would tell her afterwards, wiping his drenched body down with a towel. 'I want *more*, man,' he said, 'I want fucking *more*.'

Her songs, her work, they were making Donnie into something else. When he sang the words she wrote, it was as if she was singing them. She crossed lines in her mind. Signals got mixed.

Weeks went by, faster than clock time. Donnie's music speeded up. The obscure campus was looking more and more like a neglected movie set. August came and went. While she continued writing songs for Donnie, she could feel the end waiting for her like an open furnace. Everything was falling apart. A gun went off during one of Donnie's shows, tearing the finger off some kid's hand. They found the bullet lodged in a wooden beam above the ceiling. Donnie was sure it was meant for him, that Anna had sent someone to do it. In awaiting his death he became desperate, prone to hysterical fits that began with shouting and ended with bloodshed. His skin became even more transparent, showing through to the very blood speeding through his veins. If he were naked you could see the architecture of his circulatory system, the crazy activity around his heart, the nothingness around his limbs. He went to greater and greater extremes to provoke the audience, hurling insults at them, taunting them, inviting them to fight him on the stage. The concerts become tight, right riots of anarchy as Donnie — bald, shirtless, hopped up on who knows what — fended off angry, drunken fans who charged the stage as he tore his way through my songs, which he was playing faster and faster, pushing his drummer and guitar player to the limit, to the brink of exhaustion. He grew more hateful and disdainful of the fans, even turning his back on them during some numbers.

By fall they were barely hanging on. The spirit of the times was changing in ways that made the type of songs she was writing for Donnie seem irresponsible, even dangerous. Her songs — which had always been received by the audience as darkly funny, ironic tales of obsession — now seemed serious and threatening in all the wrong ways, as if they were actually a part of the context from which the new violence had arisen. They weren't funny anymore: it was fine to glamorize violence in the abstract, but not when the images in my songs too closely matched images from the real world.

And Donnie felt more hunted than ever, convinced that someone near him would be the one. In his paranoia, he began to suspect his songwriter. One night, after a particularly brutal show, Donnie confronted our songwriter at her table, his eyes sped up like a rabid dog's, blaming her for his impending ruination, going on and on about how her songs were all surface and shock and had no depth to them, and then suddenly reversing himself, berating her because her songs were too complex and difficult.

He showed her an unfired bullet that he said he found in his shoe one morning, shaking it in her face like proof.

She shrugged it off but she knew it was true: they were tied into this thing together somehow, all of them. How did they let that happen? And then within a week they became untouchable. The songwriter's mother was killed in a bloody, limb-severing car wreck on the way home after visiting her. Donnie's old maths teacher jumped off the roof of a parking garage, splattering himself onto storefront windows. Our songstress: all the electricity in her flat went out for nearly a week. Her plants withered and died. Donnie's nephew fell through the ice in Canada and drowned. Everything they touched they shattered. It confounded Donnie most of all. He was certain he was next. One moment he was all sound and fury, stomping around and gesticulating wildly, like a reborn Mussolini, the next he was all whimpers and tears, as soft as a marshmallow, collapsed with his bald head on his arms at her table. When she reached into her purse he jumped back like he had already been shot.

That's when the guy with the gun in his pocket came walking over, a blackened figure dragged out of the Old Testament. Then the gun was in his enormous hand, so real it looked fake. The bullet was screaming to get out. The man's finger was the most important thing in the world. In the mirror above the bar she watched it unfold like a movie trailer: the plotted-out sequence of steps, the Jack Ruby extension of the man's arm, the swift sly slick move of Donnie's hand over her beer, the man's sudden veering away and through the crowd and out the door.

Who knows what Donnie slipped in his songwriter's beer. The songwriter with those sharp black bangs that just would not quit. Donnie practically begged her to drink. Perhaps the man in black with the gun was just a diversion, an excuse. She took a sip, and was sick for a week, the inside of her stomach burning like acid. She curled up on her couch like an anthrax victim. But it could have been anything.

And then, for weeks, all she heard was gunshots. All the time. All around her. Everywhere. She wanted to write a song about it but the song kept sabotaging itself. The sky above campus was full of flying bullets. And everyone she saw — every person on the street — looked at her like they had just murdered somebody. Do you know that look? And these people... there wasn't anything she could do to stop this. It wasn't one of those things she could just call off.

She recovered, convinced that Donnie had poisoned her to save himself.

'It wasn't Donnie who was hunted,' she said when she was better. She was sipping tea in the sun on the patio. 'It was us.'

She finally figured out how to save them. How to save them all.

But by then it was too late.

21

Some Brief and Frivolous Thoughts on a Richard Hell Reading

by Richard Cabut

Cycling down to the South Bank from Honor Oak Park, I'm water bombed by some kids in Peckham. The people at a nearby bus stop laugh, and I give two fingers to the little fuckers. I'm easily discouraged. Sod it, I think, I don't really want to go to the Hell reading much anyway. These events are invariably overlong and boring, with plenty of chin stroking, appreciative nodding and polite applause. Yawn. At the *3:AM Magazine* Horse Hospital reading, I remember getting daggers looked my way by Billy Childish's wife for laughing out of turn while hubby was giving it his moustachioed all. Show some fucking respect. So I consider turning around, going home, getting dry and simply pretending that I'd attended the reading. Perhaps write something along the lines of Paul Morley's infamous early-Eighties *NME* review of Theatre of Hate, which was all about Kirk Brandon's ears. No way was Morley at that gig. He was at home reading Barthes' *Mythologies*, while sipping cocktails, as did everyone in those louche and decadent mutant disco days. 'The writer's language is not expected to represent reality, but to signify it. This should impose on critics the duty of using two rigorously distinct methods: one must deal with the writer's realism either as an ideological substance, or as a semiological value — the props, the actors...' Or, um, ears... You could almost see the light bulb appear above Paul's head. Clearly, this style went down a treat with an Eighties *NME* readership desperate for pseudo-intellectual sensation, but would it sit with a *3:AM* crowd in love with the real world, its desperation and drama portrayed in language that circumnavigates emasculated, fussy artistry, and plunges into life itself? Hair, I think to myself with a flippant dandyism, an urbane scepticism, and epicurean sensibility, I'll simply write about Hell's hair...

The last time I'd seen Richard Hell on stage, at the Camden Underworld, he'd revealed, rather bravely (although, hey, in the future, all art will be confessional, as they say), that the closer he got to a woman's anus, the more he believed in God. I remember this when, halfway through the Meltdown reading, a young woman clacks down the stairs and walks out. 'I hope she's going to the bathroom,' quips Richard, with the slickness of a self-deprecating stand-up. He carries on reading, but soon stops, pauses for a few seconds, looks into the middle distance, shakes his head as if in wonder, brushes the hair out of his eyes, and says: 'I can't get the thought of that woman in the toilet out of my mind.' He laughs and continues reading, but to no avail, as far as I'm concerned. He's lost me because, now, what is going on in Richard's fetid, stinking mind is of far more interest than the stuff he is reading out: the shit, the stench, the horrible sounds. It is what he isn't saying that reveals more about Hell as artist and person — with those silent implications of the shit, the stench, the sounds — as well as about the ridiculous human condition, rather than the blurred words repeated from the pages of his new book, *Godlike*... the belief in whom, of course...

I'm a bit scared of Richard Hell. He seems pleasant and polite enough, but you should read his exchange with one poor chap on *Bookslut*. Hell kills him.

Critic: *As a poet now, Richard Hell is perhaps not as good as he could have been had he not spent upwards of twenty years playing music.*

Hell: *Fuck you. If you want to say something like that, say it to my face. You don't hear me making claims about how 'good' my poetry is, but who the fuck do you think you are? All this writing of yours is presented as if you're a person called upon to make judgments from some position of earned respect. That's not who you are. You're a callow kid with a job reading slush for a pretentious irrelevant 'poetry' magazine [Poetry, not Bookslut]. You sought an interview from me, I was kind enough to grant it, and now you're being an asshole by exercising some grotesquely deluded misapprehension that your role in this includes some call to fucking critically assess my skills.*

There's more where that comes from. Have a look and shudder. So, during the reading, I'm drifting, looking around checking out who's turned up... anyone I know from the old days? ...when I'm jerked back to the reading... by fear. Fear of Richard. Concentrate, you fool, what if Richard finds out you're not paying attention? Some bits of the reading I find a bit boring. I slap myself around the face. No, it's *all* good! What are you, some kind of critic! Have I earned the right to critically assess his skills? Who the fuck am I to suggest that Richard has a stinking and fetid mind? Who the fuck asked me? You fuck. Fuck you! No, I mean, fuck me!

First off, though, Hell admits to the expectant crowd — there's about a hundred of us in the posh Purcell Rooms — that he's a writer, not an entertainer. He's embarrassed about being flown all the way out here, but he'll strive to give people their money's worth. He huffs and puffs. His schtick is to give a little preliminary ramble, or an interjection, to illustrate some point or other, but he struggles to make the connections, to hit the links. And you know what? It works. It's endearing. He digresses. But so what? As remarked in Sterne's *Tristram Shandy*, digressions are incontestably the sunshine, the life and soul of reading. Especially this reading. His stories frustrate our sense of tidy form by refusing to end properly, just like Chekhov, I think, stroking my chin.

The words flow over me in endless confabulation. No, really, they do. I always dug Hell's lyrics, the dopey cleverness of 'Destiny Street,' for instance. I also enjoyed the tough braggadocio of Hell's Nineties novel *Go Now* in which our man, drugged, fucks and fucks up, earns cash for nothing, like a peddle-to-the-metal hopped-up dropout crossing the States with the larger-than-life aplomb of a pulp-fiction anti-hero. Vagabond poet rogue of the open highway, as it were. Vicarious thrills are to be had here.

The new stuff, *Godlike*, is more thoughtful. It's clear that Richard has been sitting in his East Village apartment, I presume, and over a couple of coffees, scratching his head about the Big Picture. The important stuff. The philosophy of the isness of being is. How the world turns. What makes the soul sigh, the tears flow, the synapses fire. How high is the ocean, how deep is the sky (metaphorically speaking). Like a proper writer. He works things out, and comes up with some answers: 'Fuck the hippies and their emotions,' to paraphrase one of his character's sneering asides. I like such succinctness and directness in philosophical writing. Nietzsche and Adorno would agree. Brevity and speed is what it is.

Of course, Hell also continues to write about the vomit, the cocks, the cack of the city, which is probably what he's best at: malicious imagery that explores disturbing and inconsolable situations; tossed together random bleak pictures to provide some anxiety about the unbearable pathos of life; an atmosphere laden with fucked-upness and failure relaying some long-distance loneliness, all jittery and wired. It's all very rock 'n' roll in that respect.

Afterwards, a bunch of people hang around for a signed copy of *Godlike*. There's some frazzled rockers present soaking up the NYC Ramones/Thunders/smack connections, relics from the Speakeasy circa 1977, swaying and tottering, weighed down by tattoos, living the bleakness and smelling of gin, Benson & Hedges and regret — or, is that me? I sniff my armpit. Then Hell pops up to make his mark wearing a voluminous black-and-white striped shirt and some serious strides; quite retro, Truffaut-esque, perhaps. He's put on some weight, maybe. Certainly some gravitas. And, well, there's the hair to consider. So, I think, yes, let's plug, and plug into Richard Hell's luminous brilliance because, you know, even though his locks are now as lank and long as a 19th-century Symbolist poet's, his thoughts remain as spiky as his hair used to be.

22

Leaving the 21st Century

by Andrew Gallix

I am perhaps the king of failures, because I'm certainly the king of something.
— Arthur Cravan, *Notes*

Better a spectacular failure, than a benign success.
— Malcolm McLaren's headstone inscription

Circa 1974, Malcolm McLaren toyed with the idea of rebranding his boutique Modernity Killed Every Night. In the event he chose SEX, but the slogan ended up being sprayed on a wall inside the shop. It was an abridged quotation from a letter Jacques Vaché had addressed to André Breton — the future founder of Surrealism — during the so-called Great War. Despite his bovine-sounding name, Vaché (1895-1919) was a dandified anglophile, who enjoyed walking the streets dressed as a loose woman or a Napoleonic soldier. Choosing to be an actor rather than a puppet, he subverted army life, by — as he put it — deserting within himself. There, in that Switzerland of the mind, he would pretend that his superiors were under his orders, or that he was fighting for the other side. It was gun in hand, sporting an English pilot's uniform, and threatening to shoot at random, that Vaché inter-rupted the premiere of Guillaume Apollinaire's *The Breasts of Tirésias* (1917) on account of its arty-farty production. Apollinaire had coined the word 'surrealist' to describe his play, but it was Vaché's radical brand of criticism that embodied the true spirit of the forthcoming movement. A couple of years later, he died of an opium overdose, which may have been an accident, but is commonly regarded as a defiant parting shot to everyone and everything — the ultimate artistic statement. For André Breton — who befriended him during the war and always claimed that he was the true originator of Surrealism — Vaché was poetry incarnate. After listing his early literary influences — Rimbaud, Jarry, Apollinaire, Nouveau, Lautréamont — he added, 'but it is Jacques Vaché to whom I owe the most.' His stroke of genius, Breton maintained, was 'to have produced nothing.'

In avant-garde circles, suicide came to be seen as a form of inverted transcendence, a rejection of the reality principle, an antidote to literary mystification, as well as a fashion. For Jacques Rigaut (1898-1929) — who famously wrote that his 'bedtime reading [was] a gun' — it was clearly 'a vocation' rather than an affectation. In his *Anthology of Black Humour* (1940) Breton explains that he had 'sentenced himself to death at about the age of twenty, and waited impatiently for ten years, ticking off the hours, for exactly the right moment to put an end to his existence.' He was in rehab for heroin and alcohol addiction when the time came to complete this process of self-erasure. 'You're just a bunch of poets and I'm on the side of death,' he spat, bidding adieu to the Surrealists, whose provocations were far too contrived for his liking. Like Vaché, with whom he shared a world-weary detachment and a nice line in gallows humour, his influence far exceeded his (largely posthumous) literary output. Pierre Drieu La Rochelle, a close friend, wrote a short story and two novels revolving around him, including *Will O' the Wisp* (1931) which Louis Malle turned into a classic film (*The Fire Within*, 1963).

'Try stopping a man who travels with suicide in his buttonhole': Jacques Rigaut's aphorism fits Arthur Cravan like a (boxing) glove. You may never have heard of him, but Cravan was one of the most influential writers and artists of the 20th century. The fact that he produced precious little — and certainly nothing of any lasting value — should not be held against him.

Quite the contrary, in fact. The poet with the shortest haircut in the world, as he often described himself, put all his genius into his life, turning it into a magnum opus full of sound and fury, high farce and convulsive beauty. In so doing, he influenced every single major avant-garde movement from Dada onwards. Cravan was the original Sid Vicious; the blueprint for all the subsequent outrages committed in the name of art. 'Let me state once and for all: I will never be civilised,' he warned — and he meant it, man. David Lalé put it in a nutshell: 'His was a life dedicated to wanton destruction, to the extent that he elevated scandal and humiliation into an art form' (*Last Stop Salina Cruz*, 2007).

Arthur Cravan (or Fabian Avenarius Lloyd, to call him by his real name) was born in Switzerland, of British parents, on 22 May 1887. A picture from his student days in Lausanne shows him sitting pretty, looking like butter would not melt. A far cry from the agent provocateur who would write, 'I shall eat my shit.' His hand is even lodged in his waistcoat — a sign of good breeding in those days that, admittedly, may also have betrayed an ominous Napoleon complex. In another picture, probably taken a few years later, he sports the kind of haircut a young Wyndham Lewis could have flaunted on a visit to Brideshead Castle. The contrast between Cravan's delicate, almost effeminate, features — he may even be wearing make-up — and his massive lumberjack hands (in which he holds an open book) is striking. His first major brush with authority, when he was expelled from a Birmingham military academy for hitting a teacher, must have taken place at about the same time. Having relocated to bohemian Paris — where he partied hard with the likes of Blaise Cendrars and Kees van Dongen — Cravan planned to fake his own death so that he could publish his first book 'posthumously,' in a blaze of publicity. If his antics often prefigure those of Sid Vicious, as we have said, his constant wheeling and dealing foreshadows Malcolm McLaren's cash-from-chaos ethos. For instance, he always made a point of insulting as many people as possible in his journal, knowing that they would all go out and buy a copy. On one occasion, he even found a rich aristocrat gullible enough to invest in his bogus project for a rubber bicycle you could deflate and carry around in your pocket. For some reason, the fake death stunt was shelved, but Cravan pulled off the more remarkable feat of becoming France's Heavyweight Champion, in 1910, without throwing a single punch. One of his opponents got the jitters and called it quits before the match had even started. Another was suddenly taken ill. A couple of opponents were directed to the wrong venue, thus failing to show up. The last one sprained his ankle as he jumped a trifle too eagerly into the ring. The following year Lloyd reinvented himself as Cravan — a reference to Cravans, where his then fiancée, Renée Bouchet, was born.

A big bruiser of a man, Cravan certainly looked the part. His wife, the English poet Mina Loy, refers to him as 'Colossus' in the book of the same name, written after his disappearance. She beautifully captures the larger-than-life qualities of this force of nature, who never seemed to have enough legroom in our Lilliputian world: 'Cravan's truth was his oeuvre — that incipient thing for whose sustenance it appeared he must swallow the ocean and eat up the earth — that tireless tramp of continents, that scissor-like stride of the boxer which for the time that I accompanied him seemed a veritable mastication of space.' Behemoths and exotic wild beasts — rhinoceros and hippopotami — roam his unbridled imagination. He breathes 'like a whale,' deplores being stuck in Paris 'though lions and giraffes exist,' dreams of 'sleeping on tigers.' Female breasts are 'elephants of softness,' the moon dreams 'like an elephant's heart,' verses are 'carried nine years like the elephant,' and even Oscar Wilde, sitting in an armchair, has 'the air of an elephant.' In her 1999 novel, *Shadow-Box*, Antonia Logue conjures up Cravan's crazy Berlin period:

You'd dip into Cravan for a day and come out of an acid bath, your body corroding, sinuses so full of poison those inner canals in your ears would hear nothing but a high wasting moan and your balance would be all shot to hell. He strode around Berlin wearing hookers on his shoulders, them tittering and screeching down the Kurfurstendam like they were queens on a float, then leave them back where he found them, all legs and suicide.

'Genius,' Cravan declared, 'is nothing more than an extraordinary manifestation of the body.' Yet his boxing was on a par with his poetry: spirited, at best. Comically enough, he was caught up by his reputation in Barcelona, where he was unable to wriggle out of a rumble with former Heavyweight World Champion Jack Jones, an episode which left him reeling, punch-drunk. The fact that he was drink-drunk to start with probably did not help. The upside is that the fight was probably fixed — yet another moneymaking scam.

None of this prevented Arthur Cravan from flogging his 'poet and boxer' image for all it was worth. Although he was partly a fraud, he inspired a long line of literary pugilists, and even came to be seen, by some, as the ultimate adventurer-scribe: literature made flesh. Paradoxically, for one whose existence exerts such fascination, he was a self-publicist who had no self to publicise. 'I am all things, all men and animals!' he wrote in one of his better-known poems ('Hie!'), before wondering if he would ever manage to 'leave behind' his 'fatal plurality':

I would like to be in Vienna and Calcutta,
    Catch every train and every boat,
    Lay every woman and gorge myself on every dish,
    Man of fashion, chemist, whore, drunk, musician, labourer,
painter, acrobat, actor;
    Old man, child, crook, hooligan, angel and rake; millionaire,
bourgeois, cactus, giraffe, or crow;

> Coward, hero, negro, monkey, Don Juan, pimp, lord, peasant, hunter, industrialist,
> Flora and fauna:
> I am all things, all men and animals!

Arthur Cravan was large, he contained multitudes. With his 'thousand hearts,' he manifested a negative capability bordering on personality disorder: 'I wake up a Londoner and go to bed an Asian.' This probably had something to do with his rather complex origins — British, born in Switzerland, francophone — but it could also be construed as an early example of 'self-fluidization.' According to Boris Groys, this is a process whereby the contemporary artist divests herself of her public image (everything that survives one's death for a while: medical records, state archives, website passwords…) in an attempt to disappear, here and now; to merge with the material flow of time (*In the Flow*, 2016). Reflecting on his hyper-protean nature — his dizzying array of disguises, pseudonyms and personae — Mina Loy claimed that Cravan 'worked to maintain his reality by presenting an unreality to the world — to occupy itself with — while he made his spiritual getaway.' His whole life, at least from the time he first set foot in Paris, was indeed one long, convoluted disappearing act.

Cravan first gained the notoriety he so craved through *Maintenant* ('Now'), the expletive-laden journal in which he wrote everything under various noms de plume. It was partly a vanity outlet for his poems and essays, but primarily a means of courting controversy. Sourced from a butcher's shop, the very paper it was printed on highlighted his utter contempt for belles-lettres. The second issue is famous for a wickedly funny demolition job on future Nobel Prize laureate André Gide. In the third, he ran a fake interview with Oscar Wilde — his late uncle — claiming that he was still alive and had recently met him. This was discussed in the mainstream press the world over. Cravan's

Bill Grundy moment occurred when he devoted the whole fourth issue to gratuitous insults aimed at almost all the artists taking part in the 1914 Independents Exhibition. He opined, for instance, that only a good seeing-to would enable Marie Laurencin to fully grasp the true meaning of Art. As a result, her lover — the poet Guillaume Apollinaire — challenged Cravan to a duel, which he narrowly avoided by issuing a hilarious apology. He was almost lynched by a posse of avant-garde painters while selling copies of his journal from a wheelbarrow outside the exhibition room. Following this incident, he was arrested for breach of the peace. Shortly after, Cravan was sentenced to eight days of imprisonment for allegedly hitting the artist Sonia Delaunay during a drunken brawl with her husband.

Maintenant proved that writing, for Cravan, was essentially boxing by another means, as did the infamous conferences he gave in Paris. The hyperbolic sales patter used to promote them is reminiscent of a circus freak show:

COME AND SEE
the poet
ARTHUR CRAVAN
(Oscar Wilde's nephew)
boxing champion, 125 kg, 2 metres in height
THE BRUTAL CRITIC.
HE'LL SPEAK!
HE'LL BOX!
HE'LL DANCE!
The new boxing dance,
La Very Boxe.

During these happenings, he would take swigs from a bottle of absinthe (in lieu of the habitual bottle of water), read poems standing on one foot, then on the other; dance like a boxer, box like a dancer, shout abuse at the spectators and even fire gunshots over their heads. Here is an extract from a review which appeared in *Paris-Midi* in July 1914:

> *Arthur Cravan, who never fails to write 'nephew of Oscar Wilde' after his name, yesterday evening performed a spectacle in front of several hundred Englishmen, Americans and Germans, amongst whom one or two unsuspecting Frenchmen had strayed. This Arthur Cravan is a huge, blond, beardless young man who was wearing a shirt with a plunging neckline... Before speaking he fired several pistol shots over the heads of the audience and then began to expound — half smiling, half serious — the grossest insanities against art and life. He praised sportsmen, homosexuals, robbers of the Louvre and madmen, pronouncing them all superior to the artist. (Last Stop Salina Cruz)*

On one occasion, he wore nothing but a butcher's apron and concluded proceedings by mooning the audience instead of bowing in the traditional fashion. On another, he sold rotten fruit and vegetables at the entrance, so that people could pelt him during the performance should they feel so inclined (which they did). His final Parisian gig descended into pandemonium when he failed to commit suicide, as advertised — a riot that forestalled his drunken inauguration of the 1917 Exhibition of the Society of Independent Artists in New York. Francis Picabia and Marcel Duchamp (whose legendary urinal was part of the show) had plied him with gallons of booze beforehand in the hope that his antics would put Dada on the map in the United States. Cravan rose to the occasion: he stumbled on stage looking the worse for wear and started to strip — knocking over a painting in the process — only to be pounced upon, handcuffed, and carted away by security. Job done.

Cravan was a con artist with a cause. 'The world has always exploited the Artist,' he once declared, 'it is time for the Artist to exploit the world!' He prided himself on having performed 'the perfect burglary' at a Swiss jewellers in 1907. Some argue that it was his fake-painting trafficking, rather than the First World War, that initially forced him to go on the run. We know that he sold two paintings by Matisse and Picasso, at least one of which was a fake, in order to bankroll his escape from France.

As though wearing seven-league boots, he roamed the Continent, using several forged IDs, looking for 'that something the poet always seems to have mislaid,' as Mina Loy so elegantly put it. 'When I stay a long time in the same place,' Cravan explained, 'stupidity overwhelms me.' He famously described himself as a 'deserter of seventeen nations' and wrote in one of his works: 'I have twenty countries in my memory and I drag the colours of a hundred cities in my soul.'

In Barcelona, he became something of a living legend among Dadaists, who recognised him as the originator of anti-art (of his work, he once said, 'I adore it and shit on it'). Gabrielle Buffet-Picabia recalls that when her husband and Cravan crossed paths, 'it let loose, from one shore of the Atlantic to another, a wave of negation and revolt which for several years would throw disorder into the minds, acts, works of men.' David Lalé concurs: 'Dada was a prophecy and Cravan was its prophet.'

When the war seemed about to catch up with him again, he travelled to America (aboard the same ship as Trotsky) thanks to the takings from his match against Jack Jones. He left his fiancée in Spain, instructing her to join him once he had settled down, but in New York he met his future wife, Mina Loy, the author of *Feminist Manifesto* (and Marinetti's former mistress).

Cravan fled once more as soon as the Americans entered the conflict. Stealing the passport of an artist friend (who had conveniently conked out following a night on the razz) he crossed the Mexican border, disguised — paradoxically enough — as a soldier. 'Arthur Cravan dressed up as a soldier to avoid being a soldier,' wrote Francis Picabia, 'just like all those friends of ours who dress up as gentlemen to avoid being gentlemen' (*Jésus-*

Christ Rastaquouère, 1920). In Mexico, he set up a boxing school and convinced Jim Smith to take part in a fixed match culminating in Cravan's victory. He was last seen, in 1918, sailing away on a drunken boat of his own making — probably bound for neutral Argentina, where he had sent his pregnant wife — leaving behind his 'fatal plurality' forever. 'Whatever is said and done or even thought,' he had declared, 'we are prisoners of this senseless world.' Perhaps he was trying to prove himself (or rather, selves) wrong.

André Breton claimed that Cravan had achieved Rimbaud's ambition to become 'absolutely modern.' Crackling with electricity, his poem 'Whistle' is a paean to the modern world — elevators! telephones! — and New York City in particular, where he discovers 'the marriage of science / And industry / With bold modernity.' His articles — often couched in a kind of hard-boiled argot peppered with Rabelaisian profanities, and in which he always places himself firmly centre stage — read like Gonzo journalism *avant la lettre*. Equally prescient was the hybridity of his work — the blending of fact and fiction; prose and poetry. Breton is probably right in describing 'Notes' as 'pure genius, genius unrefined.' The fact that the poem is a mere draft — an unfinished one at that — means that his oeuvre (what there is of it) remains very much in that 'incipient' stage Mina Loy spoke of. As George Steiner notes in *Grammars of Creation* (2001), 'modernity often prefers the sketch to the finished painting and prizes the draft, chaotic with corrections, to the published text.' In other words, Cravan is modern because he did not leave behind a body of work. In fact, he did not leave behind a body at all, despite its gargantuan proportions. Roger Lloyd Conover believes that if he 'had totally fulfilled his quest, he would have taken his residue with him, and left only the imprint of his gestures on our imagination' (*4 Dada Suicides*). Bertrand Lacarelle considers his big boxing match against Jack Jones, not as a sporting event, but as the very first happening in art history

(*Arthur Cravan, précipité*, 2010). 'I am the prophet of a new life,' said Cravan, 'and only I am living it.' A new life in which art would evanesce into pure gesture:

> *Modern and contemporary art practices precisely the prefiguration and imitation of the future in which things now contemporary will disappear. Such an intimation of the future cannot produce artworks. Rather, it produces artistic events, performances, temporary exhibitions that demonstrate the transitory character of the present order of things and the rules that govern contemporary social behaviour. Imitation of the anticipated future can manifest itself only as an event and not as a thing.* (Boris Groys, *In the Flow*, 2016)

Arthur Cravan was just too bad to be true. He was a self-unmade man, whose biggest conjuring trick was to spirit himself away by taking elusiveness to the point of illusiveness. 'You must dream your life with great care,' wrote this outrageous six-footer, who managed to cross frontiers as though he were the Invisible Man. (Blaise Cendrars claims that he even travelled throughout Canada dressed as a woman.) No sooner had he vanished than the rumour mill went into overdrive. Some claimed that he had been stabbed in a bar or shot near the Mexican border. In the years following his disappearance at sea, he would be sighted all over the world in a variety of guises. Several people, for instance, were convinced that he was the shadowy Dorian Hope, or Sebastian Hope, or B. Holland who sold forged Wilde manuscripts to English and Irish booksellers, sometimes passing themselves off as personal secretaries of André Gide and Pierre Louÿs. There is even a theory according to which he was B. Traven, the mysterious author of *The Treasure of the Sierra Madre* (1927). More recently it has emerged that he was probably the painter Edouard Archinard (Félix Fénéon — one of Cravan's good friends — had organised an exhibition of Archinard's works in 1914). We also now know that he inspired Gide's infamous character in *Lafcadio's Adventures* (1914) who kills a man for no other reason but to exercise his free will, thus becoming a symbol of ultimate transgression for the likes of Guy Debord (in *Panegyric* he talks about the influence Cravan and Lautréamont had upon his life). The ghostly paper boat that floats above Parisian rooftops, while Duchamp and Man Ray play chess, in René Clair's *Entr'Acte* (1924), is an obvious reference to Cravan. In fact, the whole film is a homage. Since Mina Loy's 'Arthur Cravan is Alive!,' several novelists have written books premised on Cravan's survival: Tony Cartano's *Le bel Arturo* (1991), for instance, or more recently Philippe Dagen's *Arthur Cravan n'est pas mort noyé* (2006).

Dead or alive, Arthur Cravan is still at large.

23

Tales of Low-Life Losers

by Bob Short

Sleaze is easy to point a finger at. It's even easier to accidentally put your foot in it. Unfortunately, it becomes rather nebulous when you try to slap a definition onto its rather ugly posterior. One man's meat is the cliché that I'm groping for here, so help me out by filling in the gaps. It's one of those theory-of-relativity deals except no one called Einstein a sleazebag, not in New York.

I've seen guys work a room, barely able to stand upright in their oily wake. Most women see right through them in an instant. They wouldn't touch them with a double condom-wrapped bargepole. Strangely, however, the remaining twenty percent of women find such people utterly charming. These individuals rarely leave a party alone. You do the maths. Sleaze can work big time.

Some would argue that cutting a swathe of anal rampage through your fan base is inherently sleazy, but many musicians regard this as par for the course. It's the reward you have earned for all that arse-kissing the star has had to do along the way. When Pete Townsend was asked about the reason for the Who's longevity, he replied 'Sucking cock.' Whether he was being literal or figurative is beside the point.

When I first left home to explore the seedy underbelly of the rock-and-roll dream, I had a discussion with Andrew McMillan, an Australian who wrote the first articles about the Saints in the mid-Seventies. I pondered aloud why a third-rate band like The F—s could appear on local Australian programme *Countdown* whereas the Saints and Radio Birdman couldn't. McMillan smiled his crooked smile and produced a Polaroid photo from his desk in which the singer of said F—s band was being energetically spooned by the hat-wearing producer of the TV show. Those familiar with Australian pop music wouldn't be surprised by this butt cowboy's identity. This, I was informed, was the price of fame. I had no reason to doubt the assessment. Musicians were just meat for the grinder.

Whilst most record companies view ripping artists off as legitimate business practice, most artists predictably view this as typical capitalist sleaze. Looking back at the television show, *Minder*, your average informed viewer sees a comical parody of low-rent business practices. They know it isn't like real life. There are only just so many cons you can pull before Her Majesty decides you need a holiday. On the other hand, those in the business side of music see Arthur Daley as a role model; a living god. They go to the school of hard knocks just to study him. Accents are worked at and steely gazes set. Everyone claims to have a cousin who was in on the Great Train Robbery.

So, these things will happen: the pub you play in will always squeeze that one extra charge in at the end of the night for promotion. The record company you sign to will always go broke the day before your royalty cheque is due. The journalist your record company gets drunk with will always write you a decent review. If they get the editor of the magazine laid, you'll probably get the front cover.

But this petty corruption isn't what you want to hear about. You want to hear tales of filth and fury. Me? I just want the chance to start off by nailing one of those record-company scum buckets as chief amongst sleazeballs.

X was in his cups. His sorrows needed a quick dipping. Despite having the Au Pairs and the Fall on his record label, royalties would soon need to be paid and I've already explained to you what that means. Tired and emotional, he talked to me paternally (if your father was the living incarnation of Satan). 'I hate it when a girl wants to kiss you after she's sucked your dick.

Especially if you've ever screwed her up the arse.'

His label's A&R man, Y, then proceeded to detail an industry junket in Paris. He is proud of the fact that the pair had managed to split up a boy-girl duo that had a string of number ones under its belt. Given that this is the early 1980s and I've been reminded of libel laws, you'll have to work out the name of these Top of the Popsters for yourself. X and Y apparently hired a prostitute to pass the male member a nice dose of herpes. This, they thought, would break up the pair both professionally and romantically. I personally had assumed the bleached-blond fool was as bent as a three-quid note but I've been known to be wrong about these things. Probably more through luck than design, the band did indeed split up and, failing to find any kind of solo success, both went back to riding the till at the local Sainsbury's.

It's fairly unlikely that Y's story is true. It should, however, demonstrate the quality of intellect present on the business side. It all runs on a healthy diet of urban myth.

People expect the suits to be sleazy old men. You're reading this for the gossip, but the trouble with gossip is that so little of it is verifiable. Someone who's fucked someone says...

I've heard some outrageous stories, but I'm a cynic. I don't believe any of them for a minute but, strangely, true or not, they enhance your image of the people involved. I love the story about Eighties radio queen XX. At her birthday party, it was alleged that the underground stars of the day lined up to pay her more than lip service. Legend has it that this stellar cast of well-wishers included members of the Sisters of Mercy, Southern Death Cult and Theatre of Hate.

It's a stupid story. You couldn't have selected a group of more diseased-looking individuals. You'd be hard-pressed to have gotten any of those guys to line up for anything. Half of them couldn't stand up. Those who could would be having a hissy fit over who got to stand closest to the mirror. Still, it's a wonderful rock-and-roll story.

As is the tale of Billy Idol's Cinderella fetish. According to ancient lore, when Generation X were on tour, Idol took a kinky pair of thigh-high leather boots with him. Only the princess who filled those boots got to feel his royal sceptre.

The engineer of a recording session told me that he had witnessed Becky Bondage being orally pleasured during the vocal takes of an early Vice Squad single. This just has to be another tall tale. Anyone who has heard Vice Squad's recorded oeuvre can only shudder. If this was how Ms Bondage expressed her sensuality, what would PMT sound like?

Of course, most rock stars are lousy fucks. It's not so much the fact that the drugs and the booze cause their loves to lie limp. It is that appalling level of self-obsession. The only people they want to fuck is themselves. Their beautiful selves.

I remember one excruciating Tube journey to Camden's Music Machine featuring a youngish Kirk Brandon. He tried to invite anyone who would listen to attend the Pack's (his band before Theatre of Hate) performance at the Lyceum. The trouble was, he couldn't maintain eye contact with anyone. Thanks to the walls of the tunnel, the windows of the carriage were like mirrors. How could he possibly keep up this shameless self-promotion when there was such a wonderful opportunity to preen himself? Narcissism, both physical and mental, was the drug of choice for many.

Once upon a time (the late Seventies), the Scala cinema was in Goodge Street and its Saturday all-nighters were the only place to be. The stars were out. The wannabe stars were out. In fact, anyone who lived in a punk squat was out because Saturday night was the night you were most likely to have your home invaded by broom handle-wielding skinheads. You would see a pre-'Dog Eat Dog' Adam Ant wearing dark-rimmed glasses, pretending that he wasn't himself.

You would also see Marilyn, friend of Boy George and soon to be one-hit wonder. Marilyn would never leave alone. There was always some ugly old guy who couldn't believe his luck. The drugs hadn't done their worst back then and he could pass himself off quite well as a girl with that little bit of extra oomph. Of course, I'm sure the guy had a big surprise waiting for him at the end of the night (and I'm not talking about the inevitable disappearances from wallets).

That last story would be the stuff of urban legend if I hadn't witnessed it across the café so many times. The Scala was a regular den of iniquity, a little piece of *Hollywood Babylon* come to life. There were drugs. There was sex. There were really crappy movies.

Youth, bassist with Killing Joke, was a regular until his hospitalisation with hepatitis. Youth always wore this truly vile tan suit but the hospital staff who boiled it were amazed to discover that, once washed, it was white. Band hangers-on tried to put it about that he'd caught the disease from his suit rather than from a more logical explanation. That's a common ploy in the music business. I remember reading how Joe Strummer caught glandular fever from being spat on at a gig. Was it really that hard for him to admit that he might have actually kissed someone?

I remember one memorable night when Richard Morgan, the drummer in the band I was in — Blood and Roses, early-Eighties punks — had a fight with his girlfriend. It started at the top of the aisle and rolled its way down to the screen in a ball of scratching, biting and hissing. We held no fears for his partner Siobhan's safety. She could easily deck the bastard, and did quite frequently.

I should perhaps remove myself from the role of saintly onlooker. One morning, Richard came back to the squat and had forgotten his key. I was working my way into a perfectly good hangover when the bastard woke me with his banging and wailing. I wasn't a happy man as I approached the door stark naked. To make matters worse, Richard's stupid fucking dog had crapped on the floor repeatedly. Guess who put their foot in it? Right. Yours truly. Guess who was dragged in through the front door by a very large naked man and promptly had his nose rubbed into a number of dog turds? That probably doesn't count as sleazy, but now you know what kind of a guy you're dealing with. Bands are always just one big happy family.

That story also goes some way to introduce another form of sleazy behaviour rampant amongst musicians. The rock biz would like you to believe it wraps itself in the tricoloured virtues of liberty, fraternity and egalitarianism. I feel tempted to write 'Ha!' at this point. In fact, I am tempted to write several pages of 'Ha!' in double-underlined bold type.

It's bad enough that bands rip at each other's throats. In a world where the industry fills media and commercial outlets with the kind of product that gives cholera-infected shit a bad name, most independent acts spend the majority of their time trying to undercut their compatriots. 'They're all too busy fighting for a cooler place under the lighting,' wrote the Clash, with little sense of irony. I mean, the whole song is about slagging off the competition. But business is business and, with so many outside forces playing divide and conquer, such rivalry is at least explicable.

Meanwhile, within the bands themselves, this macrocosm is reflected in increasingly vicious terms. Bands market themselves as little rebel gangs fighting against a cruel indifferent world. However, their battles are often lost by swords blunted in each other's backs. Alice Cooper described his relationship to his old band thus: 'Success didn't really change us as people. It just changed what we argued about. Instead of complaining about who stole my tomato, it became get the hell out of my limo.'

The Ramones hated each other and didn't speak. Steve Jones masturbated into Glen Matlock's sandwich. Screwing your band mates' wives, girlfriends, boyfriends or pet poodles is more a sport than any kind of revelation.

When we went to record our first EP, I had to go round to pick up Jez James, our bassist. Perhaps it should have been a shock to find him in bed with the woman I'd been living with for the last year. Instead, I was particularly impressed by just how self-destructive their actions were. I mean, setting themselves up to be found with such an impeccable sense of timing. I mean, you work for years to get a record contract. Imagine that, when you finally get one, you do something that could potentially have cataclysmic effects. Talk about snatching defeat from the jaws of victory. Jez eventually went into rehab to find a cure for his many addictions. He celebrated his release by going to the Hope and Anchor, getting blind drunk and walking under a bus. He was killed. That isn't a funny story, but it still works as an analogy for how bands tend to work.

If one really wants to check out seediness, investigate bands with a heavy turnover of members. Talent vampirism is widespread and ugly. In particular, I'm thinking about Psychic TV. Genesis P-Orridge is a talented man and, despite his reputation, I have to say he's also quite likeable. He likes to work collaboratively with other talented individuals but, unfortunately, doesn't enjoy sharing the fruits of such collaborations. Until he reinvented himself in a more dance-friendly environment, PTV ate band members for breakfast. They would rehearse, tour, record and even do office duty but their time in the sunshine could be terminated rapidly. Asking about royalties was, apparently, not the most ideal question to raise.

Genesis liked to create an aura of being shocking. When his baby posited on me, his only comment was 'If you don't want kids, you have to fuck your women up the arse.' His wife and a female band member named Mouse giggled nervously. Mouse had described Mr Orridge as an ugly little sex dwarf and she intimated she had good reason to know this. Later, Mouse was to suggest that I form a threesome with herself and a large drunken Icelandic member of the band. I forget his name now, but he possessed the basic countenance and bearing of an abominable snowman. I respectfully declined. Even if I had had a sudden overwhelming urge to experiment with homosexuality, it wouldn't have involved a man who, the previous night, had snored so loudly that he could be heard four floors below the one he was sleeping on.

Some weeks later, I returned home from touring only to be told that this self-same man-mountain had borrowed my bed while I was away. I wouldn't have minded if it wasn't for the fact that he had left an army of his little friends behind him. The weird thing is, pubic lice really do look like crabs.

Meanwhile, Mr Orridge had sown the wind once too often and was about to reap the whirlwind. Christian lunatics had taken on the task of exposing child abuse in satanic cults. Seizing on a PTV video, this crusade announced proof of their allegations. Ignoring the fact that the woman shown was in her twenties and more than willing to participate, a literal witch hunt began. Social services were called in and the Orridge clan had to relocate offshore. After all, not all sleazy tales are based on fact.

24

Positive Punk

by Richard Cabut

I wrote the Positive Punk article for the NME in January/February 1983. At that time there were three distinct groupings in the punk scene. The Oi-sters and Herberts, who traded in basic forms of music, fashion and behaviour; the anarchos, a mass of black in terms of clothes and demeanour; and a loose, nameless collection of punks and former punks who were colourful, and full of, it seemed, vim, dash and go-ahead spirit. I wrote about many of the bands and places associated with the latter grouping, from the Batcave and the Specimen, to the Mob (who were sort of anarcho-plus).

It was obvious that something was going on, and the NME asked me to write a piece about it. Originally, I didn't use the name 'positive punk', or any umbrella term. But the paper needed an easy hook to snag readers. Positivity, I suggested when asked, is a common denominator, so hey presto… a little alliteration goes a long way. Of course, Positive Punk was a disaster. As soon as something is named, people have a target to attack. Also, factions within the scene quickly appeared.

The style magazine **The Face,** *for instance, ran a Positive Punk piece, but the Sex Gang Children refused to become involved — because they couldn't control it. Their noses had been put out of joint. The bigwigs in the scene, your Sex Gangs and Southern Death Cults, had suddenly been usurped, or so they thought, by upstarts like Brigandage and Blood and Roses.*

Overnight, the atmosphere changed from togetherness to suspicion, jealousy and loathing. This would probably have happened in any case, but the Positive Punk article greatly accelerated the process. As far as I am concerned, Positive Punk described the 'Passage of a few People (wearing make-up and top hats) through a Rather Brief Moment in

Time.' I think it was accurate. In hindsight, the music wasn't great, which was probably the real downfall. And then it turned into goth, with even worse music.

Part one

Don't dream it, be it.
— Rocky Horror Show

The Boy sits before the staring mirror and ponders his clean-shaven reflection. Smiling, he selects a carefully-compiled tape and slots it into his machine. 'Fatman' is the first track: Southern Death Cult excite him and he dances in his seat while unscrewing a tube of foundation cream.

He's got to look good tonight — and it's becoming every night — because he's off out to a gig. He's going to see one of *his* bands, one of the groups he regularly sees. Brigandage, Southern Death Cult, Danse Society, Ritual, Rubella Ballet, Virgin Prunes, Specimen, the Mob... They're the only ones that mean anything to him anymore.

Tonight it's Blood And Roses at London's Moonlight Club and all his friends will be there. One of their tracks, 'Your Sin Is Your Salvation,' comes up on the tape and the boy remembers the last time he saw them.

The blur of colour, the heady atmosphere, the fun, the collective feeling of motion — *forward!* It made him feel alive, positive, and then he formed a group the next week.

Finishing his make-up, the boy turns his attention to his dyed blue hair, carefully back-combing it into disarray. Last week he was beaten up by some skinheads because they didn't like the look of him. He remembers their fury but shrugs: he enjoys his appearance and is proud to look different. In a way he's almost glad that his clothes and attitude provoked the attack — their mindlessness wrapped in a dull, grey, lazy uniform of bitterness gives him a reason to be their opposite.

He feels bright and optimistic about the future, slipping into a pair of leather trousers, noticing he's only got a few quid left in his pocket. It doesn't matter though, the dole gives him time to *do* things, like his group.

A Brigandage number blares out: 'Hope,' it seems to sum things up for him. With its message on his lips the boy half-dances across the room, through the door and out.

Part two

I don't like the word movement, but there's now a large collection of bands and people with the same positive feeling.
— Andi, singer with Sex Gang Children, speaking on the opening night of Son of Batcave

Hail Eris, Goddess of Discord, and pass the ammunition: as the heavy drumbeat rolls and the harsh chords crash and sometimes even tingle, it's then that the boys and girls come out to play.

Playpower!

With wild-coloured spiked hair freezing the eye, and even more vivid clothes to spice the imagination — faces, thoughts and actions — the atmosphere's infused with a charge of excitement, an air of abandon underlined with a sense of purpose.

Something stirs again in this land of fetid, directionless sludgery, this land of pretend optimism and grim reality. Theory and practice are being synthesised under the golden umbrella of a twenty-four-hour-long ideal.

Welcome to the new positive punk.

Although it's not the purpose of this article to create any kind of movement or cult, any easy or accessible bandwagon to be tumbled onto, it is indisputable that a large number of bands and people involved in the culture called rock, have sprung up at approximately the same time, facing their lifestyles in the same direction. Maybe unconsciously so, it's a huge collective force that we *can* call the new positive punk — a re-evaluation and rejuvenation of the ideals that made the original outburst so great, an intensification of and expansion of that ethos of individuality, creativity and rebellion. The same *buzz* that burned our streets, hearts and minds in 76/77 is happening again.

The Industrial Revolution is over, a new era has begun, and the current mood is an affirmation of that point. The natural energy that for over two hundred years has been poured into the physical, the rational and the materialistic, has now all grown crooked. The mental/magical power has been lost: it was simply not needed — steam engines, radios, electricity were so much easier and they worked. But now the glamour is wearing off; we can see the strings and wires, the clockwork squeaks... the radiation is beginning to corrode the pretty box.

All the darkness and light, all the forces are still there deep underneath, bubbling, steaming, fermenting. The instinct, ritual and ceremony are rising again in everyday life; many people are starting to use the tarot and I-Ching. And the new punk groups are a reflection of this feeling; their use of mystical/metaphysical imagery and symbolism is a striking common denominator. Not in the way of dumb-dabbling and superficial posturing of, say, a Black Sabbath with their (gasp) black-magic kick.

Nor is it a silly hippy Tolkien-fantasy joyride, or even a Killing Joke stench-of-death gloomier-than-thou slice of fanaticism. It is, instead, an intelligent and natural interest in mystery, rather than history, that is a sign of an open mind.

These groups are aware: UK Decay (positive-punk forefathers), using the dark to contrast and finally emphasise the light; Sex Gang Children, taking us into the sub-world of the Crowleyan abyss; while Blood And Roses are pushing the symbols a whole lot further, their guitarist Bob being a serious student of the Art.

The mystical tide we are talking about here refers, if nothing else, to the inner warmth and vital energy that human beings regard as the most favourable state to live in. The new positive punk has tapped into this current.

And if all this sounds a touch heavy, let's consider the humour, style and inherent *fun* that are essential parts of the movement. Let's look at groups like Specimen, who are more *Rocky Horror* than Aleister Crowley, preening themselves in a glam-soaked traipse among the ruins. Or the Virgin Prunes' cheeky onstage oral-sex send-up. The real humour is intermixed with the sheer sense of *joie de vivre* present at such gatherings.

Here is a glow of energy and life that overcomes the need for artificial stimulation. Unlike the heroin- or barbiturate-sodden club scene or the glue-swamped Oi!/punk arena, the emphasis here is not on drugs. Although illicit substances are not unknown, the desperate desire to nullify boredom is not present, and therefore there is no narcotic edge to the scene. Members of several groups (such as Southern Death Cult, Sex Gang Children and UK Decay) do not even drink.

For perhaps the first time, an active and flourishing dissenting body will not go down with its hind legs kicking as the drug takes over.

Money and time *are* tight: so both of them are being spent on something far more enjoyable and important: style. There's a veritable explosion of multi-coloured aestheticism. So different from the bland, stereotyped Oi!/bootboy punk fare of jeans, leather jacket and studs, this is an individualist stance even if it tends towards a common identity. A green-haired spike-topped girl wearing a long black pleated skirt, white parachute top and bootlace tie passes a tasselled, black-haired mohawk in creepers, white socks, red pegs and self-made, neatly-designed T-shirt. Something clicks. They smile in acknowledgement.

We are fireworks.

Part three

*I think that our influence comes from the fact that there are so many
negative bands around. We're not — so away we go!*
— Bob, guitarist with Blood And Roses, Stoke Newington

If the bands absorb, reflect and present (not necessarily in that
order, it's a give-and-take thing) the attitude of their fans and the
tone of their surroundings — and I think that the important ones
do — then we can trace the whole thing back to its roots,
travelling through the erotic politics of the influential Doors and
the tense dusky danger of the Velvet Underground, and then
coming to the Sex Pistols, who operated under a vicious amalgam
of style and direction.

Projecting a perfect combination of distorted but relevant
aesthetics, music and suss, their all-important effect was the
provocation of thought.

Then, veering away from 1002 misdirected cardboard copies,
we come to the Banshees and the Ants. These two are important
to the new positive punk: the Banshees because of their sheer
power of imagination, and the Ants because of their promotion of
sensuous 'black' style.

Both had an adventurous and rebellious air about them that
cut through the regressive dross. Their outlook, musically and in
angle of thought, went beyond the proscribed boundaries of
behaviour at the time. They explored the edges of light and dark
and some of the areas in between. They were a progression and
they are the two clearest reference points to this recent outburst
of energy.

Back at the tail-end of 78 and beyond, punk spun into a
nosedive of tuinal-dazed tiredness. A pause. Trends came and
went: dead ends such as mod, new romanticism — up to and
including the funk craze — all took their toll on the vital energy.
And those who stuck with the essence of their punk were faced

with the development of Oi! punk, under the guidance of certain lobots, gathered itself around a banner of no brains, no style, no heart and no hope. Heads buried in the glue-bag of dejection and floundering away under a barrage of three-chord rubbish — this was, and is, no way to lead a life.

Some drifted with the anarcho scene which at the time (1980/81) was the only worthwhile concern going. But by 1983, when everything is said and done, that angle seems too flat and *puritan* to be of much inspirational value. Crass, although anti-sexist, were and still are extremely sexless: a stark, bleak Oliver Cromwell new model army, who have sense but no sensuality.

At the opposite end of the scale, inspired by the *feeling* of the Ants etc., come the two groups who are the immediate forerunners of today's flood. They are Bauhaus and, later, Theatre of Hate — both of whom capitalised on the idea of style and, what is more, a dangerous and sensuous style that attracted more and more fans who were sick of the bleak and macho Oi! and the shallow cult with no name.

It's these fans, reacting against the devaluation of punk, and fired by the spirit of the above-mentioned mentors, who are acting now. They've created a colourful and thriving nationwide scene — resplendent in their individuality but still linked by a progressive-punk idiom, one that says go instead of stop, expand instead of contract, yes instead of no. A new, positive punk.

Part four

Stimulating thought, bringing people together, entertaining people, creating an atmosphere of sheer exhilaration and enjoyment. These are the main things.
— Ian, singer with Southern Death Cult, *NME*, 2 October 1982

Andi Sex Gang twitches in the spotlight, the beam reflecting his harsh features and closely-cropped hair. He clenches his fists and spits out 'Into The Abyss.'

Ian Southern Death Cult flails his arms and chicken-wardances across the stage, a sharp youthful figure with black befeathered mohawk. His song is 'Moya,' the words and the power behind the words providing an insight into cultural stagnation. He howls and shrieks in defiance. Mark from the Mob, an anarcho-renegade with his bleached dread hair, stands up straight before the microphone, growling: 'Still living with the English fear, waiting for the witch hunt dear.'

All this and more as Michelle Brigandage leaps onto the amps, top hat at a rakish angle. 'As we walk in the sunlight honesty protects our eyes,' is her cry. And Bob Blood And Roses, he just grins, he knows... 'Love is the Law' — their tale underlining the truly optimistic undercurrent to this mood.

And the fans, bedecked in sparkling, inventive garb, they kick, they jump, they scream.

'A night for celebration, a night to unwind,' repeats the diminishing echo from the ghost of UK Decay. 'For celebration, celebration, celebration...'

Part five

There's nothing else. Everything else has been stripped from us. So now we're just gonna do it. There's no other choice.
— Michelle, singer with Brigandage

So here it is: the new positive punk, with no empty promises of revolution, either in the rock 'n' roll sense or the wider political sphere. Here is only a chance of self-awareness, of personal revolution, of colourful perception and galvanisation of the imagination that startles the slumbering mind and body from their sloth.

Certainly this is revolution in the non-political sense, but at the same time it's neither escapist nor defeatist. It is, in fact, 'political' in the genuine sense of the word.

Individuality? Creativity? Rebellion? The synthesis comes at the moment when you do the one thing, the only thing, when you know you're not just a trivial counter on the social chequerboard. Here are thousands doing that one thing: merging an explosive and cutting style with a sense of positive belief and achievement, and having fun while they're doing it.

The Oi!-sters and their ilk may have taken punk a few millimetres to the right or a centimetre to the left, but not one damn step forward.

This is punk — at last built on rock and not on sand.

25

1976/86

by Simon Reynolds

The following essay was written for the sixth issue of Monitor, *a 'pop journal' founded by me and some friends who'd recently graduated and were still hanging around Oxford on the dole (no Jobseeker's Allowance in those days).* Monitor's *self-chosen remit was thinkpieces and overviews, and for what turned out to be the final issue I chose as my subject the tenth anniversary of punk. This was then occasioning much hand-wringing retrospection in the music press: What happened to the revolution? Where did it all go wrong? 1986 also saw the publication of Dave Rimmer's* Like Punk Never Happened, *a book about New Pop with particular focus on Culture Club. To me, though, it seemed blindingly obvious, scanning the landscape of British music culture, that practically everywhere you looked there was ample evidence that punk had happened. New Pop itself came out of post-punk, which in turn came out of punk. I'd lived through all this in real time, but for the previous issue of* Monitor, *researching my own essay on New Pop, I decided to retrace the dialectic and visited the Bodleian Library daily for a month, ordering up back copies of the weekly music papers dating back to 1976. They arrived from the stacks in string-bound packages and I read them in chronological sequence, tracking the evolution of the discourse. This research also informed the writing of '1976/86.' (It could further be seen as the distant seeds of my post-punk history,* Rip It Up and Start Again.*) All this reading and musing about how we got to where we were fed into the polemic that I and fellow* Monitor *alumni like David Stubbs and Paul Oldfield pursued when we started writing for* Melody Maker: *the belief that late-Eighties alternative music was overdetermined by the convulsive events of a decade earlier and that there was an urgent need for the scene to be* unpunked. *For music to*

have any hope of moving forward, 76-and-all-that needed to be rever-
enced far less, perhaps even consigned like withered flowers to the
dustbin of memory. Needless to say, I loved then, and will love until the
end of (my) time, Bollocks, *Buzzcocks,* Germfree Adolescents *and the*
rest. But in 1986, the potential in punk seemed utterly played out: the
fixation with 76-77 seemed hampering, a stuck-on-repeat script that
could only ever assign us the roles of reenactors, epigones, ashen-faced
mourners.

1986, ten years on, the teeming retrospectives stress how much
we've lost. But is this really the case? Seems to me that the music
scene is still fatally hung up on punk: at this moment every
possible construction of those events, their meaning and effect, is
being lived out, carried on, by someone.

Punk haunts rock critical thinking as teasing proof that a unity
of alienation existed once, can therefore exist again. Punk's ghost
reminds us at every step of what we lack (precisely this phantom
'we'). But memory lies; to bemoan pop's present demoralisation
and drift is to forget that our division was pregnant in punk from
the off. There never was a consensus over its scope or aims or
defining actions. Punk was really the opening of a discourse
whose subject was: WHAT'S PUNK? (i.e. what's music for, what
power can art have?). Punk is best defined as 'disturbance' — a
clamour and congestion of claims and stances. People wanted
different things from 'punk.' The movement's unity existed only
on the printed page — in the music press's torrid rhetoric, in the
panic-babble of Fleet Street and TV. Since 1977 these multiple
strands of activity/ideology/grievance have simply separated out
further, each nurturing in its bosom its own version of punk, a
little myth. Let's look a little bit closer.

Punk as estrangement from normal life

A lineage from Adam and the Ants and Bauhaus to the goths and
positive punks has taken punk as inversion of values, deviance

from norms, a rallying of outcasts in a tribal underworld. The interest in Man's dark side is reminiscent of mid-Seventies heavy metal, but glam is an influence too: the way the star's remaking of herself through glamour is the model for individual liberation (collective/political hopes having died). In goth, punk's will to rise above environment, to subvert everyday life, is sublimated into fantasy: desires are so imprecise they can only be expressed in mystical language.

Punk as political responsibility

The Redskins are an ultimate group, sat painfully pat at the confluence of several orthodoxies — that there is a necessary, and simple, fit between pop culture and radical politics; that youth culture is a working-class phenomenon; that black music alone is a legitimate basis for protest. With the Redskins, soul's intensity is clenched rather than released, becomes a fist. Scrape past the Soul Man postures and you find... The Alarm.

Red Wedge is another dead end to this straight 'n' narrow path from punk — the belief that pop's value is a contribution to 'the struggle' (this single struggle). There's an implicit contempt for pop and for pleasure. Groups like the Style Council try to turn the euphoria and ecstasy of soul to CONSTRUCTIVE ENDS.

And there's the documentary realism of the Fine Young Cannibals, Elvis Costello addressing the issues of the day, senile scribes scurrying to interpret these weighty statements...

Punk as style war

An interesting development. Paul Weller, for instance, is trying to make political idealism glamorous by linking it with being a stylist. There's an idea here of consumption with integrity, the notion that certain consumer choices have a natural fit with certain political choices — hence *Our Favourite Shop*. You can find the same idea in *The Face*, where the Disinformation column snuggles next to photographs of exorbitant clothes and furniture, the assumption being that avant-garde design is part of some grand progressive thrust that also includes socialism. Then there's also the idea of glamour as the refusal to look defeated by life (the mod/soulboy creed of refusing the signs of social subordination — which unfortunately tends to look like straightforward, uncritical upward aspiration). And the *Absolute Beginners* theme of revolt into style — resistance through gaiety, a proto-revolutionary self-preening and selfishness, a riot of colour. Relevant in 58, doubtless, but these days youth is practically compulsory.

Punk as incompetence

Groups like the Membranes, Bogshed, Three Johns, et al., have contracted punk to a Northern bloody-mindedness, to a constricting equation — 'real' music = scruffy shapeless energy. Hence the Membranes' LP *The Gift of Life* — the idea that mess and muck are the sole legitimate expressions of human vitality. The arrogance! We're supposed to thrill to the knowledge that these bands are just like us, that we too could make a racket as rudimentary and joyless. Punk originally defined itself against AOR, against disco — this music seems only to exist as an anti-pop gesture, ruling out as 'fake' all grace or melody. As masochistic and macho a dead end as heavy metal.

Punk as outrage

The eternal appeal of swastikas, violence, misogyny, body openings... to the kind of male teenage vileness that always thought Sid Vicious was what punk was all about... continues today with Sigue Sigue Sputnik, the Butthole Surfers, psychobilly, Beastie Boys...

Punk as pub rock

The spirit of Stiff persists in the surprisingly dogged belief that punk was about the demystification of seeing plain Joes on stage.

Simple normality ain't enough, otherwise Phil Collins would suffice — no, it has to be an outré ordinariness, a sub-normality. So, the Pogues — a revolutionary kind of self-abasement, some would have it. Punk's radical, stylised dishevelment has very little to do with this wilful oafishness and self-neglect. Nietzsche got it right when he wrote of 'the bland degeneration which beer produces in the spirit'! What is the difference between the Pogues and Oi?

So, far from being 'like punk never happened,' our music scene is massively overdetermined by punk. (Can it be a coincidence that the best, most bearable groups of the last two years — the Smiths, Hüsker Dü, Jesus and Mary Chain — take their bearings from the Sixties?) Every conceivable demand you could make of punk is being catered for by someone. Which is the music scene's problem, the reason that no great insurrection is brewing — this great diversity that forestalls focus, this satedness that falls short of turmoil.

Just as there's a wider choice, thanks to punk, so there's a critical pluralism, and therefore disunity. Rock is no longer a monomania, but one element in a range of pleasures. The music papers grow steadily closer to *The Face* or *City Limits* in their multimedia approach. There's a diminished preparedness to expect answers from a white rock noise. The hip elite is split down the middle, because of the Rock is Dead ethos that many saw as the lasting achievement of punk, the debunking of slavish credulity in rock as salvation. On one side, the new faithless, with their import 12"s, Billie Holiday budget LPs, Charly reissues, quite decided that they'll never listen to anything with a power chord in it again; on the other side, the born-again rockists who favour either jangly soft-Velvets copyists or noisy hard-Velvets copyists. Look at the *NME* — one half wants it to be *The Face*, the other wants it to be a big fanzine.

It's the HEALTH of the music scene — eclecticism of taste, critical heterodoxy, the media's new comprehensiveness — that ensures any new revolt can only be stillborn. Punk — far from being about individuality and open-mindedness as some had it — manifested itself as the installation of orthodoxy. Actually divided, punk's impulse was anti-pluralistic, even totalitarian — witness the rewriting of rock's history which made 76 a Year Zero, discrediting most of rock's prior achievement. Punk truths were based not on theory or insight so much as the will to unity, the will to power — they were distortions, which by simplifying the world made it actionable. Of all the original punk rhetoricians only Julie Burchill has stuck with this spirit. Throughout her fitful intellectual trajectory she has lurched from one opposed orthodoxy to another — a junkie for the Categorical Utterance, not just because callous vehemence is her stock-in-trade, her living, but because she's obsessed with strength. She admires the Soviets for precisely their inflexibility; they understand that unconditional truths are the bedrock of pragmatism. Nietzsche could have been dreaming of Julie when he wrote of the 'will to stupidity' underlying any conviction. Every belief is a little blindness, a delimitation of the intellect's perception, a closure.

Remember when 'liberal' was *the* punk obscenity? The shrill likes of *NME*'s Neil Taylor instinctively understand that any future disturbance in pop must draw its strength from cruelty, blindness, the elaboration of new prejudices and dogma. Do we *want* this? The evaluation of pop in terms of 'threat' inevitably pushes us towards such a refusal of choice, of the richness of ideas and pleasures.

In a recent *Observer* article Simon Frith said *Monitor* was struggling towards a new pop aesthetic. I don't know how true this is (let alone whether we're capable of it) although this issue we do launch a concerted assault on the idea of pop as subversion (or what Frith called pop as public gesture). I'd like to close with a few thoughts on the possible shape of this 'new' aesthetic. Once we've got the punk notion of threat out of our blood, maybe two approaches are possible. First, the more modest, familiar project of studying pop culture in terms of recognition — seeing ourselves in pop artefacts, imagery, performances. This leads on to analysis of how some pop opens up the possibilities of being, where other music only confines or confirms: how sounds as much as words can enlarge the vocabulary of desire and self, perhaps even reflect dissent. Second, what's scarcely been attempted — writing about pop's fascination (rather than its meaning) — writing that attends to the surfaces of sound, the madness of rhythm, the allure of spectacle, the possibility of surprise. (The only pop critics I can think of who've tried to engage with the materiality of music are Barney Hoskyns, Richard Cook and our own Paul Oldfield and Chris Scott.) Difficult to justify such writing — why bother to *touch* the music? — except that, as Paul put it, 'words might fail, interestingly or suggestively.'

26

Camden Dreaming

by Richard Cabut

There are some photos on the Internet — *3:AM Magazine*, to narrow it down a little — of the punk band Brigandage, taken by Joan Geoffrey for *Zigzag* in the early to mid-Eighties (erstwhile *Zigzag* editor Mick Mercer places it in 1984; I'm not sure). The location is definitely Camden Town — outside the Tube station, and inside the café next-door, which was an occasional meeting place.

I suppose the pictures offer a tantalising peak at Camden before it became the youth theme park-cum-alt shopping area it is now. We can't actually see much of Camden in the pics, but if we buy into Walter Benjamin's theory that art has an aura, then from these photos, which are most definitely art, we can feel the 1984/NW1-ness of it all. Yes?

Back then, of course — and this will pique the interest of the seekers of untrammelled urbanity and unreconstructed grime, the psychogeographers or hauntologists — Camden was typically dark, dank, dystopian, and many of the other Ds, too. It was closer to the crumbling 1969 Camden portrayed in *Withnail and I* (a film Brigandage singer Michelle and I saw at the Hampstead Classic and empathised with tremendously — we would argue about which of us was Withnail and which was I) than 1990s Britpop central.

It wasn't unknown, in 1984, to come across the sort of mad Paddy that featured in *Withnail*: 'I'll murder the pair of yous!' In the Camden backstreets, the boozers were fading testaments to times past, and water passed in the form of piss up against the proverbial wall — and smelling much the same.

But Michelle and I — I was a member of the band, and the lovable spikey top in the pictures by the way — were oblivious to any of this. We were certainly not poets of the dispossessed. We strutted our Billy-the-Kid sense of cool — bombsite boys and girls from the ruins — posing our way out of the surrounding dreariness. We were living in our own colourful movie (an earlyish Warhol flick, we liked to think), which we were sure was incomparably richer, more spontaneous and far more magical than the depressing, collective, black-and-white motion-less picture that the nine-to-five conformists, or those that stumbled around with their booze-fuelled regrets, had to settle for.

We lived in a hard-to-let housing co-op gaff about ten minutes' walk from the Tube, up Agar Grove, near to York Way — on the way to Pentonville Prison or King's Cross, depending on which way the chips fell for you.

Our rehearsal studio was up there too, on St Paul's Crescent. There, the female receptionist had a thing about NME writer Paul Morley. She sent him letters and he replied in his excitable, frothy prose, enthusing about how he would like to take her to the park for some wine and a talk — no doubt about his great concepts and theorems regarding modern pop. I'm not sure if she actually did meet up with Paul, but she did become dissatisfied with her boyfriend, who she stopped shagging — but, weirdly, kept giving blow jobs to. Such was the powerful effect of Morley's words — either that, or she was living in her boyfriend's flat and felt obliged to recompense him for bed and board in some way. It was a scenario worthy of a song, but we didn't write it — too close to home probably. Anyway, she used to pass Paul's flowery letters around, to general amusement. Even better, she was mates with Martin Glover, Killing Joke's Youth, who would bring back cassette tapes he'd made in New York of the pirate hip-hop stations — which were fantastic.

Our house was around the corner, the shoddy shell of a three-storey affair that's worth an absolute fortune now. Other inhabitants included a drama student, his girlfriend and Toby Nuttall, the son of late beatnik *Bomb Culture* author Jeff, whose brother Tim would soon join our merry Brigandage band. And if we thought that the mad, the bad, the sad were outside in the gaseous pubs and on the claustrophobic Camden streets, then we should have looked a bit closer to home.

One drunken night, the drama student, jealous that his girlfriend was getting on too well with some South American guy, got up and went out of the living room where they were talking and drinking tequila. He went purposefully to the adjoining kitchen. There, on the rusty cooker that had seen its best days in the 1950s, he boiled a kettle. It took a while — he tried not to watch. He did this calmly. Coldly. It was, perhaps, the only known occasion when a kettle was boiled coldly. When it was steaming, whistling at 210 degrees F, when the water was seething in the same way he secretly was, the student dramatically took the kettle, first putting a towel around the handle so he wouldn't scald his delicate actor's hand, and carried it into the living room. There, as his girlfriend sat on the sofa, the stuffing popping out of it, laughing at some joke, he stood above her — how *dare* she laugh at someone else's jokes? — and calmly, coldly, poured the scorching water all down her front.

Strangely, her hideous screams didn't wake us up for we had gone to bed long before the actor had decided to play this, his most insane role — one that melted his lover to the core. (Years later, I saw his name in the cast of some BBC period drama. While she, after botched reconstructive surgery, became someone who looked up at you with the eyes of an old stranger if you dared ask if she was all right.)

But then it would have taken a lot to wake us up. We were still young. We were still busy dreaming in Camden Town.

27

Camera Squat Art Smiler

by Neal Brown

Go Smiler's. King's Cross. Tenement squats. Full scenic Oliver Twist look. Smiler and camera. I stay at my girlfriend's squat. Sex.

Smiler photographs staff at an early London McDonald's, High Street Kensington.

Seamus Luttman-Johnson dead. Mark Greaves dead. Sean Cooke dead. Mark Golding dead. Little Kevin dead. Soph Berens dead. Dan-I and I help carry Chris Cowen's coffin. I go to funeral of Dan-I. Dan-I's and my old friend Jake Le Mesurier dead. Jake's mother is Hattie Jacques. Sunday lunch roast with Jake, Hattie Jacques and drugs.

Age thirteen/fourteen I take LSD, Kensington Market, LSD lost-soul horror.

Seamus, Schoolhouse Squat, Shepherd's Bush Road (circa 1981-1985). 'Seamus glancing back over his shoulder... like a farewell' — Smiler, 2015.

1976. I go Hornsey Art College. I start buying *Art Monthly*. Smiler goes Hornsey 1978. George Younson head of Fine Art. Used to teach John Lennon in Liverpool.

Diane Arbus.

Thatcher, Shirley Porter, 1970s feminism. Space Invaders. Stupid table-tennis games in pubs. TV adverts for Hofmeister and Carlsberg lager. Pre-HIV/condoms.

Thatcher heroin, less a subculture more and more on the streets.

I spend time with Little Steve, truant. Hippies. *Frendz, Oz, International Times*, Portobello Road and Ladbroke Grove. Kensington Market. Biba. Black or Moroccan hashish. Older hippy women. I go visit him his children's home. Staff very kind to me. Nice building nice furniture. They give me lunch. A roast. I cannot believe the warmth and comfort, compared with own home. My father drunk, raging. Girl invites me in cupboard, lifts up skirt, flashes herself at me.

Natalya Citkowitz dead. Paparazzi photographers.

Diane. Smiler took pic of her to show her. *Diane (Two Weeks Before Her Overdose and Death)* (circa 1983).

Sex.

Wee gee.

Children. *Kids in Kings Cross Alley* (circa 1983).

Eric and I arrested election night Hornsey College Art. Graffiti. In police station I surrender all property in my bags. Over one hundred and thirty paintbrushes bought clearance-cheap from college shop. Paintbrushes individually counted in, signed for. Released after twenty-five minutes. Paintbrushes individually counted out, signed for.

Smiler born Kenya. Called a white wog. Poshboy. Scum.

Gallery House, Exhibition Road. Marc Camille Smiler's tutor for a year at Hornsey.

I saw (unless it was a dream, which it might have been) the 1972 Celebration at Gallery House as a lone sixteen-year-old truant, wandering around London, probably stoned. Gallery House was situated in a grand building, temporarily available for art exhibitions courtesy of the German Institute, but which felt more like a squat. It had a trashed interior, in which the exhibiting artists — in this case Chaimowicz, Stuart Brisley and Gustav Metzger — enjoyed 24-hour occupancy. My experience of the art and the gallery was as an exciting, anarchic trespass. The house implied wealth, power and exclusivity, and the art implied impoverishment, re-empowerment and inclusivity.

— Neal Brown writing about Marc Camille Chaimowicz. *ArtReview* magazine, issue 52, September 2011

After Gallery House finished, the building became a squat. I visit.

Tower blocks. Dixon House. *Dixon House, Squat (16ᵗʰ Floor), Latimer Road* (1980). *Dan, Dixon House, Latimer Road* (1980). Travellers help Smiler move from Dixon House to squat opposite Knightsbridge Barracks.

Little shops, pre-globalisation.

Rock Against Racism. IRA. Blair Peach. Ted Heath. Three-day week. Candles. ATM machines. Miners' strike. Wall's ice cream made from deodorised fat taken from the pigs they use for their sausages.

Methadone. DF 118s. Codeine linctus. *Studio International*.

Hornsey College of Art 1970s. Alexandra Palace. Smiler and camera. Punk. Slits, Raincoats. Smiler liked Eric Watson's work. Eric worked with Pet Shop Boys. Eric and I smashed on pastis. Smiler and camera.

Smiler worked for Dick Jewell. Dick large squat RCA. I buy remaindered copy *Found Photos*.

Slits, Raincoats, Bodysnatchers, Mo-dettes. Red Rizla. Blue Rizla. Green Rizla. Liquorice Rizla.

Smiler: Stiff Little Fingers, X-Ray Spex, Voidoids, Buzzcocks.

Neal: 101ers, Pistols, Clash, Subway Sect, Slits, Raincoats.

1970s. At Eastham College of Technology. Jon Bird: 'Neal, we can see you can draw really well. But here we're going to teach you how *not* to draw.' Peter Webb shows paedophile pornography during lecture on erotic arts. Black-and-white photograph of adult male having sex extremely small child. Looks like made with large-format plate camera. Fine grain. Webb is a loathed man. I enter the fine world of drinking culture in East London with my friend Chris Burnham.

Smiler tells me hearing Ray's voice, walking around the tenements shouting Topper's name — 'Topper, Topper, Topper.' Topper has disappeared.

Sex.

Smiler introduced to Acid House by Michael Clarke.

Mark Lebon. Charlotte Owen.

Notting Hill Riots. Sus law.

Germaine Greer.

Acklam Hall. Smiler: 'We were warned that an impending attack from bikers at the Alexandria was imminent. Security were supposedly from some martial arts club. As it turned out we were attacked by Ladbroke Grove skins instead. I was with Eric at the front door at the bar as they charged in with broken bottles, almost took Eric's eye out but luckily he just got nicked above the eye. Security were nowhere to be seen but we managed to see them out.'

Smiler mother adopted 1939 Kindertransport. Her biological parents killed in Riga extermination camps. Her father fought in First World War for Austro-Hungarians.

I got a place Hornsey lacking qualifications 'exceptional talent clause.' I get a third. Smiler fails his degree. Shortly after last day of my last term Alexandra Palace and Fine Arts Department destroyed in fire. My thesis, *Painting and Context*, destroyed. No copy, only early draft. Big squat Cranley Dene. Donkey in garden. Drunkenness. Smiler and camera.

Barry Flanagan is drunk rude to me. I am drunk rude to William Burroughs. Young alcoholic Scot woman intensely vicious says to me: 'Everyone loves you Neal, but I *hate* you.' She is offensive to two feral men in Henekey's. They snap pool cues, jab at our faces with them. Police called, caller gets name of pub wrong. I see police turn up at wrong pub, Finch's, further down Portobello Road.

I go Derek Jarman's with Slits and punks. Drunk. Jarman seems frightened.

Deeply, passionately in love, variously requited, unrequited, obsessional-compulsive. Depression.

And on one great occasion [Billy Childish's] group The Milkshakes played at a house party next to the British Museum where all us

275

students had paintings hanging in the back garden.
— Peter Doig, introduction to *Billy Childish: A Short Study* by
Neal Brown (Aquarium/L-13, 2008)

Parties, art-gallery openings, clubs, sheens. *Wrecking Crew Party*
(circa 1985). *Guests at Drug Addiction Recovery party, Chelsea* (circa
1986). *Untitled 1. Sam and Maggie's Engagement, South London*
(circa 1979).

Marc Einzig staying Monmouth Road. Asleep bitten on ear by
rat. We come back pub drunk, do a *Lord of the Flies* on the rat.

Smiler in on punk in Torquay. Saw Ramones, Clash, Talking
Heads, the Cortinas, Buzzcocks. Sex Pistols got cancelled.

Smiler left at Nigerian boarding school. When Smiler's
stepfather went to visit him, he could not understand a word
Smiler said.

I have studio in squat above Gay's the Word bookshop. I never
use it. I go sit in it, be sad. Smiler squats it, some other period.

Big squat Warren Street. Three a.m. someone points to
attractive woman says it's a man.

I leave brand new one-inch Ampex reel-to-reel tape at
dealer's. Never go back to get it. I leave some recovery literature
with dealer. Dealer bans Smiler going around. Smiler bans
someone going round to his. I ban someone going round to mine.
Smiler takes a photograph. Dickey lends car (old Ford) to some
dealers, deposit, forgets tell them brakes don't work, crashes at
first corner. I am in Blue Sky cafe with Strummer and Gillian. I
notice Strummer is wearing my blue coat that I left at Gillian's.
Strummer's hair all soft and clean. Looks wrong. Cyril who owns
the New Born bans me and Inigo after a police inspector comes in
after us because Inigo has winked at him in Westbourne
Grove. Police inspector walks around our table, dark theatrical
menace.

At age twenty-one coming of age Smiler inherited £2000 from
his father's drowning. Bought camera equipment. Lent Keith

Allen £500. Later, Keith lends me money. I lend other people money.

Mark Greaves impassioned tells me how heroin is good for his schizophrenia. Yvonne Philpotts dead. Yvonne wants go bed with me, I say no. Mick Jagger tries pick up, he is on moped, she is in taxi, her window open, summer's day, she tells him to fuck off. When she tells us we all cheer. Yvonne gives me huge speed black bomber which I do not take. Yvonne dead at about fourteen, I think. Eddy Payne dead. Charlie Kelly dead. Tom Woods dead. Nick Korner dead. Sappho Korner dead. Damien Korner dead.

Smiler's father worked with Maasai and settlers. Smiler's family spend much time under canvas.

Leaving Smiler's Judd Street I see a man knocked over by a car. The impact sends him high in the air. He gets up, I say we must get ambulance, he says no he is alright, I try insist, but he walks off. Chris has story someone dies on sofa, bad drugs, they put body on street, throw away drugs. Turns out man died because of internal injuries due car accident couple days before, not the drugs. Sadness. Chris laughs.

Depression. Oblivion.

Simon Bramley's posters. Cryptic One Club, Acklam Hall.

Cyril puts big proud sign on wall of his caff, the New Born. Says: 'This restaurant will feature in [I can't remember the name of programme] on TV tonight.' In the programme a character eats a mouthful of food, spits it out in disgust, says, 'This is the worst food I've ever tasted.'

I see elderly man fall straight down pub pavement delivery hatch left open unattended in Portobello Road. Staff come out of pub, shout abuse at him for being so stupid.

Keith Allen on a roll lends state-of-the-art recording equipment squat Fulham. Jim and Sara use it most. *Amos and Sara Go Pop.* When squat ends Jim takes Keith's studio equipment. I drink two litres of Campari, turn red.

Cherry tree in garden of squat. I think, 'those cherries will taste astringent and horrible.' I eat one, disappointment, it is delicious.

Sex, sex, sex.

Smiler photographs me and Boogie. Boogie photographs me and Smiler. Boogie's photos of Lydon, Vicious, Paul Cook etc. are great. Eric photographs me. I photograph Eric. Sunken squat, off Harrow Road. Deep in a void left by Westway.

Mad Jane lives at Strummer's squat Daventry Street. Or is it Strummer at Mad Jane's? Or was it Boogie's? Sid Vicious being filmed there and I am not let in as they do not want to be disturbed. Smiler and Mad Jane live in my place for a while. When Smiler and Jane leave mine there are Kentucky Fried Chicken boxes and bones everywhere. *Jehovah's Witnesses, Wedding, Monmouth Road* (circa 1981).

Joe lives in Monmouth Road for a few weeks, at Richard and Esp's.

Children.

Children threatened, told not to talk to the police.

Do laundry at Porchester baths. Huge old-fashioned washing machines, brass and copper and steam. See Dudanski, Esp, Paloma, Joe going in, I shyly say hello.

Smiler pic *Spotty Pete*. Nice flowery shirt. Looks like it might be from Liberty's. But not quite flower power. Art historically pleasing if the pattern was William Morris, but I don't think it is. If we're lucky it's a Burne-Jones detail. The drug is most likely heroin. Brown Persian heroin? *Spotty Pete, Lulworth House, Camden* (1991).

When I live in All Saints Road the drugs always in King's Cross. When I live in King's Cross drugs always in All Saints Road. *Man in Psychosis, All Saints Road* (1979).

My dad works on dustcarts Portobello Road. I am proud of him. Better than his two-bottles-of-gin-a-day rage stuff. Dustmen drink in the Warwick, Saturday. One day one dustman insults another dustman's dog. Big fight, broken pub windows, smashing, punching. Dog barking, dustmen swearing and cunting each other. Blood on glass. My dad gets me out. I am a little disappointed to leave.

My mother reads *Guardian*, father reads *Telegraph*, stepmother reads *Mail*, stepfather reads *Morning Star*. Stepmother on sedatives, picks her face. Every night for forty years my stepfather drinks heavily, but not so much as to be incapable of speech. But after my mother goes to bed he drinks much more, goes to bed late shitfaced. All next day hungover, rolling cigarettes, spitting bits tobacco waste out of his mouth, angry. Until evening, starts again.

Waiting to score King's Cross. Wandering I find long, eviscerated spine of some unknown creature in middle of quiet side road.

Buy heroin. Buy Kit Kat. Go public toilet, wrap Kit Kat in toilet paper put in pocket. Use foil of Kit Kat to smoke heroin off. When home put Kit Kat in drawer along with twenty-five other toilet paper wrapped Kit Kats. Once a month go on health kick and eat the twenty-five Kit Kats. Once every nine months deliver a bonnie, seven-pound, opiated baby Kit Kat turd, put its name down for Eton. Joke.

Children. *Travellers Site, Post-Eviction, Camden Town* (1985). Narrative signage, record, expression and communication to others.

Sound systems.

In the Blue Sky cafe in Westbourne Grove. Someone leaves food. Derek picks up uneaten pizza, wraps it in napkin, takes his hat off, his eyes wild, puts pizza on his head, puts his hat back on. He's been sleeping rough.

Will Self kindly gives character reference for Smiler in court. Smiler bound over to keep the peace.

Friend drunk story, goes back with woman for shag. Drunken incontinence shits himself, throws pants out window. In morning they are having breakfast woman looks out says: 'What are those underpants doing in tree?'

Heathcote Williams opens squat in Castellain Road. Opposite my mother's. I stand on marble fireplace and orate in a focal-point-of-the-room centre-of-attention kind of way.

I do life drawings in betting shops, including Lucian Freud. I invite Freud to my squat studio he agrees come look at my paintings. I give him wrong address in an excited mistake.

Lucian Freud paints Lisa.

I panic and give heroin to Dickey for safekeeping. He uses it all. Dickey beautiful girlfriend said what do you expect *daahling*. Later Dickey gave me whole unopened box Subway Sect singles. Dickey did not know they were rarities. Once a week I sell one for £20 at Record and Tape. Each one gets a quarter gram.

Chris amuses us by going to an early (1980s) NA meeting in King's Cross. We laugh and laugh and laugh.

Mark Golding repeatedly trying to get me to go to Taboo Club. I unfailingly refuse. At dealer's Mark in very straight, neat woman's clothing. Sitting on edge sofa, back prim and straight, hands clasped, good posture, eyeing me.

Children. Take clothes to launderette. Nice and clean.

Camden Town squat. Junkies all shooting up round a dark table like Van Gogh *Potato Eaters*. A lemon centre-stage for citric. The lemon pulsates a small yellow glow of pure life. My painting of this lemon used on cover of Julian Barnes book. Barnes and publisher unaware of course that it is a 'heroin' lemon. Not that it matters. Gina from the Raincoats buys the painting.

Ben Langlands in studio squat next door to my mother's in Castellain Road. Ben is tidy, hardworking and gets things done.

I spend many nights in Old Schoolhouse squat Shepherd's Bush. Mario's dog pisses everywhere. Takes it to dog healer/dog psychiatrist. Healer/psychiatrist says: 'This dog should be put down.'

Smiler taking photographs at Monmouth Road, Alexander Street, Paddington. I acquire Smiler photograph of the old

Bishop's Bridge. Years later looking closely at print I notice torn poster on bridge. It's the poster I designed for Pigbag.

Laughter. *Haley, Lulworth House, Camden* (1985). *Haley, Immac Stockings, Lulworth House, Camden* (1985).

Smiler ex-partner Lisa died. Drowned in bath. Boxing Day. Valium and heroin overdose. Absolute dismay, sorrow, sadness. Louis has lost his mother.

I drink pure, clear water. In a pint glass. I hold it up to admire its transparency. After I finish drinking it I accidentally drop glass. Surprising implosion with many small pieces. Safety glass. So as to prevent use as weapon in eighty-five thousand incidents of pub violence.

Smiler pic Ramona in Princess Royal. Her face bleached out by overexposure acetylene flash. Good cheekbones, cheekbones also in shadow. Anaglypta wallpaper behind her head. Swiss-French. A certain confident propriety in Ramona's posture. *Ramona, Princess Royal, nr Monmouth Road* (circa 1979-1982).

I come back from hospital, raw. I stand in my flat, amazed that junkies have not stripped it. Before I even sit down phone rings, police. Son of famous person, stayed in my flat, used my telephone number, ended up in address book of poor prostitute murdered in Bayswater Road. Police asked if I knew anything about the murder. I politely say no. They politely eliminate me from their enquiries. Let's hope the murderer politely admits his crime, when they call him up.

Children born. Plants grow. Sun shines. People sing. We all write songs, sing, dance, cook. Start housing co-ops. Drink tea.

Smiler pic of Aaron under bedclothes Alexander Street. Leopard head. *Aaron (with Leopard's Head)* (1978). Nice continuity between leopard's spots and Aaron's pattern woolly top. Socks on floor. Leopard reappears in the pubic hair nude with film poster over her face. *Jane, with Sophia Loren, Earl's Court* (1980). The leopard doing its best impression of a forensic-science photo-graph. It's like the leopard is the real head, partially obscured under the filmic one. Heads are obscured, masked or bleached out in Smiler's work. Also sometimes in Gareth's.

Mark Golding and I go to try and score. He has been up all night, Taboo, in some kind of drag, high-heeled shoes. Red silk material, flowing trouser-suit outfit. Looks absurd in daylight. We meet eleven a.m. Go around and around and around London all morning, all afternoon, all evening, pubs, dealers, backstreets. Fifteen hours later two am score old junkies somewhere miles and miles away end Finchley Road. The whole fifteen hours trying to score I have no money on me. Mark voids expressive sigh when I announce this, gives me small quantity. I walk all way home, treasuring my £4 worth of heroin.

Sean Oliver hassled by police. Sean kind to me. Woman slashes arms can see subcutaneous fat. Notting Hill Carnival in 1970s was great.

Street violence.

My stepfather drives me to Springfield mental hospital to see my dad. Drops me at gate. Stepfather does not want to see my dad. Father hates working classes, stepfather a working-class trade unionist. Both of them drunks. A very long, curving road from entrance gate to hospital lobby. I walk, a painfully hot summer day, no shade. In lobby my father greets me pointing to lino floor says someone slashed their wrists there last night: 'Rivers of blood, rivers of blood.' Lino looks nice and clean to me. Blue and shiny. In room nurse brings him baked beans in which float little cubes of spam. Lukewarm. Unbreakable stainless-steel plate. Nice nurse. She says: 'Do you promise to eat your dinner Mr Brown?' He says: 'Yes, I promise.' She says: 'Do you *really* promise, Mr Brown?' He says: 'Yes nurse, I *really* promise.' She closes door. He passes lukewarm beans and floating spam to me. Deep commanding voice: 'Eat this, son.' I eat.

Spencer in silly blazer and cravat at the Princess Royal. Collecting dead glasses for Mrs Moss and Clive. Spencer was nice man. Spencer dead. They scatter his ashes in the tiny pub garden.

Smiler with camera in pub. Staff mostly Irish. They do not sell draft Guinness so as 'to stop the Irish coming in.' Aaron looks good. So does Little Sean. Josephine is great. Mrs Moss, the landlady, always kind.

This Heat. Amos and Sarah. L Voag.

Viv Stanshall drunk and stoned. Susie Honeyman tearful. Viv tells me he does not like Ivor Cutler.

Smiler never went to his dad's funeral. In Kenya. Smiler's father got washed off bridge, banged head. Drowned.

Son of famous person hits his girlfriend in front of me. Repeats over and over: 'My hand slipped, my hand slipped, my hand slipped.' His girlfriend tries to get me to fuck her, I politely refuse. My friend immediately fucks her when she tells him she has shaved all her pubic hair off.

Smiler sings with my band at Porchester Hall. With Raincoats and Tymon Dogg. We sing Gary Glitter song 'Rock and Roll (Part1).' When Vincents [The Vincent Units] make single for Y Records I choose song on incorrect basis it has most chords in it so must be the best. When Tesco Bombers play Comedy Club notice sound bit weak, look around, two band members picking up cases lager walking out off stage with them, drummer so drunk he has knocked snare off rolling across stage, he is failing to catch it.

Children born. Food cooked and shared. Art made. Songs written songs sung.

Smiler loses camera on Tube. Assumes it to be completely lost. Months later, coincidentally walking past Lost Property at Baker Street, drops in, cynical, there it is.

I make drawing of gauching out mother and child. The mother uncomfortable when I remind her of this, years later. Drawing quite good. Drawings of Palmolive, Joe Strummer, David Batterham, Soph Berens, Fan Berens, Sera Furneaux.

I even take some photographs, myself.

Anthea Leeds dead. Matthew Ashton in treatment. Matthew

dead. Mole dead AIDS. Fat Anthony steals my letter runs off, I fight him in Monmouth Road.

I begin make a little film and interview of Robin Banks. Robin is articulate and funny.

Fuck off, fuck off
Fuck off you fucking cunt
I used to think you were alright
But now I think you're not
— 'Fuck off, Fuck off,' lyrics by Neal Brown, circa 1977

Fires. *Arson Attack, London's Burning* (1985).

Smiler not allowed to bring his girlfriend, Sera, home. They squat a derelict garage Torquay for the summer.

My friend drunk driving. Her boyfriend beside her. I am in back seat, with huge, stupid, dark rhinoceros skull beside me. My friend hysteric drunk laughter drives at speed wrong way up one-way street. I beg her to stop. Police come up behind, stop us, make get us out of vehicle. I offer grateful thanks to them for saving me. Back home, have a nice sleep.

1980s. Heroin £80 gram. Amphetamine sulphate £8 gram. I laugh when I buy my first amphetamine because of low cost. Ray the dealer hurt, says: 'Do you think it too expensive?' Heroin purity excellent. Little Roy was crying when he found out you could cut heroin.

Smiler pic Seamus basement of Old Schoolhouse squat. Dansette. Quite an achievement for Seamus to get a TV signal down there. And he's got not one, but two light bulbs.

At the Warwick I am flattered and elated when Seamus the landlord does not pause but immediately accepts my cheque.

Smiler knows Peter Doig at tenements. Peter remembers me. Smiler has early drawing by Peter. Peter kindly writes introduction to book I write about Billy Childish. Smiler helps me when I curate Billy's show at L-13. Billy wrote poem about sex in garden at Bloomsbury squat where I played supporting the Homosexuals. Smiler at gig. Years later I identify name of female subject Billy writing about. She has a great singing voice.

Heathcote Rough Tough squat estate agency. I go with them when they break into vicar's house. Appears premises not actually vacated.

Prostitute known as 'Blow Job,' and addressed as 'Blow.' I am never sure if this unfortunate title is part of a slightly straining, calculated theatrical effect.

Septicaemia. *Angela, King's Cross* (1983).

Patrice black Mohican hair style. French. Beautiful face. I can't remember if he was onstage when we supported the Clash. Probably. When we played Paris I had damaged hand. Had lost temper, smashed a cute little teapot, cut a tendon. Patrice did not return money I put up for his airfare. Years later gave me old bicycle, instead. *Patrice, Ladbroke Grove* (circa 1980).

Ladbroke Grove. *Sophie Young, Ladbroke Grove* (1981).

Psychosis, psychosis, psychosis.

Camden, Camden, Camden.

London sunsets. Laughter. Loving embraces. Sincerity. Children. Childbirth.

I go see Liverpool vs someone else. With James Moores and Angus Fairhurst and others. Huge crowd, singing. Angus Fairhurst dead suicide. Philippe Bradshaw dead.

Olly Olly Olly Olly Hollywood
Olly Olly Olly Olly Hollywood

Olly this, and Olly that,
And what a lot of bollocks
And what a lot of crap
I went there with my girlfriend
We took some beer and crisps
We fell asleep and missed the ending —

Because we were pissed

Olly Olly Olly Olly Hollywood
Olly Olly Olly Olly Hollywood

Olly Olly Olly
Balls in a trolley
Tits in a biscuit tin
Sitting in the dark
With a knife up your arse
Olly Olly Olly's the king

Olly Olly Olly Olly Hollywood
Olly Olly Olly Olly Hollywood

— 'Olly Olly Olly,' music by Neal Brown, lyrics by Neal Brown, Aaron Batterham, Mark Smiler Cawson, circa 1981

I lived above shebeen in Talbot Road. No, I do not mean the Globe. Open until five am. Corner shop across the road would open at six and sell alcohol. This hour between five and six am is a curious time.

Chris Courtney finds twenty bags wrapped heroin in pub toilet in All Saints Road. He uses it all. I go round to Keith's in All Saints Road. With Fan, after Soph's death. Keith opens the door completely naked cheeky chappy. Fan silent.

I am mugged underneath Anthea's flat All Saints Road. Takeaway. Mugger puts hand in my pocket, pulls out my UB40. Looks at it, carefully puts it back in my pocket. Disdain and disgust for me.

Jago Elliot dead.

Smiler pic of Jehovah's Witness at Kingdom Hall, end of Monmouth Road. Smiler stands behind official photographer. Tymon Dogg squatted in the church for a while, before Jehovah's moved in. Sold to Jehovah's for £20,000 I think.

I get given all the lost property at the Groucho. Three big black bin bags each hugely full. Fine quality hats, coats, scarves, gloves. But I look like a composite twat. Never mind. All lost again within three months.

Scallywag magazine, rent boys. *Top of the Pops*.

Working with Gareth and Smiler. The two maddest dogs. Camera vs camera. Things improved.

Smiler self-portrait beaten-up face. Can't remember what happened there. Oh yes, beating, NF. Slight Keith Moon haircut look. Beyond just physical pain. Shallow depth of field. Vest. Other NF man stubbed out cigarette in Aaron's ear. *Smiler, Self Portrait after NF Beating* (1980).

Tom Bantock dead. David Perdigue dead. Mike Evans dead. Roger Pomphrey dead. Sebastian Horsley dead. Chris Courtney dead.

Adam Green dead. Alex Baxter dead. Jay Gaubert dead. Mickey Waldorf dead.

Liam Carson dead. Groucho had been a paradise. Complimentary membership — thank you Liam.

Topper Headon kindly buys me and his friends lunch. In Whitstable. I have gone there with Jock Scott and Robin Banks. We go to Johnny Green's house first. Jock is dryly humorous, but very unwell. When we leave, Topper suggests embrace. I am very moved. Now both many years clean. No embracing with the others, unfortunately.

Smiler asks that I put the focus on me, rather than him, in this text.

Property prices go up. Squatting criminalised.

Children. Joy upon joy of intensity of love. Drinking lots of water.

Smiler doing new work. Camera. Gareth. ICA.

28

Punk Etymology

by Jon Savage

This word trace is far from definitive but is presented in the spirit of enquiry. If not actual pleasure. It's interesting to work out when a particular term comes into prominence — for naming something often brings it into being — and how that meaning may change over the years. In this particular case, the use of the word really comes into focus during the early Seventies, when fans, activists and writers were attempting to bring a truly 1970s rock music into existence. In particular, Lenny Kaye brought the whole idea into prominence in his selection and his sleeve notes for *Nuggets* (Autumn 1972):

> *The name that has been unofficially coined for them — 'punk rock' — seems particularly fitting in this case, for if nothing else they personified the berserk pleasure that comes from being onstage outrageous, the relentless middle finger drive and determination only offered by rock 'n' roll at its finest.*

From the perspective of over four decades, it tickles me that people get so macho about a form of music named after 'A boy that'll... give himself to a man' (Alexander Berkman, *Prison Memoirs of an Anarchist*).

1. Irving Shulman, *The Amboy Dukes*, 1946: '"You bastard," — Flagg tensed — "don't you call me punch-drunk! I can still lick punks like you with both hands tied behind my back!"'
2. Chandler Brossard, *The Bold Saboteurs*, 1952: '"Tell him!" I shouted at Lucille, "Straighten this punk out."'

3.   Penelope Gilliat, 'The Current Cinema,' *New Yorker*, 9 September 1967: 'Like *The Trip*, *Born Losers* was made on the West Coast; punk-uplift films these belong distinctively to California, with its appetite for consoling fad religions and easy revelation.'

4.   Bonzo Dog Doo Dah Band, 'Big Shot' from *Gorilla*, 1967: 'A punk stopped me on the street. / He said, you got a light mac? / No but I got a dark brown overcoat.'

5.   The Mothers of Invention, 'Flower Punk' from *We're Only In It For the Money*, 1968: 'Hey Punk, where you going with that flower in your hand (x 2) / Well, I'm goin' up to Frisco to join a psychedelic band (x 2).'

6.   Lester Bangs, review of MC5, *Rolling Stone*, 5 April 1969: 'Clearly this notion of violent, total youth revolution and takeover is an idea whose time has come... never mind that they came on like a bunch of 16 year old punks on a meth power trip.'

7.   Robert Somma, 'Four Stooges At The Tea Party: Rock Alienation,' *Fusion* 19, 17 October 1969: 'But the most noticeable thing is the singer. He sticks his ass in your face, struts, wiggles, spits, cocks his body, preens, writhes. He looks like he wants to look mean and tough and nasty. "Sometimes I call some punk who's been making remarks out onto the stage. But they never come."'

8.   Jim Morrison, script for *The Adept*, Summer 1969: 'Listen, my dear reader, my fine punk asshole, my dear reader, my fine punk asshole, my lovely hypocrite...'

9.   Dave Marsh, review of ? and the Mysterians, *Creem*, 1970: 'A landmark exposition of punk rock.'

10. Lester Bangs, review of *Frijid Pink* by Frijid Pink, *Rolling Stone*, 25 June 1970 (Charles Manson cover): '1970 is not shaping up as a very momentous year for rock 'n' roll... [Frijid Pink] combine the punk raunch of Detroit with the exquisitely stiff acne blues of a great teen band like The

Shadows of Knight.'

11. Suicide flyer, December 1970: 'Punk Music By Suicide' (when I went to interview Alan Vega in 1980 he provided me with several hits of amyl nitrate and proceeded to wax lyrical about ? and the Mysterians for quite some while).

12. Lester Bangs, autocritique of his *Amon Duul I* review in *Creem*, 1971: 'Well, naturally that's a great album and the guy what wrote that review was a pompous punk.'

13. John Mendelssohn, review of *Long Player* by the Faces, *Rolling Stone*, 18 March 1971: 'On the former the group is content to faithfully recite the original arrangement, which act, in these dark days of Blood, Sweat & Tears, Keith Emerson, and every last punk teenage garage band having its Own Original Approach, is awfully refreshing.'

14. 'Metal' Mike Saunders, review of *Teenage Head* by Flamin' Groovies, *The Rag*, April 1971: 'My girlfriend had seen them about a half-year before that, and said they were a mediocre punk band with a singer who thought he was Mick Jagger, but wasn't.'

15. John Mendelssohn, review of *Love It To Death* by Alice Cooper, *Rolling Stone*, 15 April 1971: 'Nicely wrought mainstream punk raunch and snidely clever lyrics.'

16. Greg Shaw, review of *In The Beginning/The Guess Who: Sown and Grown in Canada* by The Moody Blues, *Rolling Stone*, 15 April 1971: 'Guess Who. "Use Your Imagination", "Clock on the Wall", "Gonna Search" and "Don't Act So Bad" fit into this mold — good, not too imaginative, punk rock and roll.'

17. Lester Bangs, 'James Taylor Marked For Death,' *Who Put The Bomp* 8, Fall/Winter 1971: 'All right punk, this is it.'

18. Ed Sanders, *The Family*, 1971: 'In August of 1968, Brother Ely and his girl friend casually watched some members of the Gypsy Jokers slam a car door repeatedly upon the head of a middle-aged man who had called one of the bikers a punk.'

19. 'Metal' Mike Saunders, review of *Grand Funk* by Grand Funk

Railroad, *Rolling Stone*, 6 January 1972: 'The spirit of American punk rock certainly lives on in GFRR.'

20. 'Metal' Mike Saunders, review of the US music press, *The Rag*, January 1972: 'The loosely defined purpose of *Who Put The Bomp* is to cover the 1958-66 years of rock: forthcoming special issues will be on the English Invasion, Surf and Hot Rod Music, and 1966-7 American Punk Rock.'

21. Charles Shaar Murray, 'Teenage Outrage in Croydon: The MC5,' *Creem*, March 1972: 'Lead guitarist Wayne Kramer is wearing a striped Lurex drape jacket that would bring tears to the eyes of any self-respecting Ted, and he looks the total epitome of the nasty little rockanroll punk, hoodlum, reveling in the applause.'

22. Dave Marsh, 'Bob Seger: Doncha Ever Listen To the Radio...,' *Creem*, May 1972: 'The powerful vocal was charged with echo and energy not unlike a punk's idea of what Phil Spector should've sounded like.'

23. 'Metal' Mike Saunders, review of *Keep The Faith* by Black Oak Arkansas, *Rolling Stone*, 25 May 1972: 'Black Oak Arkansas have the distinction of being possibly the last punk psychedelic rock group in existence.'

24. *Flash Magazine*, June/July 1972: 'Punk Rock Top Ten.'

25. Dave Marsh, article on Jerry Lee Lewis, *Creem*, July 1972: 'The songs are almost all familiar... the spirit of each is purely vigorous, and the ambience is just punk enough to make you think you're listening to rock record even when you know that you aren't.'

26. Nick Kent, review of *Ziggy Stardust* by David Bowie, *Oz*, July 1972: 'Bowie is now working in new areas, having been studying the art of punk rock poetry from Lou Reed.'

27. Greg Shaw, review of Grand Funk Railroad, *Rolling Stone*, 22 June 1972: 'Their downfall as a punk group was oddly enough Terry Knight.'

28. Dave Laing, review of *Bolan Boogie* by T. Rex, *Creem*, July

1972: 'Ever since the demise of the Troggs, the label marked "British Punk Rock" has been lying unused in my Do-It-Yourself Rock Critics Kit. It's true that there've been lots of teenybopping bands around since then, but genuine Punk Rock is more than music to throw jellybabies to. It's quintessentially adolescent in its emotional and musical simplicity, and in the obsessive energy with which that simplicity is expressed.'

29. Nick Kent, 'Punk Messiah of the Teenage Wasteland' feature about Iggy and the Stooges, *Creem*, September 1972: 'Now this story is about a certain Detroit punk-kid and his buddies who all started out as fine, upstanding examples of the synthetic leather jacket syndrome and great to become veritable Zarathustras arising from the quagmire of acne and downers to embrace still untouched areas of teenage debauchery.'

30. I.C. Lotz, review of *All Time Greatest Hits* by Paul Revere and the Raiders, *Fusion*, September 1972: 'Heads up punk rock fans. These are the kings of the pack.'

31. Ben Edmonds, review of 'School's Out' by Alice Cooper, *Creem*, October 1972: 'This kind of macho/punk presentation is essential to the Alice Cooper process of ditching the drag image.'

32. Lenny Kaye, *Nuggets* sleeve notes, Autumn 1972: 'The name that has been unofficially coined for them — "punk rock" — seems particularly fitting in this case, for if nothing else they personified the berserk pleasure that comes from being onstage outrageous, the relentless middle finger drive and determination only offered by rock 'n' roll at its finest.'

33. 'Metal' Mike Saunders, review of the 13th Floor Elevators reunion, 1972: 'And they look like punks too: Roky, his brother Donnie, and drummer John like all look as if they'd never seen 1967, coiffed as they are in stunningly short haircuts by 1972 standards.'

34. Lester Bangs, overview of Detroit's rock culture, *Phonograph Record*, December 1972: 'Pure punk shit, but one of the best fantasies of the decade.'

35. Glenn O'Brien, interview with Ray Davies, January 1973: 'Ray: (Imitating Brando) "Let's face it. That's all I am. Just a punk."'

36. Greg Shaw, review of *Nuggets* compilation album, *Rolling Stone*, 4 January 1973, by Greg Shaw: 'Punk Rock at its best is the closest we came in the Sixties to the original rockabilly spirit of Rock 'n' Roll, i.e. Punk Rock The Arrogant Underbelly of Sixties Pop.'

37. Lester Bangs, review of the Raspberries, *Rolling Stone*, 4 January 1973: '*Nuggets*... proves that psychedelic and punk zap are just as much a real cool time now as they were when we might have invested some emotional space-born significance in them.'

38. Bud Scoppa review of *No. 1 Record* by Big Star, *Rolling Stone*, 1 February 1973: 'The group was a vehicle for the ideas of the producer-writer, Dan Penn, and Chilton's raspy, young punk voice was the focal point.'

39. Greg Shaw, review of *Reunion* by Dion and the Belmonts, *Rolling Stone*, 29 March 1973: 'Dion was the original punk.'

40. Mark Shipper, liner notes for *Explosives Compilation* by the Sonics, April 1973: 'It's like if delta blues oughta be played by old black men, and if fag rock oughta be played by real queers, then it stands to reason that punk-rock oughta be played by punks!'

41. 'Metal' Mike Saunders, review of *Approximately Infinite Universe* by Yoko Ono, *Phonograph Record*, April 1973: '"I Felt Like Smashing My Face In A Clear Glass Window" may be the punk rock song of the month.'

42. I.C. Lotz, review of *16 Greatest Hits* by Steppenwolf, *Fusion*, May 1973: 'Mitch Ryder figured out how to make punk rock a viable commercial sound.'

43. Simon Frith, review of *Billion Dollar Babies* by Alice Cooper, *Let It Rock*, May 1973: 'McGovern's election theme is translated (its vacuousness exposed) into the language of punk.'

44. Lenny Kaye, review of *Raw Power* by Iggy and the Stooges, *Rolling Stone*, 10 May 1973: 'Iggy similarly benefits, double and even triple-tracked, his voice covering a range of frequencies only an (I wanna be your) dog could properly appreciate, arch-punk over tattling sniveler over chewed microphone.'

45. Simon Frith, review of *Tubular Bells* by Mike Oldfield and *Raw Power* by Iggy and the Stooges, *Let It Rock*, August 1973: 'For once, all this punk noise and contempt has got a focus — Nixon's America.'

46. Ben Edmonds, review of *Greatest Hits Vol 1* by the New York Dolls, *Creem*, October 1973: 'Their punk swagger, "Kick 'em in the ass" attitude and the overpowering hardness of the music might seem better suited to skull-laced leathers and a Harley-Davidson, but this volatile marriage of primped flash and toughness is the source of their strength.'

47. Dave Marsh, review of *New York New Wave* compilation album, *Melody Maker*, 6 October 1973: 'The Blue Oyster Cult members do solos; their songs are heavy metal and long; their dress is grubby motorcycle punk; their lyrics are a cross between beat poetry and a Skylab press release.'

48. Charles Shaar Murray, article on Suzi Quatro, *NME*, 13 October 1973: 'Let me leave you with this as you're turning the page: Suzi Quatro is, to my knowledge, the world's only female punk rocker. Meditate on *that* mantra.'

49. Greg Shaw, review of *Goat's Head Soup* by the Rolling Stones, *Phonograph Record*, November 1973: 'They're going through the motions, and it shows, ugly and pathetic under the crumbling façade of their punk image.

50. Lester Bangs, 'Lou Reed: A Deaf Mute in a Telephone Booth,' *Let It Rock*, November 1973: 'Listen kids, you may think

you've got your identity crises and sexual lateral squeeze plays touchdown cold just because you came out in rouge 'n' glitter for Dave Bowie's latest show, but listen to your Papa Lou. He's gotta nother think for you punk knowitalls.'

51. Lenny Kaye, review of *Quadrophenia* by the Who, *Rolling Stone*, 20 December 1973: 'In seeking to understand Jimmy, he [Townshend] apparently is also trying to understand the roots of The Who, its attraction as rallying point and its eventual rejection by such as Jimmy ("The Punk Meets the Godfather") and — more appropriately — himself.'

52. 'Metal' Mike Saunders, 'Blue Cheer: More Pumice Than Lava,' *Punk*, Fall 1973: 'Cruising down Telegraph Avenue trying to score some STP early one February morning, Dickie ran into Randy Holden (brother of Stephen Holden), a guitarist who had fronted one of the better SF acid-punk albums of the era, *The Other Half.*'

53. Chris Salewicz, 'Troggs Have It Taped,' *Let It Rock*, April 1974: '...the image of the Troggs-As-Punks. The discovery of punk-rock has undoubtedly been of major importance in the re-birth of the Troggs.'

54. Mick Farren, article on Eddie Cochran, *NME*, 20 April 1974: 'Cochran had to wait over a year before he got another chance at stardom when "Summertime Blues" made the charts. The lower-middle-class, put-upon punk formula was adopted — and the series of singles that included "C'Mon Everybody", "Something Else", and "Weekend" poured forth at a rapid rate.'

55. Mick Gold, review of *Rock 'n' Roll Animal* by Lou Reed, *Let It Rock*, May 1974: 'Each time Reed returns to the classic punk credo "I guess... I just don't know," they explode in a gothic arpeggio of sound.'

56. Gary Sperazza, review of *Stranded* by Roxy Music, *Shakin' Street Gazette*, May, 1974: 'Punk-rock in space.'

57. Greg Shaw, review of *School Punks* by Brownsville Station,

Phonograph Record, 1 July 1974: '*School Punks* is an extension of that song, a concept album dealing with the attitudes of an archetypal high school hoodlum.'

58. Jerry Gilbert, 'It's Hard To Be A Saint In The City' feature on Bruce Springsteen, *Zigzag,* August 1974: 'Springsteen does it all. He's a rock 'n' roll punk, a Latin street poet, a ballet dancer, an actor, a poet joker, a bar band leader...'

59. 'Metal' Mike Saunders, 'The *Shakin' Street* Punk Survey,' *Shakin' Street Gazette,* 7 November 1974: 'This is your big chance! Yes, it's all coming back. Following the rock & roll revival, the surf music revival, and the reggae revival, the punk music revival is now in full swing.'

60. Alan Betrock, 'Know Your New York Bands: The Ramones,' *Soho Weekly News,* 1975: '1-2-3-4! The Ramones run through their originals: "Judy is a Punk", "I Want To Be Your Boyfriend", "I Don't Care"...'

61. Mick Farren, *NME,* 15 February 1975: 'Gene Vincent: Po' White Punk from the Pool Hall.'

62. Anthony O'Grady, *RAM,* 19 April 1975: 'Australia has Punk Rock bands too y'know.'

63. Mick Farren, 'The Pink Fairies: Looking Back,' *NME,* 26 April 1975: 'A thrilling tale of Ladbroke Grove, loose aggregations, hanging out, and falling about — recounted in loving detail by an actual participant in those glorious halcyon days of punk rock.'

64. Caroline Coon, 'Bryan Ferry: Putting On The Style,' *Melody Maker,* 12 July 1975: 'There are basically two breeds of rock and roll musicians. Some are working class and have exploited their inarticulate but expressive origins to the full with an uncompromising punk-image and sound, like Family, Status Quo and Ian Hunter.'

65. Gene Sculatti, article on the Troggs, *Creem,* October 1975: 'Any half-assed aficionado knows the Troggs' "Wild Thing" and "I Can't Control Myself" virtually wrote the pamphlet

on drooling leer-rock of the punk-swagger school.'

66. Charles Shaar Murray, 'Are You Alive To the Jive of 75' article about the CBGBs scene, *NME*, 8 November 1975: 'CBGB, a small club on the Bowery round about the Bleecker Street intersection, is to the New York punk band scene what the Marquee was to London rock in the '60s.'

67. Greil Marcus, '*Horses*: Patti Smith Exposes Herself,' *Village Voice*, 24 November 1975: 'The concepts that lie behind Smith's performance — her version of rock and roll fave raves, the New York avant-garde, surrealist imagery and aesthetic strategy, the beatnik hipster pose, the dark night of the street punk soul, and so on — emerge more clearly with each playing, until they turn into *schtick*.'

68. Mick Houghton, 'White Punks on Coke,' *Let It Rock*, December 1975: 'The term punk is bandied about an awful lot these days. It seems to describe almost any rock performer who camps it up to any degree, on or off-stage, or who displays an arrogance and contempt for his audience.'

69. John Holmstrom, editorial, *Punk* 1, January 1976: 'The epitome of all that is wrong with western civilization is disco. Educate yourself. Get into it. Read *Punk*.'

70. Mary Harron, article on the Ramones, *Punk* 1, January 1976: 'This is an outsider's view. I just want to make that clear. I knew that I was an outsider from the moment I walked into CBGB's because I kept falling over my high-heeled boots. People who knew were wearing sneakers. One of the *Punk* magazine editors explained: "We don't believe in love or any of that shit. We believe in making money and getting drunk."'

71. Andy Childs, 'The Re-Emergence of the Flamin' Groovies,' *Zigzag*, February 1976: 'The first article in this occasional series concerns the Flamin' Groovies, the eternal garage punk-rock band, outcasts from the San Francisco music scene of the late '60s.'

72. Neil Spencer, 'Don't Look Over Your Shoulder, But The Sex Pistols Are Coming,' *NME*, February 1976: 'Punks? Springsteen Bruce and the rest of 'em would get shredded if they went up against these boys.'

73. Caroline Coon, 'Slik Forever!,' *Melody Maker*, 13 March 1976: 'By Saturday night we knew. A hero's welcome in their home town was to be expected. As Salvation, they were a top road band in Scotland, even before they changed their name to Slik. But the band proved at New Victoria that they can play solid, potentially inspiring, music. They are about to boogie us into a Golden Age of Punk Pop.'

74. Jonh Ingham, 'The Sex Pistols are Four Months Old,' *Sounds*, 24 April 1976: 'Allan Jones of the *Melody Maker* described it: "Their dreadfully inept attempts to zero in on the kind of viciously blank intensity previously epitomised by the Stooges was rather endearing at first... The guitarist, another surrogate punk suffering from a surfeit of Sterling Morrison, played with a determined disregard for taste and intelligence."'

75. Front-cover strap, French magazine *Rock News*, May 1976: 'Special Punk issue: London, Paris, USA 65/68.'

76. 'Punk Psychedelic 65-68,' *Rock News*, May 1976: 'Punk Gold: Count Five / "Psychotic Reaction" / "They're Gonna Get You" (Pye) ? and the Mysterians' "96 Tears" / "Midnight Hour" (Cameo Parkway) and many more.'

77. Ben Edmonds, article on the Runaways, *Phonograph Record*, May 1976: 'Punk rock archivists whose nirvana would be a double bill of the Troggs and the Count Five.'

78. Giovanni Dadomo, preview of Sex Pistols gig, *Time Out*, 7 May 1976: 'The sound is a mean cacophony not unreminiscent of Bowie's early Spiders, the material a mixture of Anglo-American teen/punk classics.'

79. Miles, 'Pink Floyd: Games For May,' *NME*, 15 May 1976: 'Ten years ago the Pink Floyd were a semi-formed idea in the

mind of one Syd Barrett. Nine years ago they were the darlings of the Flower Punks and playing games for May at the Queen Elizabeth Hall.'

80. Mick Farren, 'Elvis: Well, Bless-uh Muh Soul, What's-uh Wrong With Me?,' *NME*, 22 May 1976: 'The girls in the front row were jerked from their Bible Belt upbringing into scramming hysteria. They fought to get at the larger than life stud in the gaudy suits and longer sideburns than any hot rod punk.'

81. Greg Shaw, 'The Sex Pistols at the 100 Club, London,' *Phonograph Record*, June 1976: 'Rotten has Tom Verlaine's charismatic intensity, though without the avant-garde pretentions that put me off in so much of the New York scene. Their sound is a straight blast of tortured punk rock.'

82. Ron Ross, *Phonograph Record*, June 1976: 'Dr Feelgood: Frighteningly Authentic Punk Posture.'

83. Mick Farren, 'The Titanic Sails At Dawn,' *NME*, 19 June 1976: 'It's okay if some stars want to make the switch from punk to Liberace so long as they don't take rock and roll with them.'

84. Vivien Goldman, '*Sounds* Girl In Sweet Nude Bathing Horror,' *Sounds*, 19 June 1976: 'Thousands of minute German teenyboppers are creaming in excitement at seeing four would-be punk yobbos from Middlesex tell it like they think it is.'

85. Max Bell, 'Flamin' Groovies/The Ramones/The Stranglers: Roundhouse, London,' *NME*, 10 July 1976: 'Maybe it was no accident that the hottest, steamiest, dirtiest night of the year was reserved for July 4. It's not every day that we get to see one *bona fide* legendary band, *and* a squad of *recherché* New York punksters gunning for similar status, *and* a home grown outfit who exhibit enough moody madness to take them somewhere close to the pinnacle of nasty infamy, all playing on the same bill in one of the seediest halls in

London.'

86. Max Bell, 'The Ramones: Waitin' for World War III Blues,' *NME*, 17 July 1976: 'The room is cluttered with punk ephemera: leather belts and garbage pulp mags full of archly self-conscious interviews with Big Apple street runts trying desperately to outdo each other. The Ramones are a definite part of that schtick; manager Danny has several fingers in both *Punk* and *16*, and those mags like The Bay City Rollers, so you can tell where they're at.'

87. Jonh Ingham, 'Anarchy in the UK' review of Sex Pistols, Buzzcocks and Slaughter and the Dogs gig in Manchester, *Sounds*, 31 July 1976: 'Just how the Dogs see themselves as being like the Pistols, which is how they approached the group, is an entertaining mystery. It is said that on a local radio show they defined "punk" as being a cross between David Bowie and the Rolling Stones. But fuck definitions, Pete Shelley reckons they're an offence just to the word itself.'

88. Gene Sculatti, review of *Ramones* by the Ramones, *Creem*, August 1976: '*Ramones* reads like a rock 'n' roll reactionary's manifesto. The kind of driven, primal, mindblasting r 'n' r that fueled Stooges fanclubs and formed the editorial backbone of fanzines from *Who Put The Bomp* to *Punk* comes alive in "Blitzkrieg Bop", "I Wanna Be Your Boyfriend" and "Chain Saw".'

89. Caroline Coon, 'Punk Rock: Rebels Against the System,' *Melody Maker*, 7 August 1976: 'Johnny Rotten looks bored. The emphasis is on the word "looks" rather than, as Johnny would have you believe, the word "bored". His clothes, held together by safety pins, fall around his slack body in calculated disarray. His face is an undernourished grey. Not a muscle moves. His lips echo the downward slope of his wiry, coat-hanger shoulders. Only his eyes register the faintest trace of life. Johnny works very hard at looking

bored. Leaning against a bar; at a soundcheck; after a gig; making an entrance to a party; onstage; when he's with women. No, actually, *then* he's inclined to look quite interested. Why is Johnny bored? Well; that's the story. This malevolent third-generation child of rock 'n' roll is the Sex Pistols' lead singer. The band play exciting, hard, basic punk rock. But more than that, Johnny is the elected generalissimo of a new cultural movement scything through the grassroots disenchantment with the present state of mainstream rock. You need look no further than the letters pages of any *Melody Maker* to see that fans no longer silently accept the disdain with which their heroes, the rock giants, treat them.'

90. Pete Greenwood, 'Pros and Cons of Punk,' letter in the *Melody Maker* letters page, 21 August 1976: 'Thanks for the article on "Punk Rock": it is refreshing to hear about new talent for a change. There is a great need for this sort of good rock/no frills.'

91. Chas de Whalley, review of the Kursaal Flyers and the Clash at the Roundhouse, September 1976: 'The Ramones out of an East End squat? Indeed, many of the leather-clad Strummer's new songs were little more than rewrites of this year's punk classics. But "I've Got A Crush On You", "Janie Jones", and the apocalyptic "London's Burning" proved there was still power in Strummer's right arm.'

92. Paul Morley, article on the Sex Pistols, *Out There* fanzine, Summer 1976: '...Lesser Free Trade Hall. There to see a youthful contemporary quartet play the street avant-garde music of the Sixties in its properly repressed Seventies setting. The Sex Pistols. Plenty of ripe s's in the name, the surging s rock very much inbred into the Pistols' controlled chaotic punk muzak.'

93. Paul Morley, article on the Buzzcocks, *Out There* fanzine, Summer 1976: 'For iggypops sake take note of your struggling local "s" rock band. Who merely want to WAKE YOU

UP, shake you about. Take a sluiced scoot Buzzcock.'

94. James Johnson, 'The Rotten Rock and Roll Band,' *Evening Standard*, 23 September 1976: 'Punk and punk rockers alike appear to place great emphasis on being against everything except themselves. The establishment, hippies and intellectuals are all equally despised.'

95. Chris Welch, 'Eddie and the Hot Rods: Punk? — We Just Do It,' *Melody Maker*, 25 September 1976: 'Forget tags like "punk rock." They are too real and earthy to be associated with such essentially esoteric imagery.'

96. Caroline Coon, 'Parade of the Punks,' *Melody Maker*, 2 October 1976: 'The 600-strong line, which last Monday straggled across two blocks outside London's 100 Club in Oxford Street, waiting for the Punk Rock Festival to start, was indisputable evidence that a new decade in rock is about to begin.'

97. Denis Cassidy, 'Look What Pop Kids Do Now,' *The People*, 3 October 1976: (Picture caption) 'CHAIN MALE: Punk Rocker Mark shows off the gear that made eyes really pop in the clubs of South Wales.' (Text) 'If you thought you'd seen it all, dig this latest line in crazy gear. As you can see, one end of that chain is actually through the nose, the other through an ear... it's the face of a Punk Rock, Britain's latest pop trendy.' (First bit of UK tabloid press found so far.)

98. 'In Decadent Key,' *New Society*, 7 October 1976: 'The scene is a sweltering basement club in London's Oxford Street, where a band called the Sex Pistols is topping the bill at an evening devoted to Punk Rock, a genre of pop music currently monopolizing the attention of music business bandwagon jumpers.'

99. 'Pistols Sign EMI Deal,' *Sounds*, 16 October 1976: 'The Sex Pistols, the leading British "new wave" group, have been signed to EMI Records.'

100. Jonh Ingham, 'Welcome to the ? Rock Special,' *Sounds*, 9

October 1976: 'I was hoping to avoid mentioning the bloody word at all, but since *Sounds* has so adamantly advertised this shebang as a Punk Rock Special, I guess there's no avoiding it. In the context of the band and the people mentioned in the following pages, I hate the word as much as they do. For a start it's (rock) historically inaccurate. Punk rock as a genre in the mid-Sixties, composed of American garage bands trying to duplicate or better their English fave raves like the Yardbirds and Them, has no relation with the viciously original music of the Sex Pistols or the Clash or the Damned. As an attitude there's basis for discussion, but consider Mark P in *Sniffin' Glue* 3: "You get the feeling at Pistols gigs that everyone's posing so they can't really be punks can they? Punks are carefree, and I mean completely... like a football who kicks in someone's head and don't care a shit. Yer, the Pistols crowd are not punks, they're too vain. But what's wrong with that so am I." John Rotten half-seriously favours "anarchy rock". Paul Morley in his fanzine *Out There* wants "s" rock. That's "s" as in "surge". The Jam mentioned the "punk rock (?) scene". Siouxsie from the Banshees reckoned that it should have been "(?) rock". And so it shall. Welcome to the ? Rock Special.'

101. 'Punks on the Road' front-page headline, *Melody Maker*, 6 November 1976: 'A big punk rock concert starring the Sex Pistols is being planned for London next month. The show celebrates the release of the band's debut single, "Anarchy In The UK", on November 12.'

102. Jonh Ingham, review of the Clash gig at Barbarellas in Birmingham, *Sounds*, 13 November 1976: 'Wednesday had been booked as Punk Night at Barbarellas, an excuse, if nothing else, for the club deejay to fall in love with the sound of his mouth flapping. It was the brainchild of the local Suburban Studs, supported by their mentors the Clash.

And here lies a story.'

103. Caroline Coon, 'The Clash: Down and Out and Proud,'
Melody Maker, 13 November 1976: 'Three weeks ago at
London's ICA, Jane and Shane, regulars on the new-wave
punk rock scene, were sprawled at the edge of the stage.
Blood covered Shane's face. Jane, very drunk, had kissed,
bitten and, with broken glass, cut him in a calm, but no less
macabre, love rite.'

104. Caroline Coon, 'Sex Pistols Rotten to the Core' interview
with Johnny Rotten, 27 November 1976: 'To those who come
on trying to impress him, he feigns the expected, sneering
punk facade, revealing nothing about himself. He rarely
opens up in public.'

105. Barbara Charone, 'Ray Davies and the Kinks at 13,'
Phonograph Record, December 1976: 'Keeping an eye on the
charts, watching the meteoric rise of London's new wave
punk bands who adolescently emulate the master originals,
Ray Davies wonders where the Kinks fit in the scheme of
things. Davies can't continue being *everyone's* favorite
songwriter, singing to a dedicated but cult-like audience.'

106. 'Rock Group Start a 4-Letter TV Storm,' *The Sun*, 2 December
1976: 'TV personality Bill Grundy was accused of encouraging the language that shocked thousands. He was talking
to the "punk rock" group Sex Pistols on Thames Television's
Today programme.'

107. 'The Filth and the Fury' front-page headline, *The Daily
Mirror*, 2 December 1976: 'The Sex Pistols, leaders of the new
"punk rock" cult, hurled a string of four letter obscenities at
interviewer Bill Grundy on Thames TV's family teatime
programme *Today*.'

108. 'Who Are These Punks?,' *Daily Mirror*, 2 December 1976:
'They wear torn and ragged clothes held together with
safety pins. They are boorish, ill-mannered, foul-mouthed,
dirty, obnoxious and arrogant. They like to be disliked.'

109. *The Daily Mail*, 2 December 1976: 'Four-Letter Punk Rock group in TV Storm.'

110. 'The Bizarre Face of Punk Rock,' *The Daily Mail*, 2 December 1976: 'The latest pop phenomenon called Punk Rock makes all the rest look like nursery rhymes. It's the sickest, seediest step in a rock world that thought it had seen it all. Leading the cult is the group Sex Pistols.'

111. 'Fury At Filthy TV Chat,' *The Daily Express*, 2 December 1976: 'A top level probe was ordered by Thames Television last night after a "punk rock" group delivered a stream of four letter words on the air.'

112. 'Grundy Goaded Punk Boys Says Record Chief,' *London Evening News*, 2 December 1976: 'The Sex Pistols were the first punk rock band, leaders of a violent and ugly pop phenomena.'

113. 'The Punks — Rotten and Proud of it!,' *Evening Standard*, 2 December 1976: '"Punk — Worthless, decidedly inferior, displeasing, rotten — Partridge's Dictionary of Slang and Unconventional English." Punk Rock, which exploded onto the screen last night in a string of four-letter words, is a bizarre movement which combines rock and rebellion.'

114. Steve Turner, 'Sex Pistols: the Anarchic Rock of the Young and Doleful,' *Guardian*, 3 December 1976: 'And then there was punk. Tonight the Sex Pistols, focal point of the newly dubbed punk generation, take off on their first concert tour of Britain complete with a £40,000 contract with EMI Records, a single entitled "Anarchy In The UK", and a reputation for being insolent and violent — a reputation which was compounded though their use of Thames Television's *Today* programme to throw out a few live obscenities which would appal the parents and therefore thrill the kids.'

115. Keith Waterhouse, 'The Punk and the Junk,' *Daily Mirror*, 6 December 1976: 'The Punk Rock phenomenon may be

manipulated by the music industry but it could not exist at all if the so-called "Blank Generation" — the unemployed, under-educated, aimless tribe of vandals to be found on every disastrous concrete housing project — had not been there to feed off.'

116. Ronald Butt, 'The Grubby Face of Mass Punk Promotion,' *Times*, 9 December 1976: 'I was just wondering whether it would be bad form to ask when Sir John Read (EMI Group Chairman) spoke at his share-holders meeting on Tuesday. He described the conduct of the "punk" group as "disgraceful" and said that EMI will "review its guidelines" on pop records.'

117. Miles, 'The Clash: Eighteen Flight Rock,' *NME*, 11 December 1976: 'Some people have made the connection between the high energy output of the punk rock groups and violence. The Clash rise up united. The kids, they say, just feel really bored and frustrated, get really drunk and then become violent.'

118. Peter Silverton, 'What Did You Do On The Punk Tour, Daddy?,' *Sounds*, 18 December 1976: 'To turn up to a Sex Pistols' show nowadays is to make a statement to the world that you care about rock 'n' roll and don't give a Bill Grundy what the yellow press thinks.'

119. Mick Brown, 'UK Report: Sex Pistols and Beyond,' *Rolling Stone*, 27 January 1977: 'London — So this is how legends are born. Not with a song, or even a death, but with an expletive. The day before, the Sex Pistols, Britain's premier exponents of punk, were interviewed on Thames Television's *Today* program they were known principally to a scattering of hard-core fans and to readers of the British music press. The day after, the Sex Pistols had become Britain's Number One "bad boys."'

120. Glitterbest, Jamie Reid, possibly Sophie Richmond and Malcolm McLaren, notes for *Anarchy In the UK* magazine

number 2 (unpublished), end of January, 1977: 'punknewwavedolequeuerock, so they call it, is only a beginning, a spark. The very nature of establishment rock industry those who control what we listen to what we pay for it and where, means for bands like the Sex Pistols and the Clash that they are fucked before they start: REF Pistols sacking by E.M.I.'

121. Glitterbest staff (Jamie Reid, possibly Sophie Richmond and Malcolm McLaren), handwritten notes for *Anarchy in the UK* magazine 2 (unpublished), January 1977: 'PUNK IS DEAD.'

122. Fantastic Lester Bangs rant, 'Everybody's Search For Roots,' *New Wave*, August 1977: 'The "roots" of punk. Hah! That's what we've come to... I am not a punk and never was (too literate, besides no jazz fan can ever be a punk) but I gained a certain amount of notoriety exploiting the phenom before *Newsweek* knew there was one so here I am beating a dead horse... Oh, but I'll show you the roots of punk. The roots of punk was the first time that a kid ended up living with his parents when he was 40... Punk may (may?) be essentially passive. Punk is stupid proud consumerism. Punk is oblivion when it isn't any fun... Punk is something worth destroying posthaste. Hopefully this article will speed that process...'

123. Sire Records, advert in *Bomp* magazine (featuring Ramones, Talking Heads, the Dead Boys, Tuff Darts, The Saints, Richard Hell and Patti Smith), March 1978: 'First it was "punk", then "new wave". As each term for the new rock 'n' roll falls by the wayside, people are getting the idea there's a wide range of rocking going on within the new sound. A new generation of rockers with as many styles and viewpoints as any other generation of rockers. They're not the same. No amount of tidy terms or slogans will ever make them the same.'

Acknowledgements and Credits

Heartfelt thanks to: all the contributors and interviewees for their time and effort; Andrew Stevens for additional proofing; and Tony Drayton for the front-cover image. We're also grateful to Peter Jones, Matt Worley, David Keenan and John A Walker.

All words and images used by kind permission.

Foreword: Punk's the Diamond in My Pocket — © Judy Nylon.

Introduction: Prose for Heroes — © Richard Cabut and © Andrew Gallix respectively.

The Boy Looked at Eurydice — © Andrew Gallix. A shorter version of this essay, commissioned by Nicholas Rombes, appeared in *Berfrois* on 17 June 2014.

Rummaging in the Ashes — © Andrew Gallix.

King Mob Echo — © Tom Vague.

Glam into Punk: The Transition — © Barney Hoskyns. Extracted from *Glam! — Bowie, Bolan and the Glitter Revolution*, Faber and Faber, 1998.

The Divining Rod and the Lost Vowel — © Jonh Ingham. An earlier version was published in *Sounds,* 29 May 1976.

Malcolm's Children — © Richard Cabut.

Boom! — © Ted Polhemus. An excerpt from *A Baby Boomer Memoir, 1947-2022.*

The Flyaway-Collared Shirt — © Paul Gorman. This is an expanded and updated version of a 2004 piece that appeared in *3:AM Magazine* under the title 'The Capri-Collared Shirt.'

SEX in the City — © Dorothy Max Prior.

A Letter to Jordan — © Richard Cabut. Originally published under pen name Richard Kick in *Zigzag,* May 1984.

Punk's Not Dead. It's in a Coma... — © Andy Blade.

Ever Fallen in Love? — © David Wilkinson. A version of this article originally appeared in *Key Words: A Journal of Cultural*

Materialism 13 (2015), published by the Raymond Williams Society.

For Your Unpleasure — © Mark Fisher. Originally published in different form on *k-punk*, 1 June 2005.

1977 — © Richard Cabut. Originally published in *3:AM Magazine*, 2007.

Sexy Eiffel Towers — © Andrew Gallix. Passages from this piece appeared in *Dazed Digital* ('Jeunes Gens Modernes in Paris,' 24 April 2008) and the *Guardian*'s website ('France's Pre-Banksy Art Provocateurs,' 14 May 2008).

The End of Music — No copyright. Originally published in *The End Of Music*, Box V2, Glasgow 1978. Also available in *Like a Summer With a Thousand Julys: Collected Writings from Dave and Stuart Wise*, 1978-2008, Bread and Circuses, 2016.

Banned From the Roxy — No copyright. A different version was published as 'Crass at the Roxy,' *International Anthem*, 1977.

Learning to Fight — © Richard Cabut. ('Pet Puppies in Theory and Practice' was originally published in *Kill Your Pet Puppy*, 1980. © Tony Drayton.)

Unheard Melodies — © Andrew Gallix. Passages from this piece appeared in *Garageland* 8 (Summer 2009) as well as the *Guardian*'s website ('The Fascination of Phantom Bands,' 27 December 2007).

Punk Movies — © Nicholas Rombes.

Some Brief and Frivolous Thoughts on a Richard Hell Reading — © Richard Cabut. Originally published on *3:AM Magazine*, 2005.

Leaving the 21st Century — © Andrew Gallix. Passages from this piece appeared in *Flux* magazine ('Colossal Youth,' issue 70, Autumn 2009) and the *Guardian*'s website ('Living Poetry,' 25 September 2007).

Tales of Low-Life Losers — © Bob Short. Originally published in *3:AM Magazine*, 2005.

Positive Punk — © Richard Cabut. Originally published in a

Contributors' Biographies

Andy Blade

Andy Blade formed Eater at school in 1976, aged fifteen, with his friend Brian Chevette. After being forced by necessity to steal the guitars they needed from a local music shop in Finchley, Eater went on to recruit Dee Generate (drums) and Ian Woodcock (bass) into the band. Their debut performance was in Manchester (although the band hailed from London), with Buzzcocks supporting. After an album and several singles all made the lower reaches of the chart, Eater disbanded in 1978. As Blade explained, 'The scene has turned to shit, horrible bands all over the place, and everyone's taking heroin.' He has released four solo albums, including 2016's *Plastic Penny & The Strange Wooden Horse*. The highly anticipated follow up to his memoir, *The Secret Life of a Teenage Punk Rocker: The Andy Blade Chronicles* (Cherry Red Books, 2005) is due in 2017 — 'To avoid tying in with the 40th year anniversary!'

Neal Brown

Neal Brown is an artist, musician and writer. He has written about art for most UK and many international art magazines, is the author of books on Billy Childish and Tracey Emin, and wrote an introduction to Bill Drummond's *45*. He was editor and publisher of *Nineteen Raptures*, a literary study of addictive compulsivity and obsession. His work for Fat Les makes him co-author of a top-thirty UK hit, and his old band the Tesco Bombers recently reappeared on the post-punk compilation *Cease and Desist*. He is proud of having written the original sleeve notes for Joe Strummer's 101'ers LP, *Elgin Avenue Breakdown*.

Simon Critchley

Simon Critchley is Hans Jonas Professor at the New School for

Social Research in New York. Since *The Ethics in Deconstruction: Derrida and Levinas* (1992) he has published more than twenty books, including *Very Little… Almost Nothing: Death, Philosophy, Literature* (1997), *Infinitely Demanding: Ethics of Commitment, Politics of Resistance* (2007), *The Book of Dead Philosophers* (2008), *The Faith of the Faithless: Experiments in Political Theology* (2012), *Notes on Suicide* (2015) and *On Bowie* (2016). He is series moderator of 'The Stone,' a philosophy column in the *New York Times*.

Tony Drayton

Tony Drayton founded two legendary punk fanzines at the height of their time, *Ripped & Torn* in 1976 and *Kill Your Pet Puppy* in 1980. He chronicled the rise of punk and how it developed into a lifestyle, living the life whilst contributing to the mainstream music publications such as *Sounds*, *NME*, *Record Mirror*, *Zigzag*, *Punk Lives* and others. He left writing to perform and develop a punk circus across Europe through the Eighties, pioneering the likes of Archaos, before touring the world in his own right as a fire-breathing entertainer. Tony currently runs the Facebook pages for both *Ripped & Torn* and *Kill Your Pet Puppy*, plus their popular websites.

Mark Fisher

Mark Fisher is the author of *Capitalist Realism* and *Ghosts of My Life: Writings on Depression, Hauntology and Lost Futures* (both published by Zer0 Books). His writing has appeared in many publications, including *Frieze*, *New Humanist* and *Sight & Sound*. He is a lecturer in Visual Cultures at Goldsmiths, University of London.

Paul Gorman

Paul Gorman is a writer, curator and commentator on visual culture. He has contributed to many of the world's leading publications in the UK and US. Gorman's books include *The Look: Adventures in Rock & Pop Fashion, Reasons To Be Cheerful: The Life & Work Of Barney Bubbles, Straight* with Boy George and *Derek Boshier: Rethink/Re-entry* (ed). Current projects include *Legacy: The Story of The Face* and *Malcolm McLaren: The Biography,* both to be published in 2017.

Barney Hoskyns

Barney Hoskyns is the co-founder and editorial director of *Rock's Backpages,* the online library of pop writing and journalism. He is a former contributing editor at *British Vogue* and U.S. correspondent for *MOJO.* He is the author of, among many other books, the bestselling *Hotel California* (2006), the Tom Waits biography *Lowside of the Road* (2009) and *Trampled Under Foot* (2012), an oral history of Led Zeppelin. *Small Town Talk,* his history of the music scene in and around Woodstock, New York, was published in March 2015.

Jonh Ingham

Jonh Ingham has been helping create the future since 1976, when he wrote the first interview with the Sex Pistols. He spent the year championing them, the Clash, the Damned, Buzzcocks and others, helping to make sure punk became a dominant music force. Moving to Hollywood he directed filmgraphic TV commercials, invented The Fake Club (a weekly pop-up dance club), and managed Generation X, the Go-Go's, and the Plugz. In Tokyo he produced CD-ROMs for Pioneer Japan and created his first Internet content in 1994 while working with visionary musician Peter Gabriel. In 2000 he created and developed Europe's first commercial mobile content service in Ibiza. For the last twelve years he has been Content Director at mobile operator O2, inventing and building Internet services in London, Poland, Germany and Saudi Arabia. He is currently writing and producing *Spirit of 76: London Punk Eyewitness,* a book of his 1976 punk photography.

Judy Nylon

These days, Judy Nylon is a self-taught conceptual artist working across several disciplines. Her vision is international, feminist, avant-garde and uncompromising. She has refined punk to a portable way of being, used consciously in small everyday things. In 1976, she was co-founder, with Patti Palladin, of London punk's first-wave female DIY studio duo Snatch. She has recorded and performed with John Cale, but is perhaps best known for her role alongside Brian Eno in the genesis of ambient music. Her legendary 1982 dub album *Pal Judy* was co-produced with Adrian Sherwood/On-U to anticipate in analog what digital would make commonplace. Her audio montage of phone taps between Andreas Baader in Germany and his lawyer in France gave first insight into what would become known as 'state of emergency' presidential powers. The cut-up technique of Brion Gysin, used on these phone taps, was mixed with Brian Eno's previously recorded tapes of Brand X. to which it was also applied. This recording was released as the Snatch and Eno recording *R.A.F.* (1977).

Ted Polhemus

Ted Polhemus is an internationally recognized expert on youth subculture, style, and fashion. His books include *Fashion & Anti-Fashion*, *Bodystyles*, *Popstyles*, *The Customized Body*, *Streetstyle*, *Diesel* and *Style Surfing*. Ted worked at the Institute of Contemporary Arts, London, where his Fashion Forum series promoted the talents of emerging design talents like Vivienne Westwood and Malcolm McLaren. An exhibition of his photographs, *Posers*, was held at the Photographers Gallery, London in 1981. He was the curator of the *Streetstyle* exhibition at the Victoria and Albert Museum, London (November 1994 - February 1995) and contributed to the *Supermarket of Style* and

Engine of Fashion events and exhibitions for Pitti Immagine, Florence, Italy (1995-2000) and the *Taste* exhibition at the Bonnefanten Museum, Maastricht (2000). Ted has been a Beat, a modernist, a hippy, a glam rocker, a punk and a goth.

Dorothy Max Prior

Dorothy Max Prior is a writer and an artist working in theatre, dance and performance art. She is currently writing a collection of autobiographical stories and essays under the working title *Sex is No Emergency*. As Max, she played drums in an early line-up of the Ants/the Monochrome Set (1976-77), then went on to form Rema Rema (1978-79) with Marco Pirroni, Mark Cox, Gary Asquith and Michael Allen, and subsequently formed and played drums in the Weekend Swingers and the El Trains. As Dorothy, she released a single on Industrial Records, 'I Confess' (1980). She played drums and created multi-discipline performance events with Psychic TV (1984-85). 'Sex is no Emergency' is the title of a song by Monte Cazazza, released on Industrial Records.

Simon Reynolds

Simon Reynolds is the author of eight books about pop culture, including the post-punk history *Rip It Up and Start Again* and most recently *Shock and Awe: Glam Rock and its Legacy from the Seventies to the 21st Century*. Starting out as a staff writer for *Melody Maker* in 1986, he has been a freelance contributor to numerous magazines, including the *New York Times*, the *Guardian*, the *Wire* and *Pitchfork*. He also operates a bunch of blogs centred around Blissblog (http://blissout.blogspot.com/). Born in London in 1963, a resident of New York for most of the 1990s and 2000s, Reynolds currently lives in Los Angeles.

Penny Rimbaud

Penny Rimbaud didn't go to Oxbridge. He is not married, has no children and no dog. He does not have a private dwelling in the

Home Counties nor a pied-à-terre in Hoxton. He neither drives a car nor owns a mobile phone; his landline is inoperative. Having never received one, he has been unable to return his MBE to sender, although he eagerly awaits the opportunity to refuse a knighthood. When asked, he says that he is a bread maker, this being because he realises that his bread is considerably easier to digest than his poetry and philosophy. He has been writing for all of his life, well, at least the last sixty-eight years of it. He is under no illusion that his writing days are not numbered.

Nicholas Rombes

Nicholas Rombes, novelist, filmmaker and Professor of English at the University of Detroit Mercy, is the author of *Ramones*, from the *33 1/3* series, and *A Cultural Dictionary of Punk*, both published by Bloomsbury.

Jon Savage

Jon Savage is the author of *England's Dreaming: The Sex Pistols and Punk Rock* and *Teenage: The Creation of Youth, 1875-1945*. He is the writer of the award-winning film documentaries *The Brian Epstein Story* (1998) and *Joy Division* (2007), as well as the feature film of *Teenage* (2014). His compilations include *Meridian 1970* (Heavenly/EMI 2005) and *Queer Noises: From The Closet to the Charts, 1961-1976* (Trikont, 2006).

Bob Short

Bob Short? The things that bastard has seen. Aye. The things that bastard has seen. He's heard the chimes at midnight, that one. And he's dropped a fistful of speckled blues so he could hear them again. So he's seen some things. Once upon a time, he could have been a contender. But that's pretty much true of everyone. I heard he was dead. Or in gaol. Or living in Australia.

Tom Vague

Tom Vague was the editor/designer of one of the first post-punk fanzines, *Vague*, which he co-founded with the cartoonist Perry Harris at Salisbury College of Art and Technology in 1979. He also wrote for *Zigzag*, *International Times* and *City Limits* magazines. Through the Eighties, *Vague* went from covering Adam and the Ants, Siouxsie and the Banshees, Joy Division, the Pop Group and PIL, to become a cyber-punk manual featuring Situationist and conspiracy theories, Psychic TV and the Baader-Meinhof gang. He has since worked on his London Psychogeography project in Notting Hill, including the Clash *London Calling* box-set booklet and the community-history website www.colvillecom.com.

David Wilkinson

David Wilkinson is Lecturer in English at Manchester Metropolitan University. He is the author of *Post-Punk, Politics and Pleasure in Britain* (Palgrave Macmillan, 2016). In 2014 he co-founded Manchester Left Writers, who have produced work for *Open Democracy*, *Art Monthly*, Manchester Literature Festival and Castlefield Gallery. He has also worked with LGBT History Month, The F Word and Manchester District Music Archive.

David and Stuart Wise

The Wise brothers were key members of King Mob. 'Two working class insurrectionists and dreamers slowly drowning in a sea of desertion and recuperation' (Bread and Circuses publishing).

Editors' Biographies

Richard Cabut

Richard Cabut is a writer, playwright and musician. Richard's fiction has appeared in magazines and anthologies including *The Edgier Waters* (Snowbooks, 2006) and *Affinity* (67 Press, 2015); his journalism in various national newspapers including the *Telegraph* and the *Guardian*; his music writing in the *NME* (pen name Richard North) and *Zigzag*, amongst other publications. Richard also produced the fanzine *Kick* (1979-82). His plays have been performed at various theatres in London. He was bassist in the band Brigandage, playing on the releases *FYM* (FO, 1984) and *Pretty Funny Thing* (Gung Ho Records, 1986).

Andrew Gallix

Andrew Gallix teaches at the Sorbonne and edits *3:AM Magazine*. He has written for the *Guardian, Financial Times, New Statesman, Independent, Times Literary Supplement, BBC Radio 3, Los Angeles Review of Books* and *Dazed & Confused*, among others. He divides his time between Scylla and Charybdis.

Zero Books
CULTURE, SOCIETY & POLITICS

Contemporary culture has eliminated the concept and public figure of the intellectual. A cretinous anti-intellectualism presides, cheer-led by hacks in the pay of multinational corporations who reassure their bored readers that there is no need to rouse themselves from their stupor. Zer0 Books knows that another kind of discourse - intellectual without being academic, popular without being populist - is not only possible: it is already flourishing. Zer0 is convinced that in the unthinking, blandly consensual culture in which we live, critical and engaged theoretical reflection is more important than ever before.

If you have enjoyed this book, why not tell other readers by posting a review on your preferred book site.

Recent bestsellers from Zero Books are:

In the Dust of This Planet
Horror of Philosophy vol. 1
Eugene Thacker
In the first of a series of three books on the Horror of
Philosophy, *In the Dust of This Planet* offers the genre of horror
as a way of thinking about the unthinkable.
Paperback: 978-1-84694-676-9 ebook: 978-1-78099-010-1

Capitalist Realism
Is there no alternative?
Mark Fisher
An analysis of the ways in which capitalism has presented itself
as the only realistic political-economic system.
Paperback: 978-1-84694-317-1 ebook: 978-1-78099-734-6

Rebel Rebel
Chris O'Leary
David Bowie: every single song. Everything you want to know,
everything you didn't know.
Paperback: 978-1-78099-244-0 ebook: 978-1-78099-713-1

Cartographies of the Absolute
Alberto Toscano, Jeff Kinkle
An aesthetics of the economy for the twenty-first century.
Paperback: 978-1-78099-275-4 ebook: 978-1-78279-973-3

Malign Velocities
Accelerationism and Capitalism
Benjamin Noys
Long listed for the Bread and Roses Prize 2015, *Malign Velocities*
argues against the need for speed, tracking acceleration as the
symptom of the on-going crises of capitalism.
Paperback: 978-1-78279-300-7 ebook: 978-1-78279-299-4

Why Are We The Good Guys?
Reclaiming your Mind from the Delusions of Propaganda
David Cromwell
A provocative challenge to the standard ideology that Western
power is a benevolent force in the world.
Paperback: 978-1-78099-365-2 ebook: 978-1-78099-366-9

Readers of ebooks can buy or view any of these bestsellers by
clicking on the live link in the title. Most titles are published in
paperback and as an ebook. Paperbacks are available in traditional
bookshops. Both print and ebook formats are available online.

Find more titles and sign up to our readers' newsletter at
http://www.johnhuntpublishing.com/culture-and-politics
Follow us on Facebook at https://www.facebook.com/ZeroBooks
and Twitter at https://twitter.com/Zer0Books